# Praise for *Zero Configuration Networking: The Definitive Guide*

"This book helps Zeroconf meet its promise of pain-free networking by providing hardware and software developers with the background and guidance they need in order to successfully include Zeroconf technology in their products."

> — Yaron Goland, Director of Technology, BEA Systems, Inc., and
> original network architect of UPnP

"Ever wonder why it's so hard to get two network devices to talk with each other? It doesn't have to be! If only everyone used Zeroconf services, network connectivity would be plug and play. And now, with Stuart Cheshire's wonderful and detailed new book, there's no excuse to use anything else. It's a must-read for hardware developers, software developers, and anyone wondering how Apple—and others—have built 'it just works' technology into iTunes, iPhoto, and virtually every printer on the market."

> — Jim Louderback, Editorial Director, Ziff Davis Internet

"I routinely evaluate diverse network technologies in my job. I've found that for service advertising and discovery, there is nothing out there that compares to Zeroconf—all I had to do to incorporate it into our SoundBridge Network Music Player was to insert a single c file into my project and compile it. Zeroconf, however, is not only for devices—every Windows program I write that is a network client or offers a network service now uses Zeroconf for advertising and discovery, making Bonjour an indispensable tool in my bag of tricks. Kudos to Apple and their team of network scientists!"

> — Don Woodward, Chief Technology Officer, Roku

"If my PDA is ever going to be as useful as a Star Trek™ Datapad™, it'll be because the Internet has Zeroconf."

> — Paul Vixie

"This book is so good that it will shame software authors into making their network-aware apps easy to use!"

> — Mike Bell, VP of CPU software, Apple Macintosh Hardware Division

T0256632

# Zero Configuration Networking
*The Definitive Guide*

## Other resources from O'Reilly

**Related titles**
802.11 Wireless Networks:
   The Definitive Guide
Java™ Network Programming
Python in a Nutshell

C in a Nutshell
Java™ in a Nutshell
Cocoa in a Nutshell

**oreilly.com**
*oreilly.com* is more than a complete catalog of O'Reilly books. You'll also find links to news, events, articles, weblogs, sample chapters, and code examples.

*oreillynet.com* is the essential portal for developers interested in open and emerging technologies, including new platforms, programming languages, and operating systems.

**Conferences**
O'Reilly brings diverse innovators together to nurture the ideas that spark revolutionary industries. We specialize in documenting the latest tools and systems, translating the innovator's knowledge into useful skills for those in the trenches. Visit *conferences.oreilly.com* for our upcoming events.

Safari Bookshelf (*safari.oreilly.com*) is the premier online reference library for programmers and IT professionals. Conduct searches across more than 1,000 books. Subscribers can zero in on answers to time-critical questions in a matter of seconds. Read the books on your Bookshelf from cover to cover or simply flip to the page you need. Try it today for free.

# Zero Configuration Networking
## The Definitive Guide

*Stuart Cheshire and Daniel H. Steinberg*

O'REILLY®

Beijing · Cambridge · Farnham · Köln · Sebastopol · Tokyo

**Zero Configuration Networking: The Definitive Guide**
by Stuart Cheshire and Daniel H. Steinberg

Published by O'Reilly Media, Inc., 1005 Gravenstein Highway North, Sebastopol, CA 95472.

O'Reilly books may be purchased for educational, business, or sales promotional use. Online editions are also available for most titles (*safari.oreilly.com*). For more information, contact our corporate/institutional sales department: (800) 998-9938 or *corporate@oreilly.com*.

| | |
|---|---|
| **Editor:** | Mike Loukides |
| **Production Editor:** | Matt Hutchinson |
| **Cover Designer:** | Karen Montgomery |
| **Interior Designer:** | David Futato |

**Printing History:**

| | |
|---|---|
| December 2005: | First Edition. |

ISBN:  978-0-596-10100-8
[LSI]                                                                    [2011-03-18]

# Table of Contents

# Foreword

Why can't computers in real life work like they do on *Star Trek*? I mean, it seems obvious that if you've got a lot of computing horsepower tied to your building (or your ship, or whatever), and if you've got all kinds of wireless connectivity (Wi-Fi, Bluetooth, IRDA, and so on), and if you've got a handheld "data pad" (like an Apple Newton or Nokia 770 or Treo 650), you ought to be able to see and use and share all of your digital resources. But you *can't*—not without a lot of careful handwork involving cables and IP addresses and logins and passwords. They don't have to do that stuff on *Star Trek*—it all just works! Is it just special effects, or are *we* missing something?

Of course, it's long been possible to get Hollywood-like seamlessness from your collection of gadgets, as long as all of those gadgets were produced by the same company. Consider Metaphor's desktop appliance, if you're old enough. It's also possible to "hack together" a pretty decent digital environment if you have a lot of technical skill, a lot of time on your hands, and a willingness to get those hands *very* dirty. Of course, a hand-hewn digital environment won't be very tolerant of change, nor of guests. Why can't we just buy new gadgets, take them home, plug them in (or not!) and use them? If electricity worked like communications, your house would be wired for Apple voltage or Microsoft voltage and you'd need a special step-down transformer if somebody gave you a desk lamp for Christmas that needed the kind of voltage your house didn't have.

Should we be worried by this? Embarrassed? Amused? Since I drink way too much coffee, this kind of thing just makes me angry. I understand why and how deliberate incompatibility can be a powerful tool for competition—look at Microsoft's "embrace and extend" philosophy or at Apple's closed-loop control over iTunes/iPod. But that only works for companies with monopoly power or at least market dominance. What we're getting, though, is a continuous stream of new and incompatible gadgets from companies who have nothing to gain from incompatibility—yet pursue it anyway! Why?

The answer stems from the difficulty inherent in cooperation. When a company ventures alone, variables like "time to market" or "steepness of innovation" are controlled internally—products are successful or not based on the company's ability to make and follow plans. Efficiency in operation, and a proper balance between compactness and grandness of vision, determines the fate of the venture. However, if a company wants to work cooperatively with other companies to put "interoperability" or "seamless integration" into a product, then other variables enter into the mix, variables that are harder to predict or control—for example, "conflicting visions," "conflicting interests," "competitive advantage," or even "efficiency differences." Trying to build a product that's compatible with competitors' products is *much harder* than just building a product that works.

Stuart Cheshire discovered this for himself when he began his "zero configuration networking" effort within the Internet Engineering Task Force (IETF). He found conflicts of vision and interest, and he was beset by differences in efficiency; ultimately, he was forced to admit that IETF just wasn't interested in his work. Luckily for all of us, Stuart's employer (Apple) was *very* interested in his work. Just as luckily, Stuart and Apple both saw interoperability and seamless integration as the keystones on which the Zeroconf technology would stand or fall; the technology is (as far as I know) unencumbered, and Apple's reference implementation is freely available as open source software.

Lo and behold, when I bring up a Linux data pad, laptop, desktop computer, or BSD server, all of my networked printers and file servers can see and reach one another without my having to configure anything. Even my wife's Apple laptop and my kids' Windows PC can play along.

None of the manufacturers—not SuSE, Hewlett Packard, Brother, or even Microsoft—had to license anything from Apple, and yet all of my family's digital gadgets can see one another now, and it's all because of Zeroconf. I consider it pitiful that IETF did nothing to help this effort, but that's a longer story best told over beer. We all owe Stuart Cheshire and Apple a debt of gratitude for their tenacious desire to give to all of us the technology now known as Zeroconf or Bonjour.

Let me close with the story of how Stuart and I met. He had heard that I was a DNS guy and that I'd had something to do with writing BIND, and, since he'd decided to base his "zero configuration networking" technology on DNS, he invited me to lunch and told me his plans. Having drank way too much coffee that day, I told Stuart that he was crazy, that his design was ugly, and that DNS was the wrong way to do this. I didn't say "and the gods shall surely strike you down," but I was certainly thinking it. Fortunately for all of us, Stuart just ignored my tirade, put his shoulder to the wheel, and got on with his work.

—Paul Vixie
La Honda, California, September 2005

# Preface

Two laptop computers sit less than two feet away from each other. They are so close they are nearly touching—and yet, until recently, as far as network communication is concerned, they may as well have been a thousand miles apart. Surely, communicating with a computer in the same room shouldn't have to be as hard as communicating with one on the other side of the planet? Our modern l6aptop computers bristle with an astounding array of communications technologies—Ethernet, 802.11 wireless, FireWire, USB, Infrared, Bluetooth, and so on—yet to move a file between two computers two feet apart, 99% of computer users still use physical media. They copy the file onto a floppy disk, burn the file onto a CD, or copy the file onto a USB flash-memory drive. For the 1% who do manage to move the file using networking, most do so by emailing it from one computer to another, which sometimes entails the file traveling to another continent and back, just to move two feet. To do that, the file has to traverse the slow connection to the global Internet and back, at a speed typically a thousand times slower than local Ethernet. Furthermore, a vast infrastructure of services—DHCP, DNS, IP routers, SMTP relays, email servers, etc.—all have to be working perfectly for the transfer via email to succeed. If the DSL line is down, why should that stop two computers sitting next to each other from communicating?

For computer novices, the situation is puzzling and frustrating. If you can see both computers, why can't the computers *see* each other? There are many ways of physically connecting two devices, but each way often requires its own custom software to do anything useful. If you have two computers with FireWire (also known as IEEE 1394), you can connect them with a FireWire cable, but…do you have any software for transferring files via FireWire? Do you know how to use it? You could connect two computers using the right kind of USB cable, but…would that do anything useful? You could aim the computer's infrared windows at each other, but…do you have any software for transferring files via infrared?

When we communicate across the planet, we use TCP/IP, and we don't care whether the physical connection is Ethernet or 802.11, DSL or cable modem, or a combination of those and other technologies. Could that give us the inspiration for solving the local communication problem? If we use TCP/IP, then it doesn't matter what the physical connection is, as long as it can carry IP packets.

The missing link here is that while TCP/IP is certainly *powerful* enough to solve the local communication problem, historically it was not *easy* enough to use, leading to the proliferation of different physical interfaces mentioned above. It was almost as if computer designers thought that if only we had enough different kinds of hardware, the problem would be solved. What we really needed were not more different kinds of hardware, but better software.

Zero Configuration Networking, or, as Apple calls it, "Bonjour," is that better software.

Zeroconf is the little missing link that makes TCP/IP on the local network as easy as USB. When you plug a Zeroconf camera into your Ethernet hub, it just shows up, as if by magic, in your Zeroconf web browser. It doesn't matter whether you have a working DHCP server. It doesn't matter whether you have a working DNS server. It doesn't matter whether you have a working connection to the Internet. Zeroconf works anyway, even when some or all of that infrastructure is not working. One of the benefits of FireWire and USB is that they can supply power over the cable, but with the advent of the IEEE 802.3af ("Power over Ethernet") standard, modern Ethernet hubs can do that too. A Zeroconf IP camera is as easy to use as a USB camera, except that because it uses IP, it's not tied to one particular physical connection technology. You can be sitting on the sofa with your laptop computer using 802.11 wireless, and the same Zeroconf Ethernet camera shows up in the same web browser, because even though they use different physical technologies, they speak the common language of IP. The web browser doesn't care what physical link-layer connection your computer is using. As long as it carries IP packets, it works.

Finding a TCP/IP printer on the local network is now as easy as using a directly attached USB printer. On Mac OS X, you just look in the print dialog and see a list of available network printers. Using Apple's "Bonjour for Windows," you just run the Printer Setup Wizard, and it shows you the same list of available network printers. If you visit a friend's house, one of your company's other office locations, or a hotel's business center, you don't need to ask for help finding the printer anymore. Just look in the print dialog, and there it is.

Returning to our file-transfer example, now that we know we have a working IP network, no matter what, we have a wealth of IP-based choices. Even the venerable old 1970's File Transfer Protocol (FTP) can benefit from Zeroconf. On Mac OS X, the built-in FTP server already advertises its presence using Zeroconf, and every third-party Mac OS X FTP client now uses Zeroconf to browse for FTP servers, so connecting to an FTP server is now as easy as running your preferred FTP client and picking the desired server from the Zeroconf list.

Other kinds of data sharing are easily facilitated using Zeroconf. If you want to let other machines and devices in your house play music from your computer, iTunes can advertise your music collection using Zeroconf. iPhoto can advertise selected photo albums using Zeroconf so that LCD picture frames hanging on your walls can display them. iChat can advertise your presence on the local network using Zeroconf, and—while we're talking about file transfer—dropping a file onto a Bonjour iChat window is a more direct way of getting a file to someone than emailing it via the public Internet. Finally, if you're collaborating on a document with someone, a multiuser document editor such as SubEthaEdit (which allows multiple people to simultaneously edit a file) is a much more direct way to collaborate than transferring the file back and forth all the time.

All of these data-sharing applications were, in principle, possible before Zeroconf. However, the difficulty of making them work meant that, in practice, people were going to resort to the good old floppy disk. Furthermore, software like SubEthaEdit simply didn't get written back then, even though, in theory, there's no reason it couldn't have been. Local TCP/IP networking was like a complicated machine with no oil. All the right pieces were there, and it looked like it should work, but it took so much effort to get the wheels to turn that almost no one bothered. For communication on the worldwide Internet—for the Web and for email—the pain of TCP/IP was clearly worth it, but for local-area communication people gravitated toward other solutions that offered the promise of better ease of use.

Zeroconf is not some huge, complicated piece of software. It's a small collection of simple ideas that act like the missing lubricant for the TCP/IP machine. Now that people see how easily the wheels turn, they suddenly begin to see all the useful applications of TCP/IP for short-distance communication around the home, around the office, and even around the desktop. TCP/IP is not just for the Internet any more.

Having transformed local-area TCP/IP networking, people realized that Zeroconf's DNS-based Service Discovery mechanisms could be taken back and applied to the wide-area Internet too. Being able to simply browse to find the list of printers on the local network was so useful that people wondered why they couldn't browse to find printers at a specified remote location too, and Wide-Area DNS Service Discovery was born. When staying in a hotel, Zeroconf allows you to see printers being offered by that hotel on its local network, and, with Wide-Area DNS Service Discovery, you can also see printers at your home or office, should you wish to print on one of those instead.

This book provides an in-depth look at the components of Zeroconf technology and a survey of the programming APIs that will allow you to Zeroconf-enable your product.

# Audience for This Book

This book is written for curious users, for software developers, and for hardware developers. Many of the screenshots show images taken from Mac OS X, but that's primarily a reflection of the fact that both the authors primarily use Mac OS X. Don't be misled into thinking this a Macintosh programming book. The concepts and programming examples given in this book are almost exclusively cross-platform. The Zeroconf Multicast DNS daemon and APIs are available on Mac OS X, Windows, Linux, Solaris, FreeBSD, etc. The *dns-sd* command-line tool is available on all those platforms, as are the *dns_sd.h* C programming API, the Java™ API, and the other interfaces for languages like Ruby and Python. Just one chapter, Chapter 9, covers APIs that are specific to Mac OS X.

For curious users who want to understand the technology used by iChat, iTunes, iPhoto, network printing, SubEthaEdit, and countless other applications, this book explains the Zeroconf technology.

For software developers making networking applications, this book explains how you can, with very little effort, make your software a lot easier to use. Going beyond that, this newfound ease-of-use means that previously infeasible software products now become viable. Imagine iChat's local Bonjour Window if you had to type in the IP address of each peer you wanted to chat with. It would be pointless. No one would do it, and there would have been no point even having that feature in the first place. Compare that with iChat as it is today, where it automatically discovers all the local peers on the network and displays them in a list. Now it suddenly becomes a lot more interesting, and that feature becomes worth implementing.

For hardware developers currently making IP-based hardware devices, the message is very similar. This book explains how you can, with very little effort, make your devices a lot easier to use. This translates into thinner manuals, lower support costs, and lower return rates. Those effects, in turn, mean that products that previously would not have been economically viable, because of support costs and product returns, can now be profitable. It was not so long ago that a networked printer cost over $1,000. This was not because an Ethernet chip and some IP software cost that much more than a USB chip. No, it was because of the higher support costs and return rates for these products. Zeroconf cuts those support costs and return rates, and, these days, Zeroconf-enabled Ethernet printers are available for about $100. In many cases, what Zeroconf offers is plain and simple: enhanced functionality. When devices on a network can automatically communicate, advertise, and discover services for themselves, things become possible that simply wouldn't happen if humans had to configure everything manually. Sharing idle CPU cycles on the network has long been a popular idea, yet still, as a percentage of all computer users, very few people make the effort to find out how to make that work. If, instead, all the user had to do was just click a checkbox saying "Share my idle CPU cycles," and Zeroconf automatically did the rest, then CPU sharing could become commonplace instead of remaining a rare novelty.

For hardware developers currently making nonnetworked hardware devices, this book explains how you can add the benefits of TCP/IP networking to your products without having to sacrifice ease of use. The marketplace today is full of computer peripherals that connect through serial, USB, FireWire, or similar technologies, but all of these technologies require the device to be tethered to some host computer. Devices that connect via Ethernet or 802.11 wireless interfaces can be accessed by any computer anywhere in the house, but the pain associated with TCP/IP has always been a strong disincentive. By removing that pain, Zeroconf means it's now practical for many of these serial, USB, and FireWire products to migrate to Ethernet or 802.11 wireless interfaces instead.

# The Zeroconf Technology

At a technical level, Zeroconf is a combination of three technologies. What's more important though is that at a user-experience level, Zeroconf is about making products that "just work." Setting up a network device should be as easy as setting up a new table lamp—you plug it in, you turn it on, and it works. It's important to keep that top-level requirement in mind. At the end of the day, the technologies are the means to the end, not the end in itself. While proper implementation of the specifications is important, that alone is not enough—a worthwhile Zeroconf product is one that embodies the spirit of Zeroconf, not just the letter of the specifications. With that said, our goal can't be achieved without the right technologies. For years, people wished that computers and network devices were easier to use, but wishing it were so did not make it so. Zeroconf is, therefore, about two things: it's about the top-level goal—making products that are truly easy to use—and it's also about the supporting technologies that make that possible. The three technologies that make Zeroconf work are link-local addressing, Multicast DNS, and DNS Service Discovery.

Link-local addressing is described in Chapter 2. To do any IP networking, a computer needs an IP address, and most computers today normally get one using DHCP. DHCP is a perfectly good protocol, and link-local addressing is not competing with that. Link-local addressing is better viewed as a safety net. When DHCP fails or is not available, link-local addressing lets a computer make up an address for itself, so that it can at least communicate on the local link, even if wider communication is not possible. In the case of devices with no screen or keyboard that are configured solely over the network, this is especially important. If they were to get into a state where they lost all ability to communicate, even on the local network, then there would be no way to communicate with the device to fix the misconfiguration that's causing the problem.

Multicast DNS is described in Chapter 3. Ensuring that every computer and network device always has a usable IP address, no matter what, is a good first step, but that alone is not sufficient to provide a good networking experience. Human users want to refer to computers and devices using names, not numeric addresses. On the

Internet today, devices are named using the Domain Name System (DNS). DNS is a wonderful system and works really well. Multicast DNS is not competing with that. Like link-local addressing, Multicast DNS is a safety net, so that when conventional DNS servers are unavailable, unreachable, misconfigured, or otherwise broken, computers and devices can still refer to each other by name in a way that's not dependent on the correct operation of outside infrastructure.

DNS Service Discovery is described in Chapter 4. The two technologies mentioned above get us a lot—now we can refer to a device by name and communicate with it, even when the rest of the network is broken—but we want more. Back in the 1980s and 1990s, in the days of AppleTalk, using an AppleTalk network printer didn't entail having to ask someone the name of the printer, remember it, and then type it in correctly without making a mistake. No, those old enough to remember Apple-Talk will remember that you just looked in the Printer Chooser window, saw a list of informative names, and clicked on the one you wanted to use. We want the same thing on today's IP-based networks. DNS Service Discovery provides that capability. Because it's built on top of DNS, it works not only with our new Multicast DNS (for discovering local services) but also with good old-fashioned, wide-area Unicast DNS (for discovering remote services). Using DNS Service Discovery, the printing software on your computer can conceptually ask the network questions like the following: "I know how to generate PostScript and print it over the network using the LPR protocol. Who out there is willing and able to accept that?" Each printer on the network that is able to accept print jobs via the LPR protocol metaphorically raises its hand and says its name, and that list of names is then presented on the screen for the user to choose from.

Chapter 4 introduces the concepts of DNS Service Discovery and focuses on how it applies to discovering services on the local link using Multicast DNS. Chapter 5 then shows what's involved in extending it to the wide-area Internet, using Unicast DNS. There are two facets to this: outward looking and inward looking. The outward-looking aspect is that when you're away from home or the office (e.g., sitting in a coffeehouse with your laptop computer), you can still discover services at your home or the office. The inward-looking aspect is being able to run services on your own computer and advertise them so they are discoverable and usable by others. For example, you may want to let work colleagues many miles away view and contribute to a document you're editing; you may want to let family members in distant cities view your shared photo albums; or you may want, yourself, to be able to access files on your home computer while you're at work.

Those three technologies are the foundation that Zeroconf provides. What Zeroconf offers you, as a software writer or hardware designer, is:

- The assurance that your software or hardware will always have functional IP networking, no excuses
- The ability to discover what services other devices on the network are offering
- The ability to advertise the services your device offers to the network

Zeroconf doesn't dictate how you should write your software or design your protocol. Zeroconf doesn't dictate whether your protocol should be message- or RPC-oriented, or whether it should be binary, text, XML, or something else. Because it is agnostic to protocol design details, Zeroconf provides a foundation that any IP-based protocol can use, from protocols as ancient as FTP and Telnet to future protocols and products not yet imagined. If you have an existing product that uses TCP/IP, then adding Zeroconf to it is a trivial programming task that gives a huge improvement in usability and reliability. More than once, companies have added Zeroconf to their products with as little as one day's work by one engineer.

Once you understand the ins and outs of the Zeroconf technology, you are going to want to know how to use it for yourself and how to add it to the software or hardware that you make.

## The Zeroconf DNS Service Discovery APIs

Unless you're an operating system vendor or a hardware maker, the first two layers of Zeroconf technology—link-local addressing and Multicast DNS—should be provided for you by operating system components or add-ins. On Mac OS X, they are built-in. On Windows XP, they are provided by Apple's "Bonjour for Windows." On Linux and other Unix platforms, this functionality is available using Apple's Darwin code or a variety of other implementations and is already included in some newer Linux distributions.

Understanding how link-local addressing and Multicast DNS work is valuable background information, but when it comes to actual programming, most programmers will interact with Zeroconf through the DNS Service Discovery APIs in their chosen language.

Chapter 6 introduces the *dns-sd* command-line tool that lets you experiment with Zeroconf service advertising and discovery before you actually write your first line of Zeroconf code.

Chapter 7 introduces the C API for advertising and browsing for services. The same C API exists on Mac OS X, Windows, Linux, and all the supported Unix platforms. In Apple's implementation, all the other APIs are layered on top of the C API. In much the same way as Java sockets on most platforms are implemented by making use of the kernel's native sockets support, Java's DNS-SD API is built on top of the common C API that exists on all supported platforms.

Chapter 8 explains the Java API, which lets you write portable cross-platform programs that will run on any supported platform that has Java and Zeroconf installed.

Chapter 9 describes two of the Bonjour APIs that are specific to Mac OS X: CFNetServices and Cocoa's NSNetServices.

Chapter 10 rounds out the review of APIs, outlining the Zeroconf support appearing in some unexpected languages like Ruby and Python. In fact, the Python support for Zeroconf was built using a technology called Simplified Wrapper and Interface Generator (SWIG, *http://www.swig.org/*), so that single piece of work means Zeroconf service discovery is now accessible from a wide variety of well-known and lesser-known programming languages, including Tcl, Perl, Scheme, PHP, Objective Caml, Pike, C#, Allegro Common Lisp, and Modula-3.

## Conventions Used in This Book

The following typographical conventions are used in this book:

Plain text
> Indicates menu titles, menu options, menu buttons, and keyboard accelerators (such as Alt and Ctrl).

*Italic*
> Indicates new terms, URLs, email addresses, filenames, file extensions, pathnames, directories, and Unix utilities.

`Constant width`
> Indicates commands, options, switches, variables, attributes, keys, functions, types, classes, namespaces, methods, modules, properties, parameters, values, objects, events, event handlers, XML tags, HTML tags, macros, the contents of files, or the output from commands.

**`Constant width bold`**
> Shows commands or other text that should be typed literally by the user.

*`Constant width italic`*
> Shows text that should be replaced with user-supplied values.

> This icon signifies a tip, suggestion, or general note.

> This icon indicates a warning or caution.

## Using Code Examples

This book is here to help you get your job done. In general, you may use the code in this book in your programs and documentation. You do not need to contact us for permission unless you're reproducing a significant portion of the code. For example, writing a program that uses several chunks of code from this book does not require permission. Selling or distributing a CD-ROM of examples from O'Reilly books *does* require permission. Answering a question by citing this book and quoting example code does not require permission. Incorporating a significant amount of example code from this book into your product's documentation *does* require permission.

We appreciate, but do not require, attribution. An attribution usually includes the title, author, publisher, and ISBN. For example: *"Zero Configuration Networking: The Definitive Guide*, by Stuart Cheshire and Daniel H. Steinberg. Copyright 2006 O'Reilly Media, Inc., 0-596-10100-7."

If you feel your use of code examples falls outside fair use or the permission given above, feel free to contact us at *permissions@oreilly.com*.

## Comments and Questions

Please address comments and questions concerning this book to the publisher:

> O'Reilly Media, Inc.
> 1005 Gravenstein Highway North
> Sebastopol, CA 95472
> (800) 998-9938 (in the United States or Canada)
> (707) 829-0515 (international or local)
> (707) 829-0104 (fax)

We have a web page for this book, where we list errata, examples, and any additional information. You can access this page at:

> *http://www.oreilly.com/catalog/bonjour*

To comment or ask technical questions about this book, send email to:

> *bookquestions@oreilly.com*

For more information about our books, conferences, Resource Centers, and the O'Reilly Network, see our web site at:

> *http://www.oreilly.com*

## Safari Enabled

 When you see a Safari® Enabled icon on the cover of your favorite technology book, that means the book is available online through the O'Reilly Network Safari Bookshelf.

Safari offers a solution that's better than e-books. It's a virtual library that lets you easily search thousands of top tech books, cut and paste code samples, download chapters, and find quick answers when you need the most accurate, current information. Try it for free at *http://safari.oreilly.com*.

# Acknowledgments

## Stuart Cheshire

My thanks go to Dan, my able coauthor, without whom this book would not exist. Thanks also to Mike Loukides, our editor, for striking the right balance between patience and impatience, without which this book would never have been finished. Thanks especially to Tim O'Reilly, who saw the promise of Bonjour/Zeroconf (or Rendezvous, as it was then) from the very start and persuaded me to publish an O'Reilly book on the subject.

Thanks to all the people who, through their own initiative, enthusiasm, and efforts, helped make Bonjour a success. Thanks to Kiren Sekar, for his work on the conformance test, the C API, and wide-area Bonjour; to Marc Krochmal, for immeasurable contributions in countless areas; to Craig Keithley, for his tireless evangelism efforts; and to Angie Sticher, Vincent Lubet, and Howard Miller, for their organizational contributions. Thanks to Josh Graessley and Dieter Siegmund, for providing the necessary kernel support, including IPv4 link-local addressing; to Quinn, for the initial Linux support; to Roger Pantos, for the mdnsd daemon for Linux and for the Java APIs; to Bob Bradley and Scott Herscher, for Bonjour for Windows; to Rich Kilmer, for the Ruby APIs; to Thomas Uram, for the SWIG interface definition file; and to Erik Guttman and Bernard Aboba, my coauthors on RFC 3927, the IPv4 link-local addressing specification.

Thanks for their various contributions are also owed to: Mike Bell, Richard Blanchard, Leigh Blankenship, Rob Braun, Joyce Chow, Mike Culbert, Paul Danbold, Moe Gharahgouzloo, David Harrington, Dave Heller, James Higa, Arthur van Hoff, Joe Holt, Jordan Hubbard, Brian James, Deep Jawa, Bryan Johns, Rod Lopez, Jim Lovell, Kevin Marks, Rob Newberry, Juliette Noh, Chris Parker, Eric Peyton, Jeff Robbin, David ("Lefty") Schlesinger, Bud Tribble, Andrew White, James Woodyatt, and Jeremy Wyld.

Thanks to my wife, Pavni, and daughter, Ishani, for their patience while I worked on the book.

Thanks to Lewin, Marta, Ed, and the rest of the staff of the Progresso coffeeshop on Portobello Road, for my twice-daily cappuccinos while I worked on the book.

Thanks also to Simon Patience, Bertrand Serlet, and the rest of my Apple management and colleagues, for giving me this opportunity.

## Daniel H. Steinberg

My biggest thanks go to Stuart Cheshire for creating such a nice piece of technology and for coauthoring this book. I remember seeing the demo of Bonjour (then under a different name) at Apple's Worldwide Developers Conference. It was immediately compelling. Bonjour was one of those ideas that was both obvious and groundbreaking. The underlying ideas were solid and the implementation was impressive. In addition to his contributions as an engineer, he is a careful author who explains precisely what he means to say in an easily understood manner.

Thanks also to Apple employees: Marc Krochmal, for answering all of my questions and for providing code samples that illuminated the corners of the technology; Roger Pantos, for his work with the Java API and his cheerful answers to questions; Bob Bradley, for his help with the examples for the Windows event loop; and David Gleason, for being such a helpful member of the Apple Developer Connection.

As always, many thanks to my wife, Kim. No book project would be possible without her help and support. My daughters, Maggie Rose and Elena, tested the software examples in this book and showed that Bonjour can be intuitive to a six- and an eight-year-old. As we were preparing to write this book, I was hired by O'Reilly Media to launch the java.net web site. Thanks to the great team on the O'Reilly side for making that site, and our onjava.com and dev2dev.com sites, so successful. In particular, thank you Sarah Kim, Tony Stubblebine, David Lents, Jon Mountjoy, Derrick Story, Miky Vacik, and Greg Dickerson. Bruce Stewart is the best boss I've ever had. I wish I'd learned earlier in my career the importance of having such a great manager. I have also worked closely with his boss, Nancy Abila, and appreciate how she also makes it possible for me to do my best work.

Chris Adamson and I have worked together on the O'Reilly Java web sites during the entire writing of this book. He has written two books during that time and has supported me during the writing of this book. Finally, thank you to Mike Loukides, who edited this book with the right amount of pushing and encouragement.

# CHAPTER 1

# Introduction to Bonjour and Zeroconf

You walk in a few minutes late to a meeting and want to know what you've missed. You open your text editor and your computer automatically discovers a shared document in which one or more attendees are taking notes. You have a couple of colleagues who are busy in another meeting but are interested in the topics being discussed in your meeting. You invite your colleagues to view the notes being taken and to contribute their comments and questions. A presenter announces that anyone wanting a copy of his slides should let him know. You open your local Instant Messenger application and see his name in the list of available names, even though you have never met before and he is not in your buddy list. A moment later, he has placed his presentation in your drop box in your Public folder, which he has discovered in his network directory.

The meeting comes to an end. Before anyone erases the whiteboard, someone snaps a quick picture or two and puts it in their photo-sharing library so that anyone interested can download it. You notice a new entry in your audio software that announces that the person who was recording the session has already posted it in her shared audio library. Before you save the notes on the session, you decide to print out a copy to read on the plane ride back. In the print dialog, you discover several printers and choose the one labeled "Third Floor Meeting Rooms."

This is not a fantastical glimpse of the elusive future. It is a concrete description of what is available today using Zeroconf. In this chapter, you will get a quick overview of the various components that make up Zeroconf. In the following four chapters, these details will be fleshed out. The second half of this chapter examines the Zeroconf design principles that build on two decades of experience with the AppleTalk Name Binding Protocol.

## Service Discovery with Zeroconf

None of the examples that took advantage of Zeroconf began with someone thinking, "You know what I could really use right now? An IP address." Certainly, it's a

## Zeroconf's Many Names

The seeds of Zeroconf were planted in some postings by Stuart Cheshire on the Net-Thinkers mailing list in 1997. This led to the IETF holding two "Birds of a Feather" (BOF) sessions at the March and July 1999 IETF meetings on the subject of "Networking in the Small" (NITS), co-chaired by Stuart Cheshire and Peter Ford.

Out of the NITS BOF meetings, the Zero Configuration Networking (Zeroconf) Working Group was formed in September 1999.

In May 2002, Apple announced its trademark "Rendezvous" for the Zeroconf technologies, a little like the way Apple uses its trademark "AirPort" for IEEE 802.11 wireless networking.

Unfortunately for Apple, another company also had a networking product by the name of "Rendezvous," and in April 2005, Apple announced the new Apple name for the Zeroconf technologies: "Bonjour." Other third-party products can also carry the Bonjour name and logo. Apple doesn't charge any money to license the name and logo; the products just have to pass Apple's Bonjour Conformance Test to verify that they do in fact implement the specifications properly.

Meanwhile, other open source implementations of the Zeroconf technologies have also been created, including Howl and Avahi.

The terms "Bonjour" and "Zeroconf" are often used interchangeably, but as a general rule, this book uses the term "Zeroconf" when referring to the technology in general and "Bonjour" when referring to it in an Apple-specific context. For example, iChat on Mac OS X doesn't have a "Zeroconf" window; it has a "Bonjour" window (it says "Bonjour" at the top of the window).

rare person who takes the time to say, "Now that I have an IP address, I could use a friendly domain name. I should learn how to set up DNS on my laptop." A typical user of Zeroconf should not be aware of the infrastructure required. She just wants to use a printer, stream music, exchange photos, or use some other service.

The architecture of Zeroconf is built around simplicity. It should be as easy for an end user to connect to a printer or locate streamed music as it is for him to turn on a light bulb. The simplicity extends to implementers as well. A vendor of an inexpensive device who desires to use Zeroconf should not find it hard to implement Zeroconf, even in devices with extremely limited memory capacity.

## Service Discovery

To the end user, the most important facet of Zeroconf is the ability to *easily browse for available services*. It is worth taking a moment to appreciate the significance of the concepts encapsulated in that short phrase. Start with these five highlighted words as the prime directive for Zeroconf.

## Browse for services

With Zeroconf, you browse for services, not for hardware. The reason for this is simple but important: if you want to print, there is little benefit to discovering hardware that doesn't do printing. Similarly, there is little benefit to discovering things that *are* printers but speak only a printing protocol that your client does not support, since you wouldn't be able to use those printers. Conversely, suppose that there is a device on the network in a legal office that functions, protocol-wise, as a printer, but instead of printing on paper, it archives documents as date-stamped PDF files on recordable CDs. You *would* want your printing client to discover this service, since it's a service your printing client can use. Suppose there were an inexpensive USB printer (which doesn't have Postscript or networking) connected to a desktop computer (which does), with software making Postscript printing service available to other machines on the network via IPP (Internet Printing Protocol). You *would* want your Postscript IPP printing client to discover this service, since it's a service you can use. What is it that your printing client is discovering, in this case? The USB printer? The desktop computer? The software? No. The insight here is to realize that what your printing client is discovering is the aggregate service offered by the computer, the printer, and the software working in concert, and it is that aggregate service that is being advertised as a logical entity on the network in its own right. The USB printer could break and be replaced, and the logical service being offered would remain the same. The desktop computer could break and be replaced, and the logical service being offered would remain the same. Even the software could be upgraded or replaced, while the logical Postscript IPP printing service being offered to network clients would remain unchanged. The important principle here is that when you're looking for services on the network, the relevant question is not "What are you?" or even "What do you do?" but "Do you speak my language?"

## Available services

The list that the user gets should be services that are currently available to them. They should be able to see the list of currently available printers, select one, and use it. As with all such network protocol designs, there is a trade-off between timeliness of information and network efficiency. Continuously querying the network to find what services are available gives accurate, up-to-date information but can impose an unreasonable burden on the network. Querying the network just once is much more efficient, but the client's information soon gets out of date, necessitating a "refresh" button in the UI, which then puts the burden on the human user to keep clicking the refresh button (which puts a burden on the network). Zeroconf solves these problems using a variety of techniques. For efficiency, clients query the network infrequently, as little as once per hour. To avoid long delays before new services are discovered, when a service starts up it sends a few multicast announcement packets, so clients become aware of the new service even before performing their next scheduled query. IP Multicast addresses are special destination addresses that cause packets to be delivered to all interested parties on the local network, rather than just to a single machine. When services go away, they send multicast "goodbye" packets, so they are promptly removed from all clients' UI lists. In the event that a service is unceremoniously disconnected without getting a chance to send its "goodbye" packet, stale data may remain in lists for a while, but even this case is handled by Zeroconf. When a client attempts to contact a stale service that is no longer present, the failure is noted, and the service is promptly removed from the list of available services. This prompt removal occurs not only on the client that directly experienced the failure but also on all the other clients on the same network link, which passively observe the failure and update their own lists too. Zeroconf uses these and a variety of other techniques to provide timely, accurate information while keeping the network traffic to a minimum.

This kind of peer-to-peer, multicast-based protocol is great for small networks because it is very reliable and requires no dedicated service-discovery infrastructure, but no matter how efficient the protocol, there will come a network size where it no longer makes sense. In an organization with thousands of machines, having every single machine multicasting to every other machine all the time would not be reasonable. Beyond a certain size, every service-discovery protocol has to transition from using peer-to-peer multicast to some kind of centralized repository to hold service information. Services and clients communicate with the centralized repository using a wide-area protocol. In Zeroconf, the centralized repository is one that most companies already have—a DNS server—and the wide-area protocol is the standard DNS protocol with two small extensions, Update Leases and Long-Lived Queries. Update Leases allow a DNS server to expire server records if the service that created them crashes, and Long-Lived Queries allow a client to be notified as services come and go, rather than having to keep polling the server to find out what's new.

### Easy browsing

Zeroconf would never have been so widely adopted if using it required popping open a terminal window and typing in obscure commands. Command-line tools are great for developers and network administrators, but end users will be browsing for services within a context. They are not conscious that they are requesting a list of services that implement a protocol. For example, when running iTunes, users simply see a list called "Shared Music." They don't need to be aware that iTunes is performing a query for Zeroconf service type _daap._tcp to find the list of local servers offering the Digital Audio Access Protocol (DAAP) service.

Another thing you'll notice is that the names of shared music sources displayed in iTunes don't need to look like "thing.company.com," all lowercase with no spaces or other punctuation. In the example at the beginning of this chapter, the printer was named "Third Floor Meeting Rooms," not "f3mr.company.com." In command-line user interfaces, you want names to be short and quick to type. In graphical user interfaces, you don't need to type names because you just select them from a list of choices, so they can be long and descriptive and can contain rich punctuation, accented letters, and non-roman characters, such as Kanji.

## Names and Addresses

Although service discovery is the most visible element of Zeroconf, Zeroconf is more than just that. Zeroconf is a three-layer foundation for IP networking, with service discovery sitting atop the two lower layers, addressing and naming.

### Claiming an IP address

The first requirement for IP networking is an IP address. There are existing mechanisms for IPv4 address allocation, such as using manual configuration or a DHCP server, but when neither of these is available, Zeroconf-capable devices will use a self-assigned IPv4 link-local address instead. In brief, the mechanism behind self-assigned addresses is that the device selects an address at random within a prescribed range, sends some ARP requests, and then, if no answers are received, proceeds to use that address. Self-assigned IPv4 link-local addresses are discussed in detail in Chapter 2. IPv6 also has self-assigned link-local addresses, though sadly, at the present time—even though Mac OS X, Windows, and Linux all support IPv6—most of the low-cost peripherals that they talk to, such as printers and cameras, don't yet support IPv6.

### Claiming a name

The second requirement is that the typical usage model for IP networking expects hosts to have names, not just numerical addresses. Having to remember and type numerical addresses is cumbersome at best, and when the addresses are being picked randomly, it may not even be possible. We need a way to associate a stable name with each device, in order to determine what address it has picked for itself, at this instant. The Internet's existing mechanism for associating names with addresses is a DNS server, but when no DNS server is available, Zeroconf-capable devices will use Multicast DNS (mDNS) to achieve substantially the same effect on the local link, without having to set up and maintain a dedicated DNS server. In brief, the mechanism behind mDNS names is very similar to self-assigned addresses: the device sends a few mDNS queries for its desired name, and if no answers are received, the device can then use that name. Multicast DNS naming is discussed in detail in Chapter 3.

# Replacing the AppleTalk Name Binding Protocol

At the end of any software engineering effort, the developers have a deep understanding of the problem they were solving. Imagine how much better the finished product would be if they had time to start over with the benefit of the experience they have gained. The DNS Service Discovery (DNS-SD) layer of Zeroconf builds on years of experience with AppleTalk and its Name Binding Protocol (NBP) and improves on the earlier technology while building an all-IP solution.

---

## Why IP?

Over the last 30 years, many protocols have competed in both the wide-area networking (WAN) and local-area networking (LAN) arenas. In the WAN arena, it is clear that IP won, and even in the LAN arena, IP is rapidly gaining ground. When people have networks within their homes today, using Ethernet or IEEE 802.11 wireless, it is generally IP that they use most over those networks, rather than other protocols like AppleTalk or NetBEUI. The last remaining place where non-IP protocols still thrive is in short-distance links tethered close to the computer, but even these are showing signs of migrating to IP. USB, FireWire, and Bluetooth all now have ways to carry standard IP packets in addition to their own various task-specific protocols. To illustrate with just one example, when using the native file copying protocols, copying files between two computers using Bluetooth uses different software and a different user interface than copying over FireWire, which is different than copying over USB, and so on. In contrast, when using IP over those same physical links, any given software application (e.g., FTP) works exactly the same way, regardless of whether the underlying hardware is USB, FireWire, Bluetooth, Ethernet, 802.11, or something else.

What made USB and FireWire attractive compared to IP for short-distance communication is that they are relatively easy to use and hassle-free. With Zeroconf bringing the same convenience and ease of use to IP, one of the last remaining objections to using IP for short-distance communication, as well as wide-area communication, has been eliminated.

---

AppleTalk NBP communicated the available services in a way that was logically consistent with an end user's perspective. Additionally, NBP allowed users to perform an action using a connected device without needing to know the device's address and without needing to become their own network administrator. Although DNS-SD is not simply a rewrite of AppleTalk NBP, there are many things that NBP got right, and DNS-SD brings those properties to IP networking.

## Name Services, Not Hardware

In AppleTalk NBP, the primary named entity is not a piece of hardware or even a piece of software but a logical service with which you can communicate using a particular specified protocol. There is little benefit for the average user in being able to locate and connect to a device if she cannot communicate with it. The implication is that it is most useful to name entities with which you can communicate. DNS-SD maintains the same philosophy, naming logical services as the primary entity on the network. Continuing this philosophy further, it is important not only what the service does, in a

---

human sense, but what network protocol it uses to do it, since there's no use discovering it if your client can't talk to it. For example, when you use a web browser to view a web site with the URL *www.example.com*, you generally do not know or care much which particular device is answering your request. What you care about is that it speaks Hypertext Transfer Protocol (HTTP), and that the content it sends you is something your web browser knows how to decode and display, typically Hyper Text Markup Language (HTML), and that the content relates to the *example.com* domain.

Suppose you are interested in locating web sites hosted on your local network. Suppose you could find the IP addresses of all nearby machines. Then what? You could try to contact them with your web browser using the well-known port 80. But it is certainly possible for a single device to host more than one web site, listening on different ports. What you really want is a different sort of browser that could locate all local services that offer HTML over HTTP. Zeroconf's DNS-SD allows these services to advertise themselves as offering HTML over HTTP and provide their name, IP address, and port number.

---

### Reaching a Device Versus Using It

In the early days of computers, files saved from one word processor couldn't be read by another. Merely having access to the file was not enough—to properly interpret it, the software had to also understand the language used to encode all of its formatting and other information. Similarly, merely being able to create a TCP connection to a device is not sufficient to use it. The client and the service need to speak the same language (i.e., network protocol) to communicate usefully.

---

Historically, Internet protocols have assumed so-called "well-known" port numbers. When you look up the address of *www.example.com*, the Domain Name System tells your computer the IP address of the machine to contact but not the TCP port number. The historical solution to this problem is that your web browser assumes that the desired web server must be listening on TCP port 80. If it's not (e.g., because two web server processes are running on the same machine and they can't both use the same TCP port), then blindly assuming TCP port 80 won't work. You have to manually override the default port, as in *http://www.example.com:1234*. While that may superficially seem to work, it has problems. Once you've published that URL, if you change the port number the server is listening on, the URL will stop working. It's fragile, like publishing a URL with a fixed dotted-decimal IP address embedded in it instead of a DNS name.

Another problem with "well-known" port numbers is that if every new protocol gets its own reserved number, we're in danger of running out. You can see the currently assigned port numbers at *http://www.iana.org/assignments/port-numbers*. Thousands are already reserved for applications you will probably never run on your computer.

Zeroconf's DNS-SD solves this problem by using DNS "SRV" records, which tell the client the service's port number as well as its IP address, obviating the need for pre-allocated "well-known" port numbers. Any service can use any available port on your computer and advertise its port to prospective clients along with its IP address.

## Late Binding

AppleTalk NBP has a mechanism for browsing the network for services, but, as its name emphasizes, it is primarily a Name Binding Protocol. Its primary function is binding human-meaningful names to computer-meaningful network addresses. A human user will use the browsing capabilities to locate a service initially, such as selecting a default printer, but every time the name service is used subsequently, the Name Binding Protocol is used to find out the current network address and port number for that service. This means that even if the printer address changes, clients will still be able to connect to it at the new address without disruption.

This late binding of a name to an address is an important feature of a technology intended to replace AppleTalk. If a service is available on a network that uses DHCP or link-local addressing, there is no guarantee that the device hosting the service will have a consistent IP address. When ports are allocated dynamically, there's no guarantee the service will always be running on the same port. Late binding ensures that the client attempts to connect to the current IP address and port number.

## Finding Named Services

Service requests consist of asking for a service of a particular type in a particular domain. This builds on the AppleTalk convention of using names structured as Name: Type @ Zone. The Zone in AppleTalk NBP corresponded to some logical grouping based on location ("Third Floor") or organizational classification ("Sales"). The equivalent concept in DNS is a subdomain, such as *sales.example.com* or *thirdfloor. example.com*. These replacements for zones provide an independent namespace so that there is no confusion in printers with the same name that are located in different zones.

In AppleTalk NBP, the Type identified the protocol that the service speaks. So, for example, the NBP Service Type "LaserWriter" denotes a service that speaks Post-Script over AppleTalk Printer Access Protocol over AppleTalk Transaction Protocol over AppleTalk Datagram Delivery Protocol. The equivalent DNS-SD service type might be _ipp._tcp, which indicates a printer that speaks the Internet Printer Protocol (IPP) over TCP over IP.

## Built to Last

Application-layer protocols come and go. A service discovery protocol is a more foundational technology and cannot be built on a faddish technology. There are Zeroconf APIs for a wide range of languages to support programmers using everything from C, C++, Java, and C# to Perl, PHP, and Ruby. The Zeroconf daemon runs on Mac OS X, Linux, Windows, and various flavors of Unix. Zeroconf is agnostic to application protocol design; it can advertise any kind of application protocol, from ancient ones such as Telnet and FTP to future application protocols not yet imagined.

The Name portion should be a user-friendly name. With this approach, the names are both long and descriptive. The end user will be employing a browser of some sort to select named services from a list. As they will not have to type the service name every time they want to use a service, the names should not be cryptic for the sake of making them shorter. So, for example, there could be a service with the full name 3rd Floor Meeting Rooms._ipp_tcp.examples.com. Notice that the service name can contain spaces as well as dots, percent signs, and other symbols. The character set is also not restricted to US-ASCII; users are free to choose names using any legal Unicode characters.

## Name Conflict Detection

Without a central network administrator, there is a possibility that two devices may want to use the same name. Because Zeroconf requires that the devices be self-configuring, the devices have to be able to sort out the conflict themselves. For example, you may buy two printers and connect them into the same network. They ship from the factory with the same name, "CompanyX Printer." When the second one is connected and a conflict is detected, the second one needs to choose another name, such as "CompanyX Printer (2)." If the human user prefers to have a more descriptive name, most printers provide a web-based interface or something similar that allows the user to enter a descriptive name of his choice to identify the printer. On devices such as laptop computers, which are designed for human interaction, a dialog is typically shown to inform the user if a name conflict occurs and to give him the opportunity to select a new name, if desired.

## Ease of Use

When a device is first connected to a network, it must manually or automatically gather information about the local network. With mobile devices, this happens often enough that it is unreasonable to require that a human configure the device every time the device joins a new link. For example, where a site offers one or more DNS domains with services available for browsing, the device should be able to learn this from the network, rather than requiring it to be manually configured by the human user.

The list of services displayed in the browser should be dynamic. You have seen discovery mechanisms that use an icon or dialog to indicate that the list of services is being updated. After some unacceptably long delay, a static list of results is displayed. The only way to refresh this list is for the user to press a refresh button or for the client application to regularly poll for available services. In a Zeroconf-based service browser, less than a second elapses from the time that a user initiates browsing to when she is presented with a list of results. The browser will not burden the network with frequent polling for available services. The list will update to add or remove services based on announcements from the services, from non-renewed leases, and from multicast messages from other devices attempting to use a listed service.

## Summary

Zero Configuration Networking—Bonjour, as Apple calls it—provides a three-layer foundation to enable hardware and software makers to produce great products. Zeroconf doesn't do printing. Zeroconf doesn't do network music. Zeroconf doesn't do photo sharing or multiuser document editing or instant messaging. What Zeroconf does is provide the rock-solid foundation so that those great products can be built without worrying that, from time to time, TCP/IP might fall apart and let them down.

Chapter 2 describes the first layer of the three-layer foundation: getting an IP address when there's no working DHCP server. Chapter 3 describes the second layer: being able to refer to hosts by name when there's no working DNS server. Chapter 4 describes the third layer: discovering what's available on the network without having to ask the person sitting next to you for help. Chapter 5 extends Chapter 4's local service discovery out to the global Internet. The second half of the book, Chapters 6 and onward, presents the APIs in various different languages that allow you to use local- and wide-area service discovery in your hardware and software products.

# IP Addresses Without DHCP

Each device on an IP network will need at least one unique IP address. Until you run your own network, you may not think very hard about how this works. You or someone from the IT staff most likely configured your computer at work to use a specified IP address or to use the company DHCP server, but the days when networks existed only at a few large universities and companies are behind us. Nowadays, there are small networks popping up everywhere. Computers and devices need to communicate. Your home may have a computer or two, a printer, a scanner, a digital camera, and a phone. You do not want to learn to be a network administrator just to get these devices to play nicely together, and there's no reason you should have to—just like there's no reason you should have to learn to be a car mechanic before you can drive a car.

You will see even more of these small local networks connecting various devices pop up at homes, coffee shops, or while on a walk. If we are to standardize on IP for communication among devices, it needs to be easier for them to obtain IP addresses. Suppose you take a bunch of pictures with your digital camera and wish to print them, save them to your computer, or transfer them to a friend's. When you cable that digital camera to a printer or a hard drive, or you connect your computer to your friend's wirelessly, you don't really want to have to depend on a DHCP server being present, and you don't really want to have to configure each device manually with an IP address. You would like there to be an automatic configuration of IP addresses that provides each device with a unique address.

In this chapter, we present three different ways in which a device may obtain an IP address: manual, DHCP, or self-assigned. As a motivating analogy, imagine that you want to enter a 65,000-seat auditorium to attend a networking lecture. At the moment, several seats are occupied. There are a variety of strategies that could be used:

- We could require that every student attending the lecture obtain a seat assignment in advance from an auditorium administrator. Each student arrives at the auditorium with a preprinted ticket and will refuse to sit in any seat other than his assigned one. If, by mistake, two students have been assigned to the same seat, then one of two things will happen. The first possibility is that if either of the two students behaves like Mac OS or Windows, one of the two students will leave the auditorium and complain to the administrator about the mistake. The administrator is expected to correct the mistake. The second possibility is that if both of the students behave like some other operating systems, a violent fistfight will ensue, not stopping until either at least one participant is dead or the human administrator intervenes and forcibly drags one or the other combatant (or both) from the auditorium against their will. This is analogous to manual address assignment. It is heavily dependent on the auditorium administrator never making a mistake.

- We could provide a ticket window. When each student arrives at the auditorium, she goes to the ticket window and requests a ticket. The ticket seller hands her a ticket for a seat that is supposed to be (as far as the seller knows) unoccupied. If the student finds some antisocial person already sitting in her seat, then rather than getting into a fight, she simply returns to the ticket window and requests a different ticket. This is analogous to using a DHCP server. This has some advantages over manual assignment but does require that we provide a ticket window and staff it.

- We could expect the students to find vacant seats for themselves. In this case each student arrives equipped with some kind of personal random-number generator, and each seat is equipped with a load sensor that can determine if someone is sitting there. Before entering the auditorium, each student uses the personal random-number generator to select some seat number at random. They then enter that number on a keypad outside the auditorium door. If the seat is occupied, a red light above the keypad illuminates and the student picks another random number and tries again. If, after a second or two, the red light has not illuminated, the student enters the auditorium and takes his seat. This is analogous to self-assigned link-local address assignment.

Analogies between computers and day-to-day life generally should not be taken too literally, and this one is no exception. In this last analogy, it would seem that a student might have to try many times before finding a vacant seat. In reality, the density of usage of self-assigned link-local addresses is intentionally kept very low, for precisely this reason. Even though 65,000 addresses are available, it would be rare to have a single Zeroconf network with more than 1,000 hosts on it. In fact, 10 might be a more typical number, and the network could be as small as just two devices. Even in the extreme case of 1000 devices on a single Ethernet, still less than 2% of the available addresses would be in use, so a new device joining the network would have a 98% chance of finding a free address on the first try. This example is given for IPv4 link-local addresses, but IPv6 also has link-local addresses, and even more are available. With IPv6, there are $2^{118}$ link-local addresses (RFC 2462), which is more than $10^{35}$, so the chance of an address conflict is tiny.

As described in Chapter 1, the Zeroconf technique for obtaining a unique IP address is as simple as practically possible. Choose an IP address and check that no one else has already claimed it. If someone has, then choose another address. If the address has not yet been claimed, then claim and defend it. In this chapter, you will look at some of the details glossed over in this simplified description.

# Obtaining an IP Address

There are two components to choosing an IP address for a given network. You need to find a legitimate address and you need to confirm that you are the only one using this particular address on this network. A network administrator can manually assign your IP address. In this case, the administrator is responsible for ensuring the assigned address is available and unique. If there is a DHCP server configured for your network, you can use it to obtain a unique IP address. Zeroconf allows you to automatically select an IP address in the absence of a DHCP server or network administrator.

## Manual Assignment

Whatever your platform of choice, there is usually some way to configure your network settings by hand. Often, there is a GUI that makes it easy for you to enter your IP address, subnet mask, and gateway/router information. In Mac OS X 10.4, you either select Network after choosing Apple Menu → System Preferences… or by selecting the Apple Menu → Location → Network Preferences… item.

### Entering an IP address

In the example shown in Figure 2-1, the IP address 192.168.1.123 has been selected. For now, this discussion is limited to IPv4 addresses. These are 32-bit values that are usually written as four positive integers, each between 0 and 255, separated by dots. This familiar format is known as *dotted decimal*.

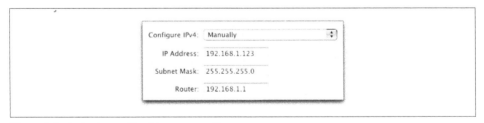

*Figure 2-1. Assigning an IP address manually*

The second number that you enter is the *subnet mask*. This is also a 32-bit number and is used to indicate which portion of the IP address contains information about the network and which portion contains information about the host. The network information corresponds to those bits that are turned on in the subnet mask. In the example shown in Figure 2-1, the first 24 bits are on and the last 8 bits are off. You can also represent the information contained in the IP address and subnet mask fields together by writing 192.168.1.123/24. The forward slash and the 24 at the end indicate that the first 24 bits are reserved for the network information, so the remaining 8 bits are for the host information. The host uses this information to determine how to deliver IP packets. When sending a packet, the host checks the network number (the first 24 bits, in this example) in the destination address, and if that exactly matches the network number in its own address, that means that the destination is on the same subnet and the packet is sent directly to the destination machine. Otherwise, the destination is not on the same subnet, so the packet is sent to the default gateway for forwarding on to its eventual destination.

The third number you enter is your local router or gateway. This is the router's address within your subnet. In other words, within the 256 possible 32-bit addresses that begin with 192.168.1, the router has host address 1 and the machine currently being configured will have host address 123. The router also has an IP address on its upstream interface connecting to the rest of the Internet. Whenever your machine wants to communicate with a host that it can't reach directly (see the sidebar "Link or Subnet?"), it needs to send the packet to the router, which will forward the packet on to its eventual destination. A certain kind of router, called a Network Address Translation (NAT) router, will also rewrite the packet header while forwarding it, to make it appear that all packets actually originate from its single external IP address. This allows several hosts to appear to share a single public IP address, but header rewriting is not a perfect technology, and hosts that are stuck behind a NAT router are limited in the things they can do. Web browsing, email, and a few other things work, but there are many less well-known IP applications that do not survive header rewriting and cannot be used by hosts stuck behind a NAT router. Technology to overcome this limitation is described in Chapter 5, in which we discuss service discovery beyond the local link.

There are other numbers not shown in Figure 2-1 that you may also need to enter. For example, if you want to resolve URLs—such as *http://www.oreilly.com*—to their corresponding IP addresses, you will need to have the address of one or more DNS servers. You will learn more about DNS in Chapter 3.

### Choosing an IP address

If an IP address is to be entered by hand, this address should be obtained from a network administrator. The administrator will know which subnets have been set up and which IP addresses are currently available on each. A central authority is responsible for assigning the addresses and avoiding conflicts. The example shown in Figure 2-1 is fairly typical for a home or otherwise small network with a single, external (and possibly dynamic) IP address. Some operating systems will display a message if you try to assign an address that is already in use. Figure 2-2 shows an example of an address conflict message.

## Link or Subnet?

Computer networking professionals often use the terms *link* and *subnet* interchangeably, which is not always accurate.

A *link* is a physical-layer concept. Using Ethernet as an example, when you send an Ethernet broadcast, all the devices that receive that broadcast are on the same link.

A *subnet* is a network-layer concept. A subnet is a range of IP addresses that are all mutually reachable from one another, directly, without going through a router.

In an ideal world, there would be an exact one-to-one correspondence between links and subnets. However, as new computers are added, sometimes all the available addresses in a subnet are exhausted. At this stage, the right thing to do might be to enlarge the subnet, but that would involve changing the subnet mask on all the existing machines, which could be something of a hassle. Because of this, network administrators will often just add a second IP subnet to the same Ethernet, so that there are *two* IP subnets on the same link. This means that when a computer in subnet A sends a packet to a computer in subnet B, it could, in principle, send it directly, but it doesn't know that. When it consults its routing table, it finds that the destination is not in its subnet and sends the packet to the router for forwarding. The router *does* know that both subnets are on the same link, so it turns the packet around and sends it back on the same Ethernet to its destination. This is obviously inefficient, in terms of both network bandwidth and utilization of router resources, but it is nonetheless more common than it should be. One solution to this problem is provided by RFC 3442, "The DHCPv4 Classless Static Route Option," which allows a DHCP server to tell the clients that they have more than one subnet that's directly reachable without going through the router, but it may be many years before RFC 3442 is widely implemented and deployed.

If a link can have more than one subnet, is the converse true? Can a subnet span more than one link? Generally, the answer is no. When a device wants to send an IP packet to a destination address on the same subnet, then instead of sending the packet to a router for forwarding, it broadcasts an IPv4 ARP (or IPv6 Neighbor Discovery) packet asking "Who has this address?" and waits for the response, then sends the IP packet directly to the recipient as the payload of a link-layer packet. The prerequisite for this to work is that both the link-layer broadcast and the subsequent link-layer unicast have to reach the relevant host, which means that for practical purposes, it has to be on the same logical link.

In addition to preventing you from accidentally entering an existing address, this also helps a network administrator identify a device causing a conflict. The hardware information can be used to lock this device off the network if it is being improperly configured.

In many cases, when you are running a small network, you will be happy to have IP addresses assigned by DHCP. There are, however, times when you will want to

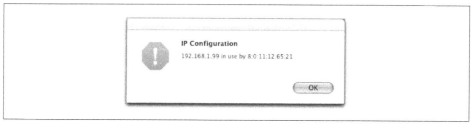

*Figure 2-2. In-use message*

manually set an address. The best example of this is a DNS server. Normally, it is best to access hosts and services by name, using a name server. However, the one service you can't look up by name is the name server itself, since you can't send it DNS queries to map names to addresses unless you already know its IP address.

Another example is an old legacy printer. Strange as it may seem today, there was a time when printer vendors actually sold network printers that didn't have Bonjour/Zeroconf. These printers usually did include a DHCP client, so they could be configured to get an address from a DHCP server, but it's not clear why. If you set the printer to use DHCP, you would probably end up being unable to use it because you wouldn't know what IP address the DHCP server had assigned to it. For this reason, these printers were more commonly used with a fixed, manually assigned, static IP address. If you have one of these old pre-Bonjour IP printers, then to print on it you need to tell the computer what IP address you manually configured into the printer, as shown in Figure 2-3.

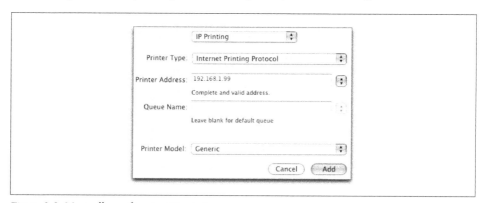

*Figure 2-3. Manually configuring IP printing*

Configuring the printer with a fixed, manually assigned, static IP address means that even after a power outage, when the printer powers back on, you know it will come back with the same IP address it had before.

Hardcoding an IP address is labor-intensive and error-prone. If you ever need to change the address of the printer, every computer has to be updated to use the printer's new IP address. Using Zeroconf, you can discover what printers are available on the network, pick one, and then subsequently access it by name, even if its IP address changes.

## Using DHCP

You can obtain an IP address from a Dynamic Host Configuration Protocol (DHCP) server if one exists on your network. The basic idea is that there is a pool of addresses that can be assigned by the DHCP server. The server is responsible for allocating the addresses in its pool so that each active requestor has a unique and valid IP address.

### DHCP-provided address

A DHCP server can be configured so that you specify the number of addresses available to be served, as well as the starting address for the block. In Figure 2-4, you see the web-based user interface to a typical low-host home gateway product that includes a DHCP server. In this case, the home gateway has been configured to be responsible for the 40 IP addresses beginning with 192.168.1.151.

*Figure 2-4. DHCP server configuration*

You can view the DHCP clients table to see a snapshot of the IP addresses currently managed by the DHCP server. Figure 2-5 shows light use by five devices. Note that the DHCP Server IP Address is the address we saw before for the router. For each device in the table with a name, the name is displayed.

The hardware address is also displayed in this table, in the column headed "MAC Address." In this case MAC, is not an abbreviation for Macintosh but rather an acronym standing for Medium Access Control. The Medium Access Control is the part of the software or firmware responsible for controlling access to the physical transmission medium. In the case of Ethernet, the MAC address is therefore the Ethernet

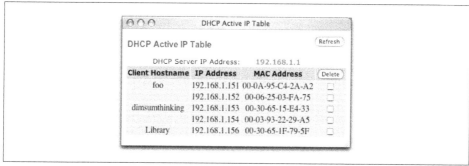

*Figure 2-5. DHCP Active IP Table*

address, and with Ethernet being the predominant networking medium in use today, many people use the terms MAC address and Ethernet address almost interchangeably or the generic term "hardware address." In the warning message illustrated in Figure 2-2, it is the MAC (or Ethernet) address that is shown to help identify the device currently occupying the desired address.

The Dynamic Host Configuration Protocol is specified in RFC 2131. Broadly speaking, it can treat clients in two ways. One way is to treat clients anonymously, handing out available IP addresses on a first-come, first-served basis to any client that asks for one. This is the easiest and most common way of using DHCP. A DHCP server can also be configured to hand out a specific IP address and other per-client specific configuration parameters to clients it has been programmed to know about in advance. The DHCP server can identify clients by their MAC address or by the *Client ID* supplied by the client. Note that there is usually no security associated with this—any impostor can impersonate a known client simply by putting that client's hardware address and/or Client ID in the DHCP request packet.

A client requests the use of an IP address for a specific length of time. The client can renew and extend the lease at any time. If the lease is not renewed before it expires, then the DHCP server returns that address to the pool of available addresses. RFC 2131 explains how DHCP allocates addresses to hosts for some period of time:

> The basic mechanism for the dynamic allocation of network addresses is simple: a client requests the use of an address for some period of time. The allocation mechanism (the collection of DHCP servers) guarantees not to reallocate that address within the requested time and attempts to return the same network address each time the client requests an address. In this document, the period over which a network address is allocated to a client is referred to as a *lease*. The client may extend its lease with subsequent requests. The client may issue a message to release the address back to the server when the client no longer needs the address. The client may ask for a permanent assignment by asking for an infinite lease. Even when assigning "permanent" addresses, a server may choose to give out lengthy but non-infinite leases to allow detection of the fact that the client has been retired.

Most DHCP servers allocate addresses sequentially, as can be seen in Figure 2-5, though RFC 2131 allows servers to allocate addresses in any order they choose. When a server has been running for a while and all addresses have been used at least once, it is common for the server to allocate a new client whichever address has been unused for the longest time.

Figure 2-6 shows a Macintosh configured to use DHCP. Note the text field for the user to enter the DHCP Client ID. Most of the time, there's no need to enter anything here. Also note the button Renew DHCP Lease. There is almost no occasion when clicking this button has any effect. Whenever your DHCP lease is close to expiring, the computer renews it for you, automatically. Any time your computer wakes from sleep, it automatically checks that its lease is still valid and gets a new one, if necessary. Any time you connect an Ethernet cable or join an AirPort network (if the interface is set to use DHCP), it automatically does everything necessary to get a valid lease for that network. If there's a working DHCP server on the network, then you'll already have a valid lease; if there isn't, then clicking the Renew DHCP Lease button won't help. However, Microsoft Windows 98 didn't do things like this automatically and, instead, made the user click a button. Because Windows had a button to click, customers insisted that Mac OS X have one too, even though on the Mac it isn't necessary and doesn't really do anything.

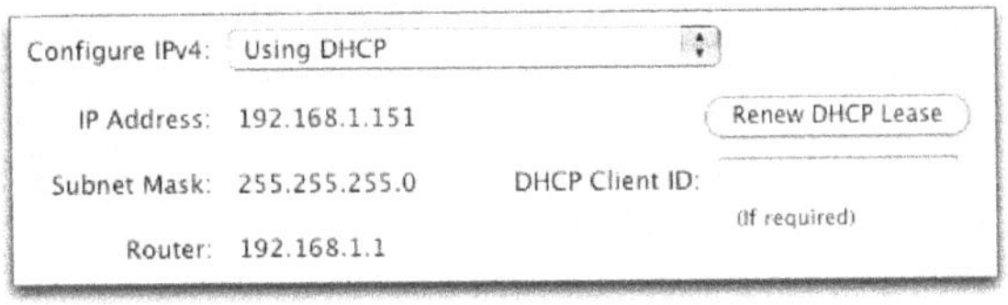

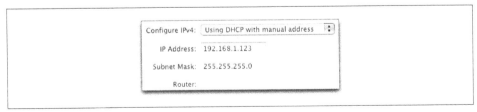

Figure 2-6. Dynamic allocation of an IP address with DHCP

## DHCP with manual addresses

Another mode that DHCP supports is where the host has a manually configured IP address, but other networking parameters (subnet mask, router address, DNS server address, etc.) are obtained from the DHCP server. Most operating systems support this mode, though it is not widely used. Figure 2-7 shows a Macintosh configured to use DHCP with a manual address.

Configure IPv4: Using DHCP with manual address
IP Address: 192.168.1.123
Subnet Mask: 255.255.255.0
Router:

Figure 2-7. Using DHCP with a manual IP address

As before, you are responsible for managing any address that you manually assign. If appropriate, you should check with a network administrator before handing out an address.

---

### Private IP Addresses

If you run a router at home, the address 192.168.1.1 may be familiar. This is often the default for the local area network (LAN) IP address for such a device. If you run a wireless network using Apple's AirPort, the default address is 10.0.0.1. These are popular choices because these addresses should never be used by any host on the "public" Internet. These addresses are reserved for private, internal network use. Thousands or even millions of hosts and devices may all use the IP address 192.168.1.1, but since they never try to communicate with one another, it doesn't matter that they all have the same address. Some of the IP addresses listed in RFC 3330 as being reserved for local private use are:

- 10.0.0.0 to 10.255.255.255
- 172.16.0.0 to 172.31.255.255
- 192.168.0.0 to 192.168.255.255
- 169.254.0.0 to 169. 254.255.255

This last set of numbers is the range that Zeroconf uses when no DHCP server is available.

---

## Zeroconf Selection of IP Address

In the case of DHCP or manual selection, there is assumed to be some sort of central authority for policing the allocation of IP addresses. With DHCP, there is a pool of available addresses, which that authority is allowed to manage. With manual configuration of IP addresses, it is assumed that the person performing the assignment is authorized and competent to do so. With Zeroconf, the selection of addresses is done in a distributed manner. Each device is responsible for choosing its own address and then verifying that it can use the selected address.

### Link-local range

In the sidebar "Private IP Addresses," you saw the four ranges of IP addresses that are officially reserved for use on local networks not connected (or not fully connected) to the worldwide public Internet. The first three ranges, described in IETF RFC 1918, are known as the *private use* IP address ranges, and the fourth, described in RFC 3927, is known as the *link-local address* range.

You may have had the experience of thinking you have a working connection to the global Internet when, in fact, you don't. You are configured to use DHCP to obtain an IP address, but what you get is something like what is pictured in Figure 2-8, an

---

address that starts with 169.254. In the early 1990s, if your computer got no response from the DHCP server, you would fail to get any working networking at all. Since 1998, though, Macs and Windows machines have at least configured a link-local address if they couldn't get anything better. Although this address is no use for global communication, it is good enough for local communication—say, to print a document. Perhaps more importantly, this address is good enough for local communication with a faulty DHCP server, so you can connect to it with your web browser and correct whatever misconfiguration or other error was preventing it from handing out IP addresses. Without the ability to do at least local network communication, you can end up in a Catch-22 situation: you need to connect to your home gateway to correct its DHCP server configuration error, but you can't because it hasn't assigned you an address. Automatic self-assigned link-local addresses, which are guaranteed to work even when everything else has failed, provide the solution to that dilemma.

*Figure 2-8. Self-assigned IP address*

In fact, not all of the range of 169.254.0.0 to 169.254.255.255 is available for general use today. The first 256 and last 256 addresses have been reserved for future use and what is left are the 65,024 addresses in the range from 169.254.1.0 to 169.254.254.255. Link-local addressing is not designed for cases in which you need all 65,000 addresses. If you have 65,000 computers and other network devices, then you really need a paid (or unpaid) network administrator who knows how to run a network that large. Link-local addressing is intended for two main scenarios: for tiny ad-hoc local networks where communication is desired without the overhead of setting up a DHCP server, and to provide a minimum safety-net level of service on networks where there's supposed to be a DHCP server but it's failed. Because no central authority is maintaining a list of available addresses, a device joining the network must handle possible conflicts with all of the existing hosts. Link-local addressing is primarily intended for networks of 2 devices, 10 devices, or perhaps even 100 devices, though analysis in RFC 3927 shows that even on a network with over 1,000 devices, it still works reasonably well:

> A host connecting to a link that already has 1,300 hosts, selecting an IPv4 link-local address at random, has a 98% chance of selecting an unused IPv4 link-local address on the first try. A host has a 99.96% chance of selecting an unused IPv4 link-local address within two tries. The probability that it will have to try more than 10 times is about 1 in $10^{17}$.

However, just because it works reasonably well for networks with over a thousand devices doesn't mean that it's recommended to have a network that large without any kind of administration.

### Choosing a link-local address

You now know the range of numbers in which you are allowed to choose your address. With possibly many independent devices choosing their own IP addresses independently, a strategy should be devised to minimize the number of tries each device will have to make, on average, to obtain a locally unique address. If you have already been connected to a particular network with a link-local address, then a good strategy is to try to use that address again. This depends first on the ability to retain this information while shut down, asleep, or otherwise off the network.

There is, of course, no guarantee that the previously used address will still be available. In situations where the same devices tend to be present on the same local network and this strategy is adopted by all devices, the process of obtaining unique IP addresses for all should go quickly and smoothly. As a human analogy, students in university classes tend to sit in roughly the same location class after class, even in cases where their seat location is not assigned. If, midway through the term, someone sits in another student's accustomed place, then that student has to find somewhere else to sit. It's not a major problem—normally the only effect is that the start of the class could be delayed by a few seconds while the student selects a new place to sit. In the auditorium example at the beginning of the chapter, there would be fewer conflicts if attendees agreed that, next time, they would request the same seats that they occupied at the previous event.

If the previously used address is now found to be in use on this network, then the host chooses a new one at random. Computers use pseudorandom-number generators, which means that the numbers they produce *seem* random but really they are quite deterministic. Because of this, it's important that the algorithm is chosen so that different machines each start with different initial values, so they don't proceed through the exact same sequence of pseudorandom numbers, conflicting with their neighbors on every single try. Deriving the initial value from the computer's Ethernet address is a good idea, since all computers (are supposed to) have different Ethernet addresses.

# Claiming a Link-Local IP Address

You do not have the right to use the address you have selected until you test that no one else on the network is already using it. In Figure 2-9, you see the output captured by Ethereal as the machines *foo* and *dimsumthinking* try to build a local network.

| Time | Source | Destination | Protocol | Info |
|---|---|---|---|---|
| 3.703964 | dimsumthinking.local | Broadcast | ARP | Who has 169.254.187.245? Tell 0.0.0.0 |
| 3.983703 | foo.local | Broadcast | ARP | Who has 169.254.186.86? Tell 0.0.0.0 |
| 4.004198 | dimsumthinking.local | Broadcast | ARP | Who has 169.254.187.245? Tell 0.0.0.0 |
| 4.283867 | foo.local | Broadcast | ARP | Who has 169.254.186.86? Tell 0.0.0.0 |
| 4.304479 | dimsumthinking.local | Broadcast | ARP | Who has 169.254.187.245? Tell 0.0.0.0 |
| 4.584088 | foo.local | Broadcast | ARP | Who has 169.254.186.86? Tell 0.0.0.0 |
| 4.884300 | foo.local | Broadcast | ARP | Who has 169.254.186.86? Tell 0.0.0.0 |
| 4.905167 | dimsumthinking.local | Broadcast | ARP | Who has 169.254.187.245? Tell 169.254.187.245 |
| 5.184522 | foo.local | Broadcast | ARP | Who has 169.254.186.86? Tell 169.254.186.86 |
| 5.205780 | dimsumthinking.local | Broadcast | ARP | Who has 169.254.187.245? Tell 169.254.187.245 |
| 5.485642 | foo.local | Broadcast | ARP | Who has 169.254.186.86? Tell 169.254.186.86 |
| 26.260895 | dimsumthinking.local | Broadcast | ARP | Who has 169.254.186.86? Tell 169.254.187.245 |
| 26.260929 | foo.local | Broadcast | ARP | 169.254.186.86 is at 00:03:93:ef:c4:8c |

*Figure 2-9. ARP probes on generating Zeroconf addresses*

Each machine first picks an address it thinks it would like to use. The machine *dimsumthinking* has chosen 169.254.187.245. It then sends some Address Resolution Protocol (ARP) requests asking for the MAC address that goes with 169.254. 187.245. ARP is the protocol that's used when a computer wants to talk to another machine on the local network. The computer knows the IP address it wants to talk to but not the Ethernet/MAC address of the machine with that IP address, so it broadcasts an ARP request asking for that information. In this case, we're using ARP slightly differently: we're sending an ARP request for our own address and hoping that we actually *don't* witness anyone else respond to that request. If someone answers, that means they already have the address, so we can't.

Note that, in the Tell section, the address is 0.0.0.0 because *dimsumthinking* is not yet asserting that it owns that address. These are ARP probes. After a couple of seconds without receiving any reply, *dimsumthinking* concludes that no one is using the address, so it may proceed to use it. *dimsumthinking* then sends out a couple of ARP announcements. Ethereal displays these in the "Who has" format, but in reality they are statements, not questions. The "Tell 169.254.187.245" section is saying, "I am 169.254.187.245."

Later in the trace, around the 26-second mark, *dimsumthinking* wants to communicate with *foo.local*. It sends an ARP request, saying "Who has 169.254.186.86? Tell 169.254.187.245," and *foo* replies with an ARP reply, saying "IP address 169.254. 186.86 is at MAC address 00:03:93:ef:c4:8c."

We cover this process in more depth next.

## Probing for Address Availability

Once a host has selected a candidate address, the next task is to check that no other host is either currently at that address or seeking to occupy that address. The mechanism for exchanging information about IP addresses and the devices using them is the ARP, which is is described in the IETF RFC 826. In this section, you will take a quick look at those parts of ARP that are needed for link-local addressing and see how ARP is used to probe for an available address.

## Address Resolution Protocol

You saw that each device (normally) has a unique MAC address. A single device may have more than one IP address and may also have addresses that change over time. When you send an IP packet to another device on the same Ethernet, you send it directly, in an Ethernet-level packet addressed directly to the recipient, but Ethernet packets need Ethernet addresses, and you don't yet know the Ethernet address of the recipient. The ARP protocol exists to solve that problem. You broadcast an ARP request asking what Ethernet address to use to reach your desired IP address, and the device that knows the answer sends an ARP reply telling you. The format of an ARP packet is shown in Figure 2-10. ARP requests and ARP replies use the same packet format; the Opcode field indicates if it is a request or a response.

```
Address Resolution Protocol (request)
    Hardware type: Ethernet (0x0001)
    Protocol type: IP (0x0800)
    Hardware size: 6
    Protocol size: 4
    Opcode: request (0x0001)
    Sender MAC address: 00:03:93:ef:c4:8c (foo.local)
    Sender IP address: 0.0.0.0 (0.0.0.0)
    Target MAC address: 00:00:00:00:00:00 (00:00:00_00:00:00)
    Target IP address: 169.254.186.86 (169.254.186.86)
```

*Figure 2-10. Probing for address availability*

The Sender MAC and IP addresses serve as an assertion: this is my MAC address; this is my current IP address.

The Target MAC and IP addresses serve as a question: who has this IP address? The Target IP address is specified, but the Target MAC is always all zeros in an ARP request because the sender doesn't yet know it.

When you broadcast an ARP request and get an ARP reply back, you store the Sender MAC and IP addresses in your ARP cache, so the next time you need to know what MAC address goes with that IP address, you'll already have that information at hand.

## How to probe

Because ARP is used to look up IP addresses anyway, it's the natural way to tell if an address is in use. If the machine *foo* wishes to probe the address 169.254.186.86, it broadcasts a series of ARP requests such as the one represented in Figure 2-10. RFC 3927 recommends that the host send three probe packets spaced one to two seconds apart, though other numbers and intervals could work, too.

As you can see in Figure 2-10, the Sender MAC address information is included in the ARP probe while the Target Mac address is set to all zeros. The Target IP address contains the dotted decimal of the address the host is inquiring about while the Sender IP address is all zeros. An ARP request with all zeros for the Sender IP address is known as an ARP probe. You must not fill out the Sender IP address with the address you are hoping to claim, because some other device may already have legitimately claimed it. If you put your desired IP address as the Sender IP, then other hosts on the network will update their ARP caches and send those packets to you instead of to the legitimate holder of that IP address.

## Results of probing

The purpose of the ARP probe is to determine whether or not a device can claim a particular address. Remember that, for small networks, there is a high probability that a randomly selected address will not collide with existing addresses. So what could go wrong?

- Another host might be trying to claim the same address at the same time. What indicates this is an ARP probe for the same Target address from a different host. Determining whether or not this is the case is why it is necessary to include the Sender MAC address in the probe. Suppose, while probing, you receive an ARP probe for the same Target address. If the Sender MAC address is different, then someone else wants the same address that you want. If the Sender MAC address is your own, then there is no conflict. There are various reasons you might see your own probes. For example, you might have Ethernet and 802.11 wireless active, but (unknown to you) they are both bridged together, so every time you sent a broadcast on 802.11, you see that same packet arrive milliseconds later on the Ethernet interface.

- Another host has already claimed the same address. In this case, the host will receive your ARP request asking about the specified Target IP address, and it will respond to you with an ARP reply asserting ownership of that IP address, exactly as specified in RFC 826 way back in 1982. Receiving any ARP packet (request or response) with your desired IP address specified as the Sender IP address indicates that someone else is already using that address.

If, after a few ARPs, no conflicting responses have been received, the host has claimed the address and can proceed to announce this fact. If a conflict is detected, then the host chooses another address and begins the probing process all over again.

## When to probe

Notice that, when you probe, you are asking any device that can receive your message whether the address you want is available. This implies that any time you are not able to receive such a probe, you cannot be sure that someone else has not claimed your address. Any time your network interface becomes active after a period of inactivity, you need to go through the process of trying to claim the address again.

You certainly have to probe any time your device starts up or is rebooted. If your network interface does not remain active while your device is asleep, you must probe on waking up. You must also probe if you bring up an inactive network interface, either by attaching a cable, associating with a new wireless base station, or by changing your network settings to activate a particular interface.

## Announcing

At this point, your host has finished probing and is ready to announce its claim of that IP address. The announcement is important because, moments before you arrived, some other (now departed) host may have been using that IP address. Other peers on the network could have that old IP address/MAC address mapping in their ARP caches, and when they try to communicate with you, they will send their IP packets (unsuccessfully) to the wrong MAC address. By broadcasting an ARP announcement, we ensure that all those old stale ARP cache entries are updated to point to your MAC address instead, since you are now the new legitimate holder of this IP address. You may observe that the chances are vanishingly small of there having been some other host using the same IP address just moments before you arrived. This is true, but the purpose of Zeroconf is to provide high reliability, so we want to make sure that even this rare case is handled correctly. We want a protocol that works correctly all the time, not just almost all the time.

### Announcing your address

You have chosen your address and determined that no other device is probing for the same address or has already claimed it. You have claimed the address and must now broadcast this by sending two ARP requests two seconds apart. The requests are similar to those shown in Figure 2-11.

```
Address Resolution Protocol (request)
    Hardware type: Ethernet (0x0001)
    Protocol type: IP (0x0800)
    Hardware size: 6
    Protocol size: 4
    Opcode: request (0x0001)
    Sender MAC address: 00:03:93:ef:c4:8c (foo.local)
    Sender IP address: 169.254.186.86 (169.254.186.86)
    Target MAC address: 00:00:00:00:00:00 (00:00:00_00:00:00)
    Target IP address: 169.254.186.86 (169.254.186.86)
```

*Figure 2-11. Claiming a link-local address*

As before, the Sender MAC address is included along with the Target IP address. This time, to indicate that the address has been claimed, the Sender IP address is set to the value of the claimed address. The Target MAC address is still set to all zeros, as always for an ARP request, and the Target IP Address is the same as the Sender IP address. The two effects of sending this ARP announcement are that any hosts simultaneously probing for this same address will realize they need to choose a different address, and all the other hosts on this link will update any stale ARP cache entries to reflect this new information.

## Defending Your Address

Devices can join and leave the network and try to claim addresses at any time, so the process of address conflict detection is ongoing. When a new host joins the network, if its randomly chosen address happens to be our address, when it sends its ARP probes, our host will answer them, informing the new host that its desired address is already in use and it should choose another. There's nothing special about answering ARP probes. An ARP probe is just a certain kind of ARP request, and hosts are answering ARP requests all the time anyway, as part of the normal process of IP networking.

## Late Conflicts and Misbehaving Peers

As described so far, the process works perfectly well. As long as all the hosts follow the rules, each will assign itself a unique address.

But what if some hosts don't follow the rules? What if some hosts have software or hardware bugs that mean they don't perform probing properly? What if two hosts do perform probing properly on two separate unconnected Ethernet segments (so, at the time, there's no harm in them both assigning themselves the same address), but then, without either host's knowledge, those two Ethernet segments are later connected together? What if a human user decides to *manually* assign a 169.254.x.x address on a device that doesn't implement address conflict detection for manual addresses? Or does it on a device that does implement address conflict detection for manual addresses, but the human user, for some reason, has disabled that address conflict detection?

The usual reaction to these issues is just to call them errors, out-of-scope for this protocol. If devices have bugs, the bugs should be fixed. If a human user is guilty of willful malice, then the human user should be dealt with. The Zeroconf philosophy goes beyond this typical response, though. Certainly, these situations should not arise, but if they do, is there anything we can do about them?

The answer is that when a device observes an ARP packet sent out from another machine claiming to have the same IP address, RFC 3927 specifies that the device may send, at most, a single ARP of its own, reasserting its claim on that address; if the other machine doesn't back down, then the device MUST give up its address and select another. Many people recoil against this notion. They feel that if they claimed the address, fair and square, then it's theirs and they shouldn't have to give it up, and it's the other machine that should change. The problem is that if both devices are programmed to behave this way, then neither will select a new address, and they will just continue to fight indefinitely. Meanwhile, until they get the address conflict resolved, neither device can do any useful networking.

Two devices fighting over the same IP address is like two people in a half-empty cinema fighting over the same seat. They can either sit in different seats and enjoy the film, or they can spend the entire time continuously punching each other, in which case, neither will get to see any of the film and they'll disrupt the people around them too.

The analogy of someone trying to make you move to another seat is the way many people think of the situation, and while it's accurate to an extent, such anthropomorphization of computer situations often leads people to incorrect conclusions. As a person, if you were sitting in a half-empty cinema enjoying a film and, halfway through, some thug came and hit you, then quietly moving to another seat might seem like a weak, cowardly response. The manly thing to do would be to stand your ground and refuse to move. Computers are not people, though. They have no feelings or ego. A computer programmed to meekly select a new address is not going to feel bad about it. If, instead, the computer were programmed to fight forever, then it would do just that. It would fight forever, without any regard for the consequences or benefits. Two computers programmed to fight forever over the same IP address would do just that. Neither could do anything to stop the other from trying to use the address; neither would give up trying to use the address itself. Neither would succeed in achieving anything except causing disruption on the network. They would just sit there shooting ARP packets at each other without limit, flooding the network and consuming CPU time on all the other hosts on the network, until some human intervened to stop them. This is where the human user would encounter the serious problem: if the only user interface to these devices is via a configuration page that you view via a web browser, and neither device was able to achieve stable networking, then that could make it very hard for a human to fix the misconfiguration.

The other mistake that anthropomorphization frequently encourages is the notion that a particular link-local IP address is something worth fighting over. What people don't realize is that after a few seconds of address conflict, there's nothing left worth saving. When another host broadcasts an ARP claiming your IP address, peers on the network update their ARP caches. Subsequent TCP packets go to the wrong host, which, having no record of that TCP connection, responds with a TCP RESET packet. After this point, continuing to fight over the address would be futile. The connections are all gone. It's too late to save them. It's a bad situation and it shouldn't happen, but if some thug does come and stomp on your IP address, the most productive thing for a computer to do is get a new, untainted address and get on with life, not waste time fighting over the old, dead one.

The way Zeroconf detects and handles this is by passive observation of the ARP broadcast packets it receives anyway. Every ARP packet includes the sender's MAC address and (claimed) IP address. Consider the case of your host, with IP address 169.254.187.245 and MAC address 00:03:93:ef:c4:8c, receiving the ARP packet shown in Figure 2-12. The sender of the ARP packet is seeking to communicate with IP address 169.254.186.86 and wants to know its MAC address. However, the sender of the ARP packet is also asserting that it owns IP address 169.254.187.245 (which is yours) with MAC address 00:03:65:15:e4:33 (which is not yours, so you know this probe didn't originate from your machine). This is a conflict and needs to be handled.

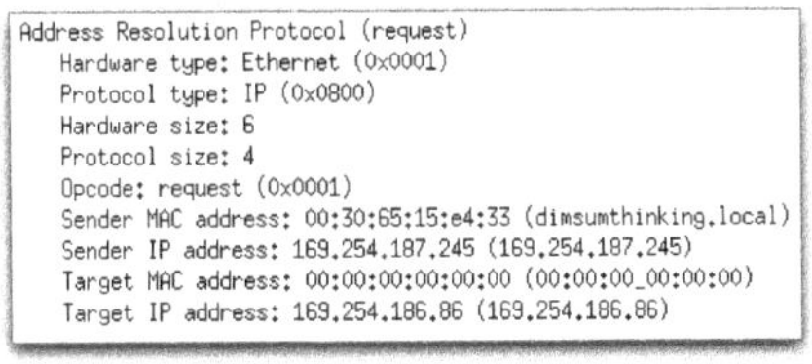

```
Address Resolution Protocol (request)
    Hardware type: Ethernet (0x0001)
    Protocol type: IP (0x0800)
    Hardware size: 6
    Protocol size: 4
    Opcode: request (0x0001)
    Sender MAC address: 00:30:65:15:e4:33 (dimsumthinking.local)
    Sender IP address: 169.254.187.245 (169.254.187.245)
    Target MAC address: 00:00:00:00:00:00 (00:00:00_00:00:00)
    Target IP address: 169.254.186.86 (169.254.186.86)
```

*Figure 2-12. Conflicting ARP packet*

RFC 3927 allows a machine to handle a conflict in one of two ways:

- It can gracefully back down and let the other host have the address. It picks a new address and begins the probing process all over again.

- If it has open TCP connections that it doesn't want to lose, then it can respond by broadcasting a single ARP announcement asserting its own ownership of that address. However, if this doesn't solve the problem, then it must back down and let the other host have the address. There's nothing to be gained by two hosts getting into a fistfight over an address. When two hosts think they have the same IP address, any open TCP connections are not likely to survive for long, so, pretty soon, the thing the hosts were each fighting to preserve will be gone anyway.

The first option, making an immediate change, ensures that the conflict is resolved as quickly as possible. The host issuing the conflicting ARP packet will most likely keep its IP address and your host will make a change. If your host has an active TCP connection, it may prefer the second option, as that gives it a chance of maintaining its IP address and forcing the other host to change.

If your host decides to defend the IP address, then the ARP announcement it broadcasts is received by the other host as a conflicting ARP packet. The other host then has the same two options: choose another address or try to defend the current one. But what if the other host will not yield? Then the other host sends out its single ARP request defending its address and now your host receives a second conflicting ARP packet. Now you've received two conflicting ARP packets in a row, in a short window of time, and the protocol specification leaves your host no choice: it must relinquish that address and pick another.

Another case mentioned before occurs when two previously separate networks are bridged together. In this case, neither host is really to blame—the network environment just changed around them. This is harder to detect because the individual hosts generally do not even know that the bridging has occurred. One solution that's occasionally suggested is to have all hosts periodically broadcast ARP packets giving their IP addresses, so that each host can detect when some other host thinks it has the same IP address. This is not a good idea because it would be a huge, ongoing waste of bandwidth, even when hosts are otherwise quiet and not communicating, to solve a problem that, in fact, occurs so rarely that many network protocol designers would be content simply to ignore it. The more lightweight solution adopted by RFC 3927 is simply to have hosts send ARP replies by broadcast instead of unicast, so that the hosts all get to see what one another are saying and can passively observe if another host asserts ownership of the same IP address. Since every unicast ARP reply would normally be sent in response to a broadcast ARP request, this can be viewed as just a little more broadcast traffic at a time when there was broadcast traffic anyway. Periodic announcements would be additional broadcast traffic at times when there was, in fact, no need for any broadcast traffic at all.

When considering these issues, it is important to remember three things:

- The problems of late conflicts, network topology changes, and buggy or misbehaving hosts are exceedingly uncommon. AppleTalk had no mechanism to detect these kinds of problems and was used successfully for two decades. Zeroconf is simply being held to an even higher standard, where even these obscure situations should be handled gracefully, too.

- With 65,000 addresses available, the chance of conflict is small. Even if two large 100-host networks are joined, there's still a better than 75% chance that not a single host on either network will suffer a conflict.

- Link-local addressing is designed for the case where no alternative is available, or the alternative has failed. In some sense, even if link-local addressing were to be unreliable or not work very well in all cases, that is still better than the alternative, which is no functional networking at all. Often, all that is required is that link-local addressing work long enough for the network administrator to communicate with the DHCP server to fix it.

## Summary

Link-local addressing, like all of Bonjour/Zeroconf, has two important goals: simplicity and reliability. Simplicity is important because this technology is not only for powerful $1,000 computers; it is for all manner of emerging ultra-low-cost devices that will use IP networking. Reliability is important because this technology is not just for today's computer experts. This technology is for use by the general public, who have neither the knowledge nor the patience to struggle with all manner of arcane and inexplicable computer failures, and indeed they shouldn't have to. Global communication on the worldwide Internet is very powerful and very useful, but there are many ways that global connectivity can fail, so it's beneficial to have an alternative backup technology that can be relied upon to always work, no matter what. Sometimes, reduced functionality—communication only on the local link—is better than no communication at all.

Consequently, following the goals of simplicity and reliability, the steps for obtaining a link-local address are designed to be as straightforward and simple as possible. Choose a potential IP address in a reasonable way. Select from the allowable addresses in the 169.254/16 range. As Zeroconf is designed for situations in which fewer than 2% of the IP addresses have been assigned, your host will almost surely obtain an address within the first one or two tries. To increase this likelihood, your best strategy is to first try to reclaim an address you have previously successfully claimed. You can then use this address to seed your pseudorandom-number generator. After selecting an address, your host ARPs three times with the target address in the ARP set to the desired IP address. If there is no response during a reasonable time period, the address is claimed by sending a further ARP with the desired IP address entered as both the source and target address in the ARP broadcast. Once an address is selected and in use, the reliability requirement calls for ongoing vigilance, to handle the extremely rare (but possible) case where conflicts are not detected until later.

# CHAPTER 3

# Names Without DNS

In Chapter 2, you saw how Zeroconf allows your device to obtain a locally unique IP address without a DHCP server or a network administrator. The next step is to obtain a name that can resolve to this address. The method you use to do that is independent of how you have obtained your IP address; for example, you may have taken advantage of link-local addressing, been assigned an address using DHCP, or manually assigned an IP address. If you need a name that is at least locally unique and there is no DNS server available, the Multicast DNS (mDNS) mechanism will help you obtain one.

This stage may feel unnecessary. After all, why not just use the IP address obtained in the last step as the device name? IP addresses may change over time, and network location and IP addresses are not a convenient form for people to remember or recognize devices. In other words, you need to assign locally unique names and not use the automatically assigned IP addresses for the following reasons:

- The IP address provided may be temporary. If you are communicating with a device at a given address, it is quite possible that, at a later time, the device may have a different address. Attempting to contact the device by connecting to its old address will not succeed. Even worse, that address could be reused by a different device, so when you attempt to connect to it, you may apparently succeed, except you're not actually communicating with the device you intended.

- With mobile devices and devices connected to many networks, the device cannot expect to keep the same IP address in every location and on every different network. In a world where IP addresses are fluid and changeable, having a persistent name that's relatively much more stable is a big benefit. Of course, names also have to be unique—two devices cannot have exactly the same name—but the space of all possible names is so much larger than the space of possible IP addresses that coming up with unique names is relatively much easier.

- An IP address is not a human-friendly way to locate a device providing a service. When we want to use a web browser to visit Apple Computer's web page, we type *www.apple.com* and not a dotted-decimal IP address. As the world moves to

IPv6, this problem becomes even more acute. An IPv4 address is just four decimal numbers, such as 17.112.152.32, which is just about possible to remember, if absolutely necessary. An IPv6 address is 32 hexadecimal characters, which is a different story altogether. Most people don't pick secret passwords that are hard to remember, not even for their most important financial accounts.

- If you need to select a device from a list of available devices, this is easier to do if the list is presented as text-based names and not a collection of IP addresses. This is similar to the previous point but is the other direction of recognizing a device, as opposed to requesting that device.

> In this chapter, *local* refers to devices on the same link. You can think of this in a *geographically local* sense. There are also people with whom you interact every day. If you work remotely, other members of your team are closer to you in some sense than the person you've never met who is working a couple of tables over from you at your neighborhood coffee shop. These remote-but-close devices cannot have a link-local address that carries any meaning. Their name must also be somehow globally unique and not just locally unique. In Chapter 5, you will see how Zeroconf's local technologies can be extended for people and devices that are not on the same link as you. In this chapter, the discussion is restricted to finding a locally unique name using Multicast DNS.

When it comes to global networking today, nothing beats the global domain name system (DNS). However, the power of the global DNS doesn't come without a price. Someone has to set up and run the DNS servers, and the globally unique names have to be assigned, allocated, and managed, usually with money changing hands. For global communications, it's worth all that effort, but if all you want to do is print on a network printer across the room, surely there must be an easier way. When all you need to do is establish names that are valid for the local link, link-local Multicast DNS (mDNS) provides a simple, no-fuss solution.

Instead of relying on a centralized authority, mDNS allows each machine to answer for itself. When a client wishes to do a query, instead of sending it to a particular DNS server, the client sends it using *IP Multicast*, which means that, a bit like a broadcast, it goes to every interested machine on the local network. Each device on the network runs a little piece of software that's listening for these multicast queries, and, when it sees a query for its own name (or other mDNS data it knows), it answers that query, much as a conventional DNS server would have done. On Mac OS X, this little piece of software is called *mDNSResponder*. On Windows, it's *mDNSResponder.exe*. On Linux and similar Unix systems, it's usually called *mdnsd*.

In this chapter, you will see the details of how to claim a locally unique name in much the same way that you claimed a locally unique IP address. Within a domain intended for this purpose, you choose a name and ask if anyone is using it. If no one is, then you claim and defend this name on the local network. If the name is in use, you choose a different name and repeat the process. The goal with mDNS is to have a system that requires minimal administration and configuration and that works when DNS is not available. We begin the chapter with a look at how DNS works.

# A Brief Tour of DNS

Your mobile telephone number is used to reach your phone while you travel from place to place and even if you switch providers. When you register an Internet domain name, you can be assured that it is unique and you can publish it so others can use it to find you. If you later move your host machine(s) to a different location or IP address, this name that you have advertised will still correctly direct people to your web site. Some central authority must administer telephone numbers and domain names if we want to ensure consistency and stability. This section provides a quick overview of DNS.

## The Namespace

Consider a typical URL, such as the one for Apple's Bonjour home page:

> *http://developer.apple.com/bonjour/*

The *http* identifies the protocol as the hypertext transfer protocol. The *developer. apple.com* identifies the machine where the resource can be found, and */bonjour/* identifies the particular resource on that machine.

A domain name read left to right moves from the specific to the general. So, *developer* is a node in the *apple.com* domain and *apple* is a node in the *com* domain. There are other domains at the same level as *com* that sit under the root of the domain name space in the same way that *bin*, *dev*, and *usr* directories sit under the root of a Mac OS X machine. On a Mac OS X or other Unix machine, you might have a path such as */usr/lib*. The leading slash (/) character is used as a separator, and we also think of the root of a Unix file system as being (/) and navigate to the root by typing **cd /** in a terminal window. When you type a filename or pathname in Unix without a leading slash, it's interpreted relative to your current working directory, whatever that might be. If you're not currently in the directory you thought you were in, then the filename or pathname might not actually refer to the file you intended. When you type a filename or pathname with a leading slash, it's an absolute name, relative to the root of the file system, so there's no ambiguity.

In the same way, a domain name that doesn't end in a final dot (.) is interpreted relative to your current DNS search list. Suppose you mistype *developer.apple.com* as *devloper.apple.com*, and there's no final dot. Your system will first look up *devloper. apple.com*. When it finds this does not exist, it will go through your list of search domains, appending each in turn, trying names like *devloper.apple.com.apple.com.*, *devloper.apple.com.starbucks.com.*, or *devloper.apple.com.whatever.org.*, depending on what's in the DNS searchlist your machine received from the DHCP server. If some joker sets up a real web server called *devloper.apple.com.whatever.org.*, then you may find you've connected to that instead of the one you expected. Just like putting a leading slash on a pathname, you can eliminate this ambiguity by making the domain name absolute (i.e., *fully qualified*) by adding a **.** to the end. So, *developer.apple.com.* is the fully qualified name.

The root doesn't really have a name. You can think of it as the null character to the right of the trailing **.** or you can think of it as the final **.** itself. However you think of this trailing **.**, a fully qualified name is complete in itself and DNS search domains will not be appended.

---

## Left-to-Right or Right-to-Left?

With Unix and DOS pathnames, you start with the top-level directory at the left, and then with each successive pathname component, you further narrow the scope until you've identified the one specific file you want.

Similarly, with telephone numbers, you start with the country code at the left, then the area code, then the exchange, then finally the last digits that identify the specific telephone you're calling.

IP addresses work the same way. When you see any IP address that begins with 17, that means the address is somewhere at Apple. Successive digits narrow the scope to the particular building, particular floor, and finally, the specific host being addressed.

Postal addresses are written the opposite way: you begin with the specific person or street address first and end with the city and country.

In the United States, domain names are written like postal addresses, not telephone numbers or IP addresses: you start with the specific and end with the general top-level domain (e.g., *com*, *edu*, *mil*) or country code (e.g., *us*, *uk*, *fr*).

For a long time in England, domain names were written like telephone numbers, starting with the country code first, so the domain name for Sidney Sussex College Cambridge was written *uk.ac.cam.sid* instead of *sid.cam.ac.uk*. These days, England writes its domain names with the root on the right, like the rest of the world, though, in an ironic twist, so-called "reverse-DNS" naming has become popular in all sorts of other areas, such as Java package names (e.g., *com.sun.mail.smtp*), so the debate over left-to-right versus right-to-left continues.

---

# Administration of DNS

DNS is robust because there is no central authority responsible for all of the nodes. From the root, there are top-level domains that can be viewed as independent sub-trees.

The top-level domains that exist directly below the root in the domain name hierarchy include the following:

- *arpa*, which is used for address-to-name mappings
- Generic domains, such as *com*, *edu*, *gov*, *net*, and *org*
- Geographical domains, which are country codes, such as *ca* (Canada) and *jp* (Japan)

Below the top-level domains are second-level domains. For example, *apple.com* is a second-level domain that sits under the top-level *com* domain. Apple Computer had to register this name and now they manage it. So, for example, Apple did not have to ask an outside authority for permission to add the node *developer* to *apple.com*. They manage their own domain as a separate zone and cannot possibly cause a name conflict with a domain outside of their zone. You can think of zones as sub-trees of the domain name space that are managed independently. The leaves of each sub-tree, such as *developer*, often correspond to a specific IP address.

When subdomains are created, they are often managed as separate zones, each responsible for their own administration. Within a university, the top-level domain may be split into domains for the different schools or departments. So, for example, the *rice.edu* domain has a subdomain for the computer science department, *cs.rice.edu*. The administrator of *rice.edu* does not need to be concerned about how *cs.rice.edu* is administered. This responsibility has been delegated. A node named *exciton* has been added to the *cs.rice.edu* zone. This information needs to be stored in a name server for *cs.rice.edu* so that the name *exciton.cs.rice.edu* can be resolved.

## Resolving Names

When you direct your browser to view *www.apple.com*, some work needs to go on below the surface to figure out where to direct your browser. In Figure 3-1, the ethereal application has been used to packet sniff to see what information is being exchanged. The figure highlights the response received from the default DNS server that the machine issuing the query is using. The query is `www.apple.com: type A, class inet`. For the domain name *www.apple.com*, a type-A query specifies that the IP address is requested and class *inet* specifies the query class is *Internet*. In principle, a DNS server could be used to store many other classes of data apart from just Internet-related data, but in practice, the only DNS class that is in widespread use today is class *Internet*.

The result of a successful DNS query gives you the DNS *resource record* associated with the requested name, type, and class. Often, you'll see a resource record's type and class referred to as the *rrtype* and *rrclass*. The resource data inside a resource record is called its *rdata*. Usually, the rdata has a particular structure that's determined by the record type. For example, the rdata for an IPv4 address record has to

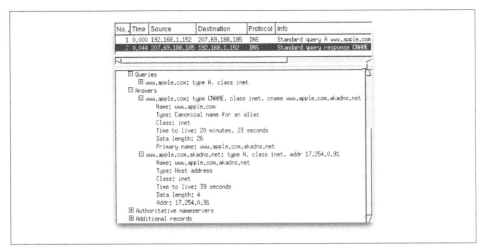

*Figure 3-1. DNS query for an IP address*

be exactly four bytes. The rdata for a PTR or CNAME record doesn't have to be a fixed length, but it does have to be a properly formatted DNS name.

In the response, you can see that *www.apple.com* is actually the name of a CNAME record, which tells us that *www.apple.com* is not the real name of the machine; it's an alias for the real, or *canonical*, name. The rdata of the CNAME record gives the canonical name, *www.apple.com.akadns.net*. The second part of the answer provides the IP address for the name, *www.apple.com.akadns.net*.

You may have noticed that not all of the available information has been displayed in Figure 3-1. Some of the sections have been collapsed. You can also see some of this information using an application such as *host*, *nslookup*, or *dig*. The Domain Information Groper, or *dig*, is a command-line tool that can be used to run various queries. For example, the query dig developer.apple.com sends a query for the IP address corresponding to *developer.apple.com*. You can see the response from *dig* in Figure 3-2. It is fairly verbose and includes the answer, as well as a list of the six authoritative name servers and IP addresses for some of those name servers, so we don't have to begin our query at root next time. For fun, you can run *dig* with *rice.edu* and *cs.rice.edu* and compare the answers and the authority sections of the two responses.

You also may want to run *nslookup* with the command nslookup developer.apple.com. Run the query more than once and the answer should be something like this.

```
Non-authoritative answer:
Name:    developer.apple.com
Address: 17.254.2.129
```

The phrase "Non-authoritative answer" indicates that the answer came from a cached value and not a fresh query to an Apple name server. As in other applications, caching

```
foo:/ daniel$ dig developer.apple.com.

; <<>> DiG 9.2.2 <<>> developer.apple.com.
;; global options: printcmd
;; Got answer:
;; ->>HEADER<<- opcode: QUERY, status: NOERROR, id: 8555
;; flags: qr rd ra; QUERY: 1, ANSWER: 1, AUTHORITY: 6, ADDITIONAL: 3

;; QUESTION SECTION:
;developer.apple.com.            IN     A

;; ANSWER SECTION:
developer.apple.com.    84630   IN     A       17.254.2.129

;; AUTHORITY SECTION:
apple.com.              172781  IN     NS      nserver.euro.apple.com.
apple.com.              172781  IN     NS      nserver.apple.com.
apple.com.              172781  IN     NS      nserver2.apple.com.
apple.com.              172781  IN     NS      nserver3.apple.com.
apple.com.              172781  IN     NS      nserver4.apple.com.
apple.com.              172781  IN     NS      nserver.asia.apple.com.

;; ADDITIONAL SECTION:
nserver.asia.apple.com. 281     IN     A       203.120.14.5
nserver2.apple.com.     430924  IN     A       17.254.0.59
nserver4.apple.com.     431682  IN     A       17.112.144.59

;; Query time: 63 msec
;; SERVER: 207.69.188.185#53(207.69.188.185)
;; WHEN: Sun Mar  7 10:24:50 2004
;; MSG SIZE  rcvd: 246
```

*Figure 3-2. Using dig to resolve a domain name to an IP address*

improves performance at the risk of passing on information that is no longer correct. DNS is a distributed database of domain names and addresses, with caching of information higher up in the tree, that provides robust and efficient resolution of persistent globally unique names to relatively long-term globally unique IP addresses.

# The Zeroconf Namespace

When you want to run a global web server that's reachable from anywhere on the planet, you need a globally unique name that's resolvable from anywhere on the planet. However, if you're setting up a web server that's only used locally, then it would be nice if you didn't have to incur all of that overhead. Running a web server on Mac OS X is as simple as just clicking one checkbox, so it would be nice if getting a name for that server were as easy. As shown in Figure 3-3, you check the Personal Web Sharing checkbox to start up the Apache web server.

The content of the computer's web site is contained in the */Library/Webserver/ Documents/* directory. The *index.html* file will appear when the browser is pointed at the provided IP address. In addition, each user can have a personal web site that is accessed using the IP address followed by *~username/*. The pages being served are in this machine under the *~username/Sites* directory.

Note that, in the Figure 3-3, the displayed URL contains an embedded IP address. This is not very memorable, nor user-friendly, and because it's a DHCP-assigned address, it may well be different tomorrow. What we need is a memorable, stable name in place of this IP address.

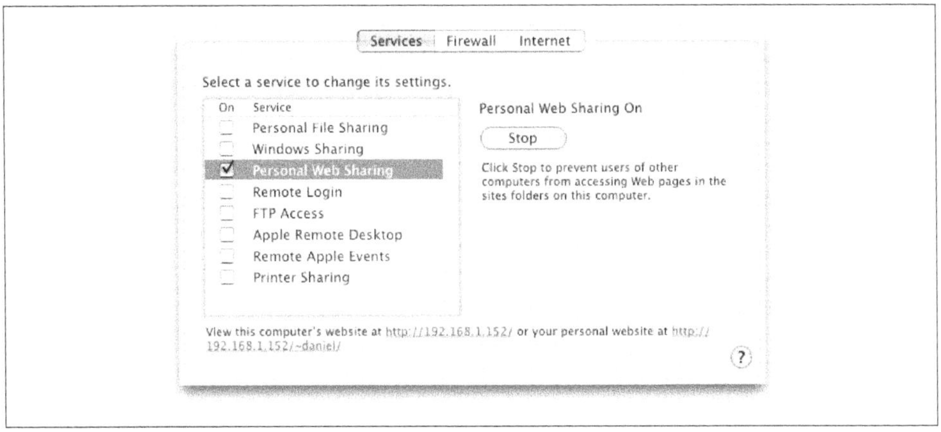

*Figure 3-3. Starting the Apache Web Server on Mac OS X*

## The local Domain

In order to distinguish local names from existing domain names, Zeroconf uses *.local.* as a pseudo-top-level domain (TLD). Just as IP addresses beginning with 169.254 are deemed special, not globally unique, and therefore only meaningful on the local link, names under the pseudo-TLD "local" are similarly deemed special, not globally unique, and only meaningful on the local link. The benefit of local names is that you don't need an arbiter who hands out names and you don't have to pay money for them. The drawback of local names is that because there's no arbiter and you didn't pay any money for your name, you can't claim unique ownership and prevent others from using that same name if they want. Instead, devices using local names have to follow a set of cooperative rules (i.e., protocol) by which they detect if two devices try to use the same name at the same time, and, if this happens, one of them voluntarily selects a new unique name. You cannot assume, if you see the name *example.local.* on a given link, that it has any relationship to an *example.local.* that you see on a different link, nor can you assume that it has any relationship to an *example.local.* you may have seen before on the same link. Of course, you should pick a name that is personalized to help others who know you have a chance of finding and identifying you.

The easy changeability of names may seem to some to be a big potential security weakness—what if I'm not really printing on the printer I intended? In reality, however, IP addresses and even Ethernet hardware addresses can be spoofed. The only sound way to provide assurance of identity is by end-to-end cryptographic means. For example, when you connect to a host for the first time using the *ssh* (secure shell) remote login command, that host's public key is saved for future reference in your *.ssh/known_hosts* file. Each subsequent time you connect, the host's identity is verified cryptographically using the public key you saved, and if you ever inadvertently connect to an impostor host that doesn't have the correct secret key matching the public key you previously saved, then *ssh* will display an error message telling you so and will refuse to complete the connection.

Names in the pseudo-TLD *local* are always looked up using multicast, but what about other names? Standard DNS names are normally looked up using unicast queries sent to a normal DNS server. (Unicast packets are the standard type of packet usually used on the Internet; they go to a single destination machine, as opposed to broadcast or multicast packets that are delivered to some collection of machines.) However, when the Internet link is down, or the DNS server is not responding for some other reason, this leaves all these names unresolvable. You may be trying to connect to *tim.oreilly.com*, sitting right next to *tim.oreilly.com*, but you can't connect because your Internet link is down and you can't reach the global DNS. (There's an old joke that *network computing* means "You can't get your work done because of a problem you don't care about with a computer you've never heard of in a building you've never been to.") In this situation, a client could choose to multicast its query locally, so that the two computers can communicate directly, peer-to-peer, and set up a connection without reliance on the external DNS. Even though the peers cannot communicate with the global DNS, they would still be using their usual global DNS names to refer to each other. While it is clearly useful, it also makes spoofing easier. The machine next to you may *claim* to be *tim.oreilly.com*, but how can you be sure? This risk could be mitigated by using cryptographic techniques like the ones described above used by *ssh*, but much of today's application software doesn't implement such strong security measures. In the future, when better security mechanisms are in place, it may become practical to begin using local mDNS as a fallback mechanism to look up global DNS names when the global DNS is inaccessible, but for now, it is safest to restrict mDNS for use with dot-local names.

---

## Names on Intranets

There's no end of names that can be chosen as a TLD for private DNS namespaces. For example, you could choose *.intranet*, *.internal*, *.private*, *.corp*, or *.home*. In "How to create local DNS names" (*http://cr.yp.to/djbdns/dot-local.html*), author D.J. Bernstein recommends using *.0* through *.9* as safe top-level local names. You should avoid *.local.* because it has been used in Mac OS 9 and Mac OS X for a long time to identify a name as being link-local, and now with Bonjour for Windows and Multicast DNS for Linux, *.local* has special meaning on those platforms also.

---

## Choosing a Name

If you are the administrator for a domain such as *example.com*, you can choose any name for a device and assign it and register it; e.g., you may choose *printer.example.com*. However, most of us don't have the luxury (or burden) of administering our own DNS domain. The impediment is not merely the financial cost of paying for your own DNS domain, but also the organizational overhead of getting it properly delegated from its parent domain and the technical burden of running a name server or getting someone else to do it for you. None of these problems is really that big, and many computer enthusiasts do run their own domains quite successfully, but the fact remains that the majority of Internet users have no idea how to do this, or even that the option is available to them. Also, even if you're the kind of person who can set up a working name server with just half a day's work, there are many situations where even that level of effort is not justified. There are many situations where all you need is some temporary communication between a couple of devices, and you want to do it with just a few seconds of effort, not a few minutes or a few hours. Zeroconf provides this "system administration for the rest of us."

As shown in Figure 3-4, you can set your computer's "dot-local" hostname by clicking the Edit… button in the Mac OS X 10.4 Sharing preference pane.

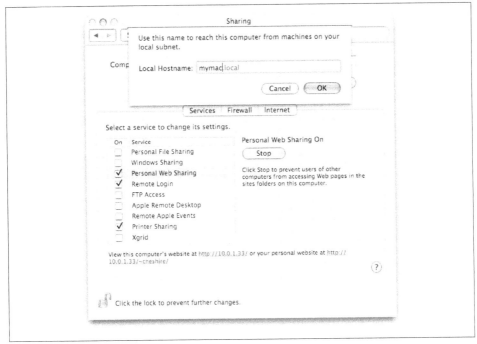

*Figure 3-4. Choosing a dot-local hostname for your computer*

Once you have made the change shown in Figure 3-4, devices on the local link can refer to your computer by the name *mymac.local*. This name can be used anywhere a normal DNS hostname would be used—such as on the command line (for example, `ping mymac.local`, `ssh mymac.local`, `ftp mymac.local`), in graphical FTP clients, in the Finder's Connect to Server dialog, or in a web browser.

The name *mymac.local* may not be a particularly good name to use on public local links since it is not likely to be (or to remain) unique. Your name can be fairly long and descriptive; however, well before you hit the formal upper limit of 63 characters allowed for a dot-local hostname, you will get to a length that is difficult to display and for potential users to easily enter. Think of how you currently react to overly long URLs. A good dot-local hostname is memorable, short, and easy to type, but unique enough that encounters with others who've picked the same name should be relatively rare.

The Mac OS X 10.4 Sharing preference pane also has a text field labeled Computer Name, which is actually used to control the default name used for services advertised on your machine. We'll cover more on this in Chapter 4. Generally speaking, you want your local hostname to be short, because it's usually entered by typing it, and you want your default service name (i.e., Computer Name) to be long and descriptive, because advertised services are usually selected from a list of choices by clicking with the mouse, never by typing. Because of this, service names can be as rich as you like, with uppercase, lowercase, spaces, accented characters, and any amount of weird and wonderful punctuation.

If two computers on the same link try to use the same hostname, one of them will automatically rename. For example, if both try to use the name *mymac.local*, one will automatically rename to *mymac-2.local*. In Mac OS X 10.3, this change happens silently, and the user is not informed. In Mac OS X 10.4 and later, the system puts up an alert to inform the user of the name change.

In principle, it's possible for each network interface on your computer to answer to a different name, or even for a single network interface to answer to a variety of different names. But in practice, this would be confusing, so Mac OS X uses a single hostname for all its interfaces.

# Multicast DNS

Most conferences have a message board somewhere where you can post and retrieve messages. The key is that there is a well-known place for you to visit to send or read items of interest to an individual or to a group. The message board is not generally secure and you cannot be assured that messages have been reliably delivered unless the target of your message replies. Other people can see the same messages you can see. Often, a friend will stop you in the hall to let you know that there is a message waiting for you on the message board. The message board is a great mechanism to announce a so-called "birds of a feather" session where people who share a common interest convene.

A multicast address is the network world's equivalent of a shared public-notice board. Using a previously agreed-upon IP Multicast address and port, messages can be delivered that will be received by all subscribed devices. Devices on a local link can use Multicast DNS to resolve locally unique hostnames. Every device on the local link listens for queries that are sent to the multicast address, and when it sees any query for its own name, it answers. In this section, you will see how the multicast part of mDNS works.

## The mDNS Multicast Address

Any DNS query for a name ending in .local is sent to the address 224.0.0.251, which is the IPv4 address that has been reserved for mDNS. For a list of assigned multicast addresses, see the IANA document "INTERNET MULTICAST ADDRESSES" at *http://www.iana.org/assignments/multicast-addresses* (IPv4) and *http://www. iana.org/assignments/ipv6-multicast-addresses* (IPv6). The IPv6 mDNS link-local multicast address is FF02::FB. The concepts of Multicast DNS apply equally, whether the data is sent in IPv4 multicast packets or IPv6 multicast packets.

Because 224.0.0.251 and FF02::FB are in the link-local multicast ranges for IPv4 and IPv6, respectively, packets sent to these addresses are never forwarded outside the local link nor forwarded onto the local link from outside. A device can therefore be sure that any link-local multicast packets it sends remain on the local link, and any link-local multicast packets it receives must have originated on the local link.

In general, the mDNS-based algorithm for claiming names and handling conflicts replaces a central authority with cooperating participants. If there are participants on the local link intent on disrupting this process, then they can do so. In principle, this could be solved by using IPSEC and/or DNSSEC signatures to identify trusted participants, though, in practice, it has not yet been a problem, and no current products implement these kinds of protection.

Queries to determine the hostname for a particular link-local IP address ("reverse lookups") can also be sent to 224.0.0.251. For IPv4, this reverse address mapping is any DNS query for a name ending in *254.169.in-addr.arpa*, and for IPv6, it is a name ending in *0.8.e.f.ip6.arpa*.

# Multicast DNS Queries

Multicast DNS Queries fall into three categories: one-shot with a single answer, one-shot with multiple answers, and ongoing.

The first category is a one-shot query. Modifying an existing DNS client to perform one-shot queries can be trivial. If the name ends in *local*, then set the destination address to 224.0.0.251, set the destination port to 5353, and send the UDP packet as usual. When the UDP response comes back, the DNS client receives it and handles it, as it would any other DNS response. If no response is received, then the query is retransmitted a few times, just as with a normal Unicast DNS query. The code doesn't have to be modified to do anything else special because it's using multicast—from the code's point of view, it is just talking to a DNS server at a particular address and port number. If all you want to be able to do is to type *http://somename.local/* into a web browser and have it work, then this level of Multicast DNS functionality is sufficient.

The second category is one-shot queries that accumulate multiple responses. The DNS client still sends a query to 224.0.0.251, but this time the DNS client is aware that there are queries for which more than one response is possible, so the DNS client both waits for more than one response and, when appropriate, retransmits its query. When the DNS client has got enough results or has waited long enough, it returns the results to the application that initiated the query. Because the DNS client may retransmit its query more than once, this could cause the same host (or group of hosts) to respond more than once, which would be a waste of network bandwidth. To prevent this, each successive query includes a Known Answer list. If a host sees its answer already in the Known Answer list, then it doesn't have to respond again. Successive queries are also not transmitted at a constant rate but at an exponentially decaying rate, with the interval between packets doubling each time.

The third category is continuous, ongoing queries. If you want to browse the network to find the list of available printers, then a query that waits for 10 seconds and then displays the results has two problems: (a) waiting for 10 seconds before you see the results is far too long, and (b) the moment you see it, the list is already beginning to get out of date. What you want is a list that appears instantly, updates immediately whenever a new printer appears, and, ideally, also shows you promptly whenever a printer goes away. Consider also an instant messenger client like iChat that shows a list of buddies on the local network. You don't want a snapshot of the list of buddies that were there when you launched iChat, and you don't want to have to keep clicking a refresh button to update the list. You simply want a list that's always up to date, from second to second, and you want a protocol that's smart enough to do this efficiently. By repeating queries, mDNS keeps the list up to date. By including a Known Answer list, mDNS reduces unnecessary traffic. By using exponential backoff instead of querying at a constant rate, the traffic rate is further reduced. The interval between queries can grow up to one hour. So that it doesn't take an hour for you to discover a new buddy on the network, new clients announce their presence by sending gratuitous responses when they arrive on the network. Every answer record that's received has a time to live (TTL) that tells the receiver how long to hold that record in the local cache. When the TTL is close to expiring, the querier queries for it again, and if no answer is received before the record expires, it is removed from the cache and disappears from the screen. The combination of these efficiency features and others results in a system that provides excellent responsiveness at a low packet rate.

For continuous, ongoing queries, responses are sent via multicast, not unicast. It may seem that multicast responses will lead to an unreasonable increase in traffic on the network. On the contrary, responses that are sent as multicast allow multiple machines to receive the same information without having to issue a query themselves. The machines on the network are all listening to queries and responses addressed to 224.0.0.251. When a machine receives a response to a query, other machines on the network receive the response too and can add it to their own caches for future use. If they later need this information, they don't have to issue a query because they already have it.

## Reducing traffic

There are useful techniques employed to reduce the sending of redundant information. The first is the Known Answer Suppression, mentioned above. Think of a teacher trying to get additional answers from a class by saying, "What might you try before you implement the State Pattern? We've already seen that one solution is *nested if statements* and another solution is *using the case statement.*" The idea is that when a Multicast DNS query is sent by a host that already knows some of the answers, the query must include the known answers in the Answer Section of the DNS message. The TTL of each known answer is set to indicate how many seconds remain before it expires from the querier's cache. A Multicast DNS responder does not respond if it sees its answer already in the Known Answer list with a TTL that's at least half the correct value. A TTL of less than half the original value indicates that the record may expire from the cache soon, so the responder responds to refresh all the neighboring caches. Because of this, the querier knows that records with remaining cache lifetime of less than half their original value needn't be included in the Known Answer list in the first place, thereby reducing the size of the initial query packet. If there are too many answers to fit in a single query packet, then the TC (*truncated*) bit is set in the DNS packet header, and the Known Answer list continues in the next packet. Information contained in the Known Answer list of the query is only used to signal information the querier *believes* to be correct and should not be taken as authoritative by other devices on the network.

Returning to our classroom example, once one student has been scolded for asking "Is this going to be on the test?" the other students get the message not to ask this same question. Similarly, if a host is preparing to transmit a query and it detects a query containing the same question, then it may not need to send the same question itself. The host that has not yet issued the query needs to check the Known Answer section to determine that there are not any answers there that this host would not have added as its own. In other words, if there is no additional information that can be learned by transmitting the query, then none should be sent.

Back in our classroom example, a student has just answered the teacher's question and all the other students who were going to give the same answer lower their hands. A similar optimization is used in mDNS. If a host is preparing a response and sees a response from another host with the same answer as its own, then it can suppress its own response.

If a host knows that certain of its resource record data has become invalid, it should send a goodbye packet. This is a gratuitous announcement mDNS response packet with an RR TTL value of 0. A host receiving this will update its local TTL for this entry to zero, which causes the cache entry to be deleted. When a service is shutting down cleanly, this goodbye packet causes it to be deleted immediately from peer caches, instead of lingering while its TTL slowly decrements all the way to 0. If the service does not shut down cleanly, or the goodbye packet is lost, the caches still converge to correctness eventually—it just takes a little longer.

# Claiming Your Local Name

This section looks at the dance that results in a device obtaining a locally unique name. The details of the Multicast DNS Querier and Responder, and other mechanics of where the messages are being sent and which devices are listening, were covered in the previous section. For now, consider a device that has an IP address that is now trying to claim a unique name in the *.local* domain. The steps and precautions parallel much of what was described in Chapter 2. The sequence is very similar: first, a name has to be chosen, then the device probes to check for uniqueness, and then it announces its chosen name.

## Probing to Check for Uniqueness

Once a hostname is chosen for a particular device and an IP address has been selected or assigned, the next step is to create a local Multicast DNS address record that maps the name to the IP address. DNS Record types are documented in the IETF's RFC 1035 "Domain Names - Implementation and Specification" (*http://www.ietf.org/rfc/rfc1035.txt*). DNS Record type A is the IPv4 address record type.

Having created our tentative address record (also known as an *A record*), we need to check to see if someone is already using an address record with that same name. (The name of the A record and our desired hostname are one and the same.)

We could send an mDNS query for our desired hostname, DNS type A, and see if we get any responses. However we may also want to create other record types for our hostname, such as host info (HINFO), so we instead send a query for DNS query type T_ANY, in order to find if there are records of *any* type with that name.

---

## DNS Query Type T_ANY

What does DNS query type T_ANY mean? Many assume it's a wildcard search that returns all matching records, but this is incorrect. The query type is called T_ANY, not T_ALL. The semantics of the T_ANY query are that if there are *any* records with that name, of any type, it will return at least one of them. Sometimes, it may return all records, but not always. This is particularly true with DNS caches. If a cache has *any* records with that name, it is allowed to return just what it has, without checking with the authoritative server to see if there may be any more records with that same name. This makes T_ANY queries less useful than they may at first appear.

In Multicast DNS, however, T_ANY queries do, in fact, return all matching records.

---

If no conflicting Multicast DNS response is received, then a second query is sent 250 ms after the first and, in the absence of conflicts, a third query is sent 250 ms after that. After waiting an additional 250 ms, or a total of 750 ms for the three queries and corresponding waiting time, if no conflicting Multicast DNS response has been received, then the host has successfully verified uniqueness and proceeds to the announcement step. If, at any point in the probing step, a conflicting Multicast DNS response is received, then the host must select a new name for each of the conflicting records that need unique names. A device may have a mechanism for selecting another name or it may, if appropriate, be set up to display an error message to prompt a human user to manually select another name.

What if two devices probe to verify the same name *at exactly the same time*? Neither will be able to answer the other's probe because neither owns the name yet. Certainly, this normally shouldn't happen very often, but the reliability goals of Zeroconf dictate that even the situations that don't happen very often still need to be handled correctly.

Multicast DNS solves this race condition by adding the desired new record to the authority section of the query packet. This usage is analogous to the way DNS UPDATE packets use the authority section to convey the new data to be added to the server.

When two hosts probing the same name see each other's probes, they consult the authority section and use the data there as a tiebreaker. This type of conflict is resolved in favor of the record with the lexicographically later rdata. The determination of *lexicographically later* is made by first comparing the record class, then the record type, then a raw comparison of the binary content of the rdata without regard for meaning or structure. If the record classes differ, then the numerically greater class is considered lexicographically later. Otherwise, if the record types differ, then the numerically greater type is considered lexicographically later. If the type and class both match, then the rdata is compared.

The bytes of the raw rdata are compared in turn, interpreting the bytes as eight-bit unsigned values, until a byte is found whose value is greater than that of its counterpart (in which case, the rdata whose byte has the greater value is deemed lexicographically later) or one of the resource records runs out of rdata (in which case, the resource record that still has remaining data is deemed lexicographically later). The following is an example of a conflict:

```
sctibook.local. A 169.254.99.200
sctibook.local. A 169.254.200.50
```

In this case, 169.254.200.50 is lexicographically later (the third byte, with value 200, is greater than its counterpart with value 99), so it is deemed the winner. The loser is expected to pick a new name and the winner proceeds as if nothing had happened. If the loser refuses to cooperate, then the conflict is still detected and resolved eventually; it just takes longer.

The reason the protocol chooses the lexicographically later data as the winner (rather than the lexicographically earlier) is because of the way some networks (particularly wireless networks) can delay and repeat old packets. After a name conflict, a host typically responds by appending "–2" to the end of its name, or incrementing "2" to "3," both of which yield a new name that's lexicographically later. Situations have been observed when a host, probing for uniqueness of its DNS "SRV" service records (described in Chapter 4), would see an old packet of its own, from half a second ago, come back from the network. If the lexicographically earlier data were to win, then, in this situation, the host could sometimes conclude that it had lost a tiebreaker *with itself* (as of half a second ago)! Declaring the lexicographically later data as the winner means that in these strange and uncommon situations, a host's current state will tend to win in comparison to its old self. It's a minor consideration, but given that there's really no other reason to prefer lexicographically earlier or lexicographically later, this one point tipped the balance in favor of declaring the lexicographically later data to be the winner.

## Announcing

After issuing three queries and waiting 250 ms after each query, if a host has not received a conflicting Multicast DNS response, it begins the announcing step. In this step, the Multicast DNS Responder sends a gratuitous Multicast DNS response that contains all of its resource records in the Answer Section. The purpose of these announcements is (just like ARP announcements) to update neighboring caches on the network that might still be holding old, stale data. This announcement is normally sent more than once to guard against packet loss. For records that have been verified unique, the mDNS cache flush bit of the rrclass is set to 1. This is the most significant bit of the rrclass, and as the mDNS spec explains:

> When a resource record appears in the answer section of the DNS Response with the "cache flush" bit set, it means, "This is an assertion that this information is the truth and the whole truth, and anything you may have heard before regarding records of this name/type/class is no longer valid".

Upon receiving this data, neighboring caches will delete all old records they have with this name and replace them with the new data.

A host needs to be able to detect conflicts anytime it is operating and advertising mDNS records, not just during the initial probing phase. Anytime a host sees another host send answer records that disagree with its own (for example, an address record with the same hostname but a different IP address), that's a conflict, which needs to be resolved. This is one of the places that the usefulness of sending replies via multicast instead of unicast is evident. When all the replies are public, you can quickly see when another host is advertising records that you don't agree with.

When two hosts see each other send conflicting answers, both hosts reset their records back to probing state. When they then proceed to send their three probe packets, each will see the other's probes, and the tiebreaking rules will be invoked to determine who has to rename and who does not.

# The Structure of the Multicast DNS Message

The Multicast DNS Message format is modeled closely on the Unicast DNS Message format. In fact, they are so similar that packet-sniffing software such as Sniffer, EtherPeek, and Ethereal can decode and display mDNS packets using the same decoder as uDNS packets. There are, however, a few minor differences:

- Unicast DNS packets are limited to, at most, 512 bytes. Multicast DNS packets are allowed to be up to 9,000 bytes, though it's recommended that implementations try to limit themselves to using packets only as large as the local link can carry without breaking the packet into multiple IP fragments. Standard Ethernet can carry packets up to 1,500 bytes without fragmentation. Subtracting 28 bytes for the IP and UDP headers, this leaves up to 1,472 bytes for the DNS portion of the packet.

- Multicast DNS uses UDP port 5353 instead of port 53.

- Multicast DNS uses UTF-8, and only UTF-8, to encode resource record names. Unicast DNS, for a variety of legacy compatibility reasons, has to use arcane encoding for non-roman text, but Multicast DNS is a new technology not saddled with those limitations, so it has the luxury of using the much simpler UTF-8 for everything.

- Unicast DNS only allows query packets to contain one question each. For efficiency, Multicast DNS allows clients to pack in as many questions as they wish. They're still treated by the receiver just the same as if they were separate packets—packing them into a single packet is just an optional optimization to save network bandwidth.

- Multicast DNS "borrows" the top bit of the rrclass field in a resource record. Remember that the only DNS class in widespread use today—out of the 65,536 possible values for this 16-bit field—is the Internet class. By repurposing the top bit, we cut the range of possible class values in half to 32,768, but that's still a lot when you consider that we're only actually using one today. In responses, the top bit of the rrclass field is called the *cache flush* bit and signals the receiver that this new data should completely replace all old records with the same name, rather than adding cumulatively to any existing data. In questions, setting the top bit of the rrclass field signals a request to have the response for that record sent via unicast instead of multicast. This is something that's occasionally done in situations where it is believed that a unicast response would be more efficient on the network, but current operational experience seems to indicate that the actual benefit is very minor, so it's possible that future versions of mDNSResponder may not use this capability.

# Summary

Zeroconf's Multicast DNS, like RFC 3927 link-local addressing, provides a safety net when the equivalent conventional infrastructure is not present or working. When there's no DHCP server, link-local addressing gets you an address that's at least good for the local link. When there's no DNS server, or there is one but you have no way to add your own hostnames to it, Multicast DNS gives you a way of referring to devices by name that at least works on the local link. This gets us to a useful level of functionality: even when DHCP and DNS are broken, link-local addressing and Multicast DNS mean that you can give your devices names, refer to them from other computers using those names, and establish working TCP connections so that you can do useful networking. Zeroconf doesn't stop there, though. With the technology described so far, you can do useful networking, but you need to know the hostname, you need to remember it, and you need to type it in correctly. If you mistype it, misremember it, or just don't know the name of the printer, you're in trouble. Wouldn't it be better if you didn't have to know the name of the printer in advance? Wouldn't it be better if you could just say, "I need to print a document. Is there anything on the network that can help me with that?" That's Zeroconf's DNS Service Discovery technology, and that's the subject of the next chapter.

# UTF-8

The American Standard Code for Information Interchange (ASCII) has long been the standard way most computers represent text in their memories and on their disks. Each letter, digit, and symbol is represented by a different seven-bit binary code. Rather than write the codes in binary, they are usually written in numerical form, as numbers from 0 to 127. For example, the code for A is 65.

The problem is that while 128 values are enough to represent English uppercase letters, lowercase letters, digits, and punctuation, they're not enough to represent all the accented characters used in European languages, and definitely not enough to represent all the characters used in Japanese, Hebrew, Indian languages, and so on.

A new standard for representing text called the Universal Character Set (UCS), or Unicode, solves this by having literally millions of possible codes. The problem is that to work directly with Unicode data, software that manipulates text has to be rewritten, which takes a long time. Also, Unicode is less efficient than ASCII for English words, making it slow to gain popularity among many English speakers who don't see much benefit from having all those extra characters if they're not using them. The word "Hello" in Unicode can take double or even four times the space to store as the same word stored using ASCII.

UCS Transformation Format 8 (UTF-8) solves this problem in a simple, elegant way. A single eight-bit byte in computer memory can hold 256 possible values, from 0 to 255, but ASCII requires only 128 values, leaving the other 128 unused. The ingenious solution is that UTF-8 uses the values 0–127 to represent exactly the same characters as ASCII—so the word "Hello" stored using UTF-8 and the word "Hello" stored using ASCII *are exactly the same in memory*. UTF-8 is a compatible superset of ASCII. So we can declare, by fiat, as it were, that every single ASCII string stored in memory or on disk anywhere in the world is actually a UTF-8 string, and not a single line of software has had to change.

The second step is how UTF-8 represents all those additional non-roman characters. UTF-8 uses those byte values in the range 128–255, unused by ASCII, to represent those characters. Depending on the character, it may be represented in memory as a consecutive sequence of two, three, or more bytes in the 128–255 range.

The beauty of this is that almost all software that works with ASCII text can work without modification with the new UTF-8 text. Of course, if you want to display UTF-8 text on the screen or print it on paper, you need software that knows how to properly decode UTF-8 and draw the right characters, but most software never needs to do this. DNS code is concerned with putting data into packets and reading it out, not with what those characters look like to humans. The little bit of user-interface code responsible for showing text on the screen has to draw UTF-8 characters correctly, but the rest of the DNS protocol code—the vast bulk of it—can just pass the data around as raw data, unconcerned with how that data might eventually be presented to the human user.

*—continued—*

UTF-8 is popular in the United States, because it allows non-roman characters to be represented using multibyte sequences in otherwise standard ASCII files. In some places outside the USA, where most characters need to be represented using multibyte sequences, UTF-8 is less popular, and many people prefer to use 16-bit Unicode characters (UTF-16) directly. Multicast DNS adopts UTF-8 as the best way to maintain compatibility with existing ASCII names, while at the same time providing the capability to represent non-roman characters, too.

# CHAPTER 4

# Browsing for Services

Once you are on a network where you have a working IP address and hostname, you are in a position to begin doing some useful networking. Your IP address may change over time, particularly if you are using IPv4 link-local addressing, but your Multicast DNS hostname generally won't. People on the local network can access services running on your machine using your mDNS hostname anywhere a conventional hostname would be used, automatically connecting to your current address, even if your address changed since the last time they connected. People can use your mDNS hostname on the command line to connect with FTP or SSH commands. If your machine is running a web server, others can connec[t to it by entering your mDNS hostname into their web browser. Note that web servers can take many forms apart from the conventional collection of static pages: if you have a typical network-connected camera with Multicast DNS, you can connect by typing its name (e.g., *netcam.local*) into your web browser. This is, of course, a big improvement over having to know the IP address to type, but in some ways we've merely moved the problem, not solved it. Instead of having to know what IP address to type, you now have to know what name to type. In the case of IPv6 addresses, which are 20–40 characters long, a short, memorable hostname is definitely an improvement, but imagine how much better it would be if you didn't have to know the name at all, and your web browser could simply instruct the network, "Show me the list of services that I know how to talk to."

This chapter introduces DNS Service Discovery (DNS-SD), the mechanism in Zeroconf that lets you discover what services are available on the network without having to know device or service names in advance via some other means. DNS Service Discovery is accomplished by building on existing standard DNS queries and resource record types, not by creating a new set of technologies and hoping they will be adopted over time. Enhancing and extending existing technologies is one of the things that has helped lead to the quick adoption of DNS-based service discovery.

The first two legs of Zeroconf allow you to fully participate in a local network in the absence of what we would have traditionally considered the enabling technologies of DHCP and DNS. Obtaining an IP address is nothing new. At work or at a café offering wireless Internet access, your computer has likely been assigned an IP address by a DHCP server. The first leg of Zeroconf provides a way to obtain a link-local IP address without a DHCP server, so that common and necessary step can now be accomplished in a new situation. In Chapter 3, you saw that however you obtained an IP address, it was desirable to obtain a locally unique hostname. One alternative is conventional unicast DNS, but setting up DNS is a lot of work, and all that work really should not be necessary if you just need to transfer a file or print a one-page document. Multicast DNS is a lightweight alternative that gives you DNS-like functionality on the local network without all the overhead and effort of conventional unicast DNS.

Thus far, Zeroconf has not provided anything that you could not, in principle, have obtained through other means. What Zeroconf has provided are alternative ways of doing the same things, ways that work when the conventional mechanisms let us down. In addition, at each step, Zeroconf is not concerned with how you accomplished the previous step. Step one: obtain an IP address by using DHCP, manual assignment, or self-assigned link-local addressing. Step two: obtain a meaningful hostname by using Multicast DNS in cases where conventional Unicast DNS is not appropriate. Step two requires that a device has obtained a working IP address but is not concerned with how. Step three: browse for the services that you need. Step three requires the availability of working DNS-like functionality, but it could be link-local Multicast DNS, global Unicast DNS, or both.

Regardless of whether Multicast DNS or Unicast DNS is being used, new services coming onto the network announce their presence via Multicast DNS, or they use DNS Dynamic Update to update a Unicast DNS server with their information; thus, clients looking for services of that type are all informed that a new instance is now available. When a service goes away gracefully (as opposed to crashing, having the network cable cut, or suffering a power failure), it sends a Multicast DNS goodbye packet or uses DNS Dynamic Update to remove its information from the Unicast DNS server, so that clients can be informed that that particular named service instance is no longer available.

In this chapter, you will see how Zeroconf's service discovery works. As the DNS-based Service Discovery Internet-Draft explains, the prime directive for the service discovery protocol is that it "should be so simple to implement that virtually any device capable of implementing IP should not have any trouble implementing the service discovery software as well."

The service discovery software has two main responsibilities: enumerating the list of names of services on the network of a given type and translating from any given name on the list to the IP address and other information necessary to connect and use it. The service instance names should be under user control but relatively persistent, so that tomorrow, the same service instance name logically identifies the same conceptual service being offered, even if the IP address has changed or the TCP port number the server is listening on has changed. Even if the hardware has been replaced or the software has been upgraded, clients should still be able to connect to that service using the same name.

You will notice a recurring theme in this chapter: you are browsing for services, not devices. The importance of browsing for services instead of devices is a lesson that was learned from the old AppleTalk Name Binding Protocol, a protocol that enjoyed two decades of success in the marketplace, and it is an important lesson. The difference between discovering *services* and discovering *devices* is subtle. The concept of a service, as a pure abstract entity in its own right, divorced from whatever hardware may be providing that service, is a fairly counterintuitive concept. Humans can touch, see, buy, and sell hardware, so from a human perspective, it seems natural that the computer would also see the network as a collection of bits of hardware. However, from a computer and network protocol perspective, the useful question to ask the network is not "What hardware do you have?" but "What can you do for me?" From a human perspective, the user thinks in terms of finding a printer, but from a protocol perspective, the software is looking for a network service that it can use to print. The difference is subtle but important. Discovering hardware is no use if you don't know how to talk to it. Discovering a service you can use is what's useful, and from a protocol perspective, it doesn't really matter what kind of hardware is providing that service.

# Zero Configuration Operation

Finding services should be as easy as turning on a lamp. If technological devices continue to be unreasonably hard to set up and use, the market for those devices is going to be stifled because the buying public simply won't be willing to expend the time and effort it takes to get them to work.

Consider a table lamp. The customer needs to plug the lamp into a live AC outlet, the lamp needs to have a working bulb properly in place, and the customer needs to locate and operate the switch. When a customer flicks a switch and the light does not come on, there are not many things that could have gone wrong. The tech support script is pretty basic: "You say the light doesn't come on. Did you try the bulb in a different lamp to make sure the bulb is good? Did you try connecting some other appliance to the outlet to make sure it's providing power? What? I see. You hadn't actually plugged the lamp into a power outlet? That may be your problem. Sure, I'll hold while you try that. Works now? Great. No, really it's no problem, your service contract allows you unlimited calls for the first year you own your lamp." This scenario is comical because, of course, no one has technical support service contracts for table lamps. We need to arrive at a world where we think of consumer electronics and networked devices the same way we think of table lamps.

# Finding Services, Not Devices

In the world of networked devices, it does you no good to locate a device with which you cannot communicate. We commonly anthropomorphize devices in ways that are not quite correct. We say that we "pinged a server," though, in fact, what we pinged was a piece of software on the server that answers ICMP echo request packets. If you take away that software, it stops answering ping requests, even though the server is still there and may still be performing other functions perfectly well.

When designing a service discovery system, it's important to remember that what network software clients need to discover are software entities with which they can communicate, not pieces of hardware. The difference between discovering services and discovering hardware may seem small and subtle, but it makes all the difference in actual use. In a print dialog, you want to see the list of things you can print to. In iTunes, you want to see the list of music sources you can play. In iPhoto, you want to see the list of photo albums you can view. In a web browser, you want to see a list of offered web pages you can view. Any given piece of hardware on the network may offer zero, one, or more of each of these kinds of resources. What you want to see is the list of resources you can use, not a list of the hardware where they may or may not reside.

# Knowing the Protocol

A visitor staying in Paris wants to know whether she should take her umbrella on her travels around the city. Standing in the hotel lobby in the morning, she sees a local newspaper, which has the day's weather forecast, but it is in French. She doesn't read French. Also in the hotel lobby is a copy of an English newspaper, which she can read, but the English newspaper doesn't include a weather forecast for Paris. This illustrates one of the challenges of network software. To be useful, a service has to (1) provide the conceptual service the client wants (e.g., a weather forecast) and (2) provide it using a language (protocol) the client can speak and understand (e.g., English). Because of this, a Zeroconf service type name conveys not just the "what" of a service but also the "how." For example, the Zeroconf service type _ipp encodes both the "what"—printing—and the "how" via Internet Printing Protocol.

When an IPP printing client browses for services of type _ipp, it is not looking for printers in a broad, fuzzy, not-very-precisely defined human sense. It is looking specifically for printers it can talk to. It is looking specifically for printers that implement IPP, the Internet Printing Protocol. There may be an old AppleTalk printer nearby, which may be a printer as far as human beings are concerned, but from the point of view of an IPP printing client that has no way to communicate with an AppleTalk printer, it may as well not exist. From the point of view of IPP printing client software, it's only useful to discover things that it can actually use. This is one of the reasons that proliferation of network protocols is a bad thing. While we may embrace the richness of variety in human languages, the same is not so desirable in network protocols. When there are 10 different ways of doing basically the same thing, there's much opportunity for incompatibility. The server may offer the *conceptual* service that the client wants, but if they have no protocol in common that they both speak, it may as well not exist.

The converse is also true. Finding entities that implement a given protocol is only appropriate when the semantic service being offered is also appropriate. It is common to borrow an existing protocol and repurpose it for a new task. This is an entirely sensible and sound engineering practice, but that doesn't mean that the new protocol is providing the same semantic service as the old one, even if it uses the same message formats. For example, the local network music-playing protocol implemented by iTunes on Macintosh and Windows is built using HTTP GET commands. However, that does not mean that it is sensible or useful to try to access one of these music servers by connecting to it with a standard web browser. The data that is being fetched via those HTTP GET commands is compact binary machine-readable data, not HTML text that a normal web browser could interpret and display as a page on the screen. If iTunes were to advertise the _http service, that would cause iTunes servers to show up in conventional web browsers like Safari and Internet Explorer, which is of little use since an iTunes server offers no pages containing human-readable content. Similarly, if iTunes were to browse for _http service, it would find generic web servers, such as the embedded web servers in devices such as printers, which is of little use since printers generally don't have much music to offer. Consequently, the DNS-SD service advertised (and browsed for) by iTunes is the Digital Audio Access Protocol, or _daap, which conveys both the "what" of the service (a collection of music) and also the "how" (read using HTTP GET commands).

# Building on DNS

As early as the 1980s, AppleTalk had an effective service discovery mechanism. Many attempts have been made to replicate that on IP, but none have been a resounding success. Zeroconf took an unconventional approach to solving this problem. Rather than inventing an entirely new protocol from scratch, it built on an existing ubiquitous standard, DNS. A scalable service discovery mechanism needs to work both on small networks, operating peer-to-peer with no infrastructure, and on large networks, where peer-to-peer multicast would be too inefficient and, instead, service discovery data needs to be stored at some central aggregation point. As pointed out in the Internet Draft on DNS Service Discovery, DNS and its related protocols already provide the properties we need:

*Service discovery requires a central aggregation server*
  DNS already has one: it's called a DNS server.

*Service discovery requires a service registration protocol*
  DNS already has one: it's called DNS Dynamic Update.

*Service discovery requires a query protocol*
  DNS already has one: it's called DNS.

*Service discovery requires security mechanisms*
  DNS already has security mechanisms: they're called DNSSEC.

*Service discovery requires a multicast mode for ad-hoc networks*
  Zeroconf environments already require a multicast-based, DNS-like name lookup protocol for mapping hostnames to addresses, so it makes sense to let one multicast-based protocol do both jobs.

By building on an existing protocol, many of the deployment and adoption problems are already solved. Just about every large company already runs a DNS server, so the required hardware and software is already in place. DNS delegation means that if the network operators don't want to support service discovery functions on their current DNS server, they can choose to delegate that responsibility to some other machine. Whether running on the company's main DNS server or delegated to some other piece of hardware, the DNS technology is familiar and the software well understood. We don't have some entirely new, unfamiliar piece of software to be installed, learned, configured, and maintained.

In the remainder of this chapter, you will see how DNS-SD builds on what exists in DNS.

# Browsing for Services

The DNS protocol family already defines a record type called SRV for service discovery, specified in RFC 2782, "A DNS RR for specifying the location of services (DNS SRV)." (The letters "SRV" are not initials that stand for something; it's just a simple contraction of the word "service.") SRV records give us a new way of finding services for a given domain. Today, to find the web server for domain *example.com*, you would look up the address associated with the pseudo-hostname *www.example.com*. The reason we call *www.example.com* a pseudo-hostname is because *www* is not really the name of a host; it is really the name of a service. The user typing *www* doesn't know or care what host they're connecting to, what they care about is that the host has web pages on it. This puts us in the odd situation where some DNS names are hostnames, and others are really service names, but the distinction is blurred and vague; for any given name, it's not always clear whether it's intended to be the name of a logical service or the name of a particular piece of hardware. This is why, in 1996, a new DNS record type was defined, the SRV record. Using the new SRV mechanism, you would do a DNS query for the SRV record with the name *_http._tcp.example.com*. This is explicitly and unambiguously not the name of a piece of hardware. What you're asking for with this query is HTTP service (i.e., web pages) for the domain *example.com*.

The *_tcp* part of the name is there for largely historical reasons. It suggests that the service usually runs by default over TCP, not UDP, though it is only a loose suggestion, and in retrospect perhaps it should have been omitted from the specification. However, the inclusion of the transport protocol label in the SRV record name does give us an accidental benefit—a DNS server operator can easily offload all the service-discovery workload from the main server by simply delegating the *_tcp* and *_udp* subdomains to some other machine.

The result of our SRV query tells us the hostname of the machine and the port number of the process on that machine offering HTTP service for the *example.com* domain. Some sites might have multiple servers running for fault tolerance reasons, in which case, we would get multiple SRV records in the response. The client then picks one of the SRV records at random. It doesn't matter which one, since all the servers are offering the same pages.

So far, we've described SRV records as specified in RFC 2782. As specified there, SRV records work for finding a company's main web page but are less useful for other kinds of service. If an employee wants to print, and there are 50 printers available at the company, then having the printing client simply pick one at random is not likely to be very useful. What DNS-SD adds to RFC 2782 is the ability to present a list to the user, so she can choose *which* printer she wants to use.

There's an old joke that the answer to every problem in computer science is to add one more level of indirection. In this case, that joke offers us the answer to our problem. Instead of having 50 DNS SRV records with the name *_ipp._tcp.example.com.*, we have 50 DNS pointer (PTR) records, each pointing to a differently named SRV record describing that printing service. By performing a PTR lookup for a name of the form *ServiceType.Domain*, you get a list of individual named instances of that service from which the client can choose. This is the key refinement that DNS-SD adds to vanilla SRV records.

## Service Instance Names

When you perform a PTR lookup for a service type in a domain, you will receive zero or more PTR records containing service instance names. A *service instance name* adds a third piece to the name contained in your PTR lookup. Your lookup sent the name `ServiceType.Domain` and returned PTR records that contain service instance names consisting of `Instance.ServiceType.Domain`. For example, a query for `_ipp._tcp.example.com` may return the service instance names `Sales._ipp._tcp.example.com` and `Bullpen._ipp._tcp.example.com`.

The `Instance` portion of a service instance name is not restricted to US-ASCII characters. Any Unicode characters may be used, up to a total of 63 bytes of UTF-8 encoded text. Of course, you are free to name your services how you choose; you can use names containing only US-ASCII if you wish, but you shouldn't feel compelled to keep names short to make them easy to type. Users select Zeroconf services by picking from an onscreen list, not by memorizing names and typing them in, so there's really little benefit in making names terse and easy to type. You can use long names, including capital letters, spaces, punctuation, and other characters, to make them more descriptive.

You can think of the *ServiceType.Domain* name structure as being analogous to a directory hierarchy containing instance names. So, the example _ipp._tcp.example.com would correspond to the directory */com/example/_tcp/_ipp*, as shown in Figure 4-1.

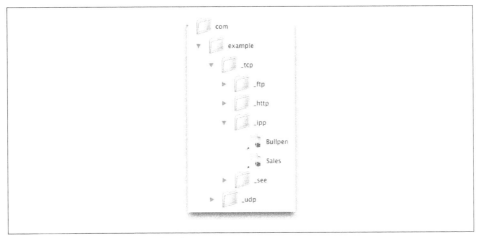

*Figure 4-1. The directory metaphor for service instance names*

Inside of this directory, you can imagine aliases or soft links to actual instances of services of the specific type. If you wanted to select the Bullpen printer, you would double-click on its alias. In the actual case of a service instance name, when a user selects the service name in a service browser, a DNS query will be sent for the SRV record with the selected name. In response, the client receives an SRV record with the host and port information for the service. Notice that this means that a host is able to allocate its available port numbers dynamically to services that need them, instead of restricting each service to run on one predetermined, "well-known" port.

In the directory analogy, you see that the most significant part of the *Instance. ServiceType.Domain* triple is the domain, with the service coming in second. The idea is that within a domain, there may or may not be services offered. For a given service type within a domain, there may or may not be instances of that type. The key in this structure is that the instances are the leaves in this tree you are navigating. In a graphical user interface, typically only the instance portion of the service instance name is displayed. In principle, the service type and domain of a discovered instance don't have to match the service type and domain of the PTR query that returned them, but in practice, they almost always do. Still, it's good programming practice to store the full name, type, and domain of each discovered service, rather than just storing the name and assuming the other two will necessarily be the expected values.

# What You See Is What You Get

One design decision in DNS-SD was that the user-visible name of a service instance is also the primary identifier for that instance. They are one and the same. If you change the name, it is conceptually a different instance. If you replace defective hardware with new hardware but continue to advertise the service using the old name, then it is conceptually the same service being offered.

There are other service discovery systems that don't work like this. In those systems, the primary identifier for a service is some hidden binary unique ID, like the MAC address of the Ethernet interface or some other globally unique ID (GUID). These identifiers are long and cryptic and practically impossible for humans to remember. Because the unique IDs are not intended to be user-friendly, a user-visible name is also associated with the service, a mere transient ephemeral attribute, changeable at any time. On paper, this flexibility might sound attractive: you can change the "name" of a service at any time without really changing its identity. Identity is defined solely by the unchangeable unique IDs, which are hidden and supposedly never seen by human users. In practice, once you use a system like that for a while, you find the flexibility is not always the benefit it seemed. If the name does not define the identity, then two things with different names might actually be the same service. Two things with apparently the same name might really be different. When problems occur, as they frequently do with networked devices, the veil is pierced. Users are forced to start being aware of the supposedly hidden unique IDs in order to diagnose what's really going on and solve the problem. With DNS-SD, in contrast, there is complete naming transparency. The true identifiers are not cryptic, secret, and hidden. What you see is what you get.

# Flagship Service Types

Normally, the namespaces for different service types are separate. For example, you could have a file server called Home Office, a printer called Home Office, and an Ethernet-attached security camera called Home Office, and there's no confusion because they all offer clearly different services.

The difficulty arises when there are several different protocols that offer conceptually similar services. For example, there are at least four different ways of printing over TCP/IP:

- Old-fashioned Unix *LPR* printing. The data transferred is often, but not necessarily, postscript. The DNS-SD service type name is _printer._tcp.
- Proprietary printer-specific command set, usually sent to TCP port 9100. The DNS-SD service type name is _pdl-datastream._tcp.

- IETF-Standard Internet Printing Protocol. The DNS-SD service type name is `_ipp._tcp`.
- Remote USB port emulation. The DNS-SD service type name is `_riousbprint._tcp`.

Suppose you have a printing client like Mac OS X's printing client that speaks all four protocols. It browses for all four DNS-SD service types. Suppose it finds, for each type, a service instance called Home Office. Should it assume that it has found four different printers that each speak one protocol or found a single printer that speaks all four and is offering four logical services on the network?

The DNS-SD convention is that it should assume it has found one single printer that speaks all four protocols. To make this assumption safe, we want to ensure that, if there actually are four different printers on the network, they don't pick the same name. Normally, for entities offering the same service type, Multicast DNS's built-in name conflict detection will ensure that two services can't have the same name. However, how should DNS-SD know that you *can* have a file server and a network security camera with the same name, but you *should not* have a service of type `_pdl-datastream._tcp` along with another service of type `_riousbprint._tcp` advertising the same name on the network at the same time? The answer is flagship service types. For each group of protocols that offer conceptually similar services, one of the protocols, usually the oldest, is nominated as the flagship of the fleet of protocols. In the case of printing protocols, the flagship protocol is Unix LPR printing (`_printer._tcp`). Any device advertising any protocol of the fleet must also advertise the flagship protocol. If the device speaks the flagship protocol, then it advertises it as a normal service it offers, and the usual name conflict detection ensures that there aren't two instances of this protocol with the same name at the same time. If the device *does not* speak the flagship protocol, then it advertises a special empty SRV record, where the target hostname is the device's hostname, but the target port number is zero. This constitutes an assertion that "I claim ownership of this name, but I don't offer the actual service." This solves the problem of ensuring mutual name uniqueness among a set of related protocols. The existence of the flagship SRV record means that attempts by other devices to create other SRV records with the same service name will register a conflict, but the *absence* of a PTR record advertising that service means that clients browsing for that particular service type won't inadvertently discover our non-service and mistake it for a real offered service. In other words, the device has reserved the name in that particular namespace, preventing others from accidentally using it, without having to actually offer or advertise a real service of that type.

Flagship protocols are used when there are two or more protocols that perform effectively the same or similar functions from the user's point of view. From our earlier example, DAAP and HTTP are not viewed as protocols in the same fleet because, even though they share a common design foundation, the functions they perform from the user's point of view are most definitely not interchangeable.

The determination of what constitutes a *fleet* of protocols is not something that the software can do automatically. That determination is made by the human protocol designers. Typically the way things evolve is that initially, a first protocol is created (e.g., LPR). At this point there is no fleet, because there's only one. Later, an improved protocol is invented (e.g., IPP), and because it does roughly the same thing as the earlier protocol, when the new service is advertised by some new device, the device also advertises the older protocol as the flagship of the newly created fleet (of two). Devices advertising only the older protocol don't need to know this—they just continue to advertise the older protocol as they always did. As subsequent new protocols are invented that perform roughly the same function, as long as each one is specified to advertise the same original flagship protocol, then that original flagship protocol becomes the conceptual rendezvous point of the whole family of protocols for name conflict detection purposes. Eventually, many years later, it's possible to arrive at the situation where the original protocol is obsolete and no longer used by anyone at all, but it retains its role as the non-service that every device registers, to ensure that different devices, advertising different protocols that perform roughly the same function, conceptually bump into one another if they try to advertise the same name.

## Subtypes of Service Types

The design of Zeroconf was intentionally kept simple, because in network design, simplicity is the best way to achieve reliability, with products from different vendors all interoperating and working correctly with one another. For this reason, DNS-SD intentionally does not include a complicated query language allowing arbitrarily elaborate queries. What it does include is a very simple filtering capability, which can be useful for some cases. Subtypes are a useful way to advertise a service when some clients will want to find all instances of that service type, but others will only be interested in finding some subset.

Subtypes are best illustrated with an example. Suppose a game developer makes a network game. The commercial version of the game supports both open games that anyone can join and password-protected games. The game developer also makes a free version of the game client available, but the free version can only join open games without a password. In this case, the full version wants to find all available games on the network it might join, whereas the free version wants to find only open games without a password, since it can't join password-protected games.

This selectivity can be achieved using subtypes. Suppose the DNS-SD service type for the game is _mynetgame._tcp. When starting a password-protected game, the service type _mynetgame._tcp is advertised. When starting an open game, the subtype open is used to convey that this game is open to all clients. In Apple's Bonjour APIs, subtypes are introduced by placing them after a comma following the main type, like this: _mynetgame._tcp,open.

When a full client browses for games to join, it simply browses for the main type _mynetgame._tcp and finds all advertised instances on the network, both open and password-protected. When a restricted client browses for games and wants to find *only* open games, it browses for the subtype _mynetgame._tcp,open and finds only those games that were advertised with this subtype.

When advertising a service, zero, one, or more subtypes may be added as a comma-separated list after the main type. When browsing for services, at most one subtype may be specified. If a client wishes to find more than one subtype, it needs to start a separate browsing operation for each one.

In the on-the-wire packet format, subtypes are implemented by registering additional PTR records. In our example above, an open game is advertised with two PTR records, one with the name _mynetgame._tcp and another with the name open._sub._mynetgame._tcp. When the full client browses for _mynetgame._tcp, it finds all games, both open and password-protected. When a restricted client browses for open._sub._mynetgame._tcp, it finds only those instances that were advertised with this additional PTR record.

Note that, in both cases, the type of the discovered service remains the same: _mynetgame._tcp. Subtypes perform a filtering operation so that only a subset of the instances is discovered, but they don't change the type being discovered.

Whether to use subtypes is a design decision for each protocol. Sometimes, subtypes are appropriate. Other times, it may be more appropriate to define two entirely separate types, with clients browsing for one or other or both as appropriate, and servers advertising one or other or both as appropriate.

To date, few DNS-SD protocols have specified any subtypes, and it remains to be seen how useful this mechanism will be. The most common use of subtypes so far has been for defining programmatic mappings from other communication schemes (e.g., Jini, UPnP, and web services) onto DNS-SD, to allow software written using those programming models to get the benefits of Zeroconf not offered by those other mechanisms, including pure peer-to-peer discovery that works even when no infrastructure is present and planet-wide discovery using wide-area DNS Service Discovery.

# Late Binding

Sometimes, when a user chooses a service from a list, it is for immediate use.

Other times, a user makes a choice, like picking a default printer, which may be used repeatedly in the coming hours, days, or weeks. In the latter case, it's important that the client software store the chosen service name, type, and domain, instead of resolving the named service to an IP address and storing that. This is because IP addresses and port numbers can change, whereas service names are the intended stable identifier for a given logical service instance. As long as the client resolves the service name at printing time, it will be sure to get the current address and port number, even if they have changed in the time since the service was first discovered.

# DNS-SD TXT Records

In many cases, all a client needs to know to contact and use a service are the hostname or IP address where that service resides and the port number on that host.

There are other cases where more information is required. For example, a print server may advertise three LPR printers. All three logical printing services are being offered on the same host. All are being offered via the LPR port. What distinguishes them is the LPR queue name. How does a client, having discovered an advertised printer, know what LPR queue name to specify when contacting the machine hosting that service? If it doesn't specify the right LPR queue name, its output may not go to the right physical printer. The answer is the DNS TXT record. In addition to the SRV record, every DNS-SD service has a TXT record, optionally containing additional parameters and attributes of interest to clients. DNS-SD uses the DNS TXT record to store a series of key/value pair attributes in the form "key=value." The TXT record is a standard DNS record type, but DNS-SD establishes some conventions about how it is used for DNS-SD service types. Those conventions are described in this section.

 The TXT record should not duplicate information that is stored elsewhere—for example, the host and port number for the service—since those are obtained from the SRV record.

## Format for DNS TXT Records

Since DNS-SD uses standard DNS TXT records, these records must conform to format rules. In particular, the data consists of one or more strings, each of which consists of a single length byte followed by 0–255 bytes of text. An example of such a string is:

```
| 0x08 | p | a | p | e | r | = | A | 4 |
```

In this diagram, the first byte of data is a binary byte with value 8. It is then followed by eight more bytes of data, each containing the ASCII (or UTF-8) codes for the character indicated. For example, the second byte contains the value 0x70, the ASCII code for lowercase P; the third byte contains the value 0x61, the ASCII code for lowercase A. Note that there is no terminating zero at the end of the string, as there conventionally is with strings in the C programming language.

According to the DNS specification (RFC 1035), a TXT record must contain at least one string. An empty TXT record with zero strings is not allowed. Because of this, you'll often see DNS-SD services advertised with a TXT record containing a single empty string (a single zero length byte, followed by no data).

The total size of a typical DNS-SD TXT record is intended to be small—200 bytes or less. If large amounts of data need to be transferred, making this part of the client protocol is better than using a large TXT record.

However, there are some cases in which we are dealing with a legacy protocol like LPR, and we are not at liberty to change the client protocol. In this case, it is sometimes necessary to use TXT records of around 400 bytes to provide sufficient information to the client. Keeping the total size under 400 bytes should allow it to fit in a single standard 512-byte DNS message. (This standard DNS message size is defined in RFC 1035.)

In extreme cases where even 400 bytes is not enough, keeping the size of the TXT record below 1,300 bytes allows it to fit in a single 1,500-byte Ethernet packet. Using TXT records larger than 1,300 bytes becomes much less efficient on the network and is not recommended.

## Content of DNS-SD TXT Records

Each component string in a DNS-SD TXT record consists of a key/value pair preceded by a byte giving the length of the string containing this information. The example given above was:

```
| x08 | p | a | p | e | r | = | A | 4 |
```

In this example, the key is paper, the value is A4, and the length of the string "paper=A4" is eight bytes, which is given by the initial length byte x08. The key component is interpreted without regard for case, so paper, Paper, and PAPER are seen as identical. Spaces are significant in keys, so the strings "Papersize" and "Paper size" are distinct. Note that this means that if you insert a space before the equals sign, it is interpreted as a trailing space in the key. So paper=A4 and paper =A4 are distinct key/value pairs. The moral is: don't add unintended spaces.

The key must consist of at least one character, while the value may be absent. The way the key/value pair is parsed is that everything after the length byte until the first equals sign is the key, and everything following the first equals sign to the end of the string is the value. This means that a key cannot contain an equals sign as one of its characters. The key is allowed to contain any printable US-ASCII character other than = (0x3D). Other UTF-8 values are not permitted in key names because they complicate things without increasing the expressive power of the protocol—key names are not intended to be user-visible. They just need to be unique identifiers— such as C variable names—that are used by the software.

If the string contains no equals sign, then the entire string is the key, which is interpreted conceptually as a Boolean attribute; it exists but has no assigned value. In general, for a key that is used to indicate a Boolean value, if the key is present the Boolean is true, and if the key is absent the Boolean is false.

A value is made up of any eight-bit binary values. In the case of textual data, UTF-8 encoding is strongly recommended, but TXT record values don't have to be readable text. If you have some binary data to store, it is much more efficient to store it as binary data than to convert it to text using hexadecimal or Base-64 encoding. For example, an IPv4 address is just 4 bytes as binary data but up to 15 when written as text (e.g., "192.168.108.221").

A string beginning with an equals sign will be ignored, as it would have to be interpreted as a key/value pair with an empty key, which is not allowed. If any key appears more than once in a TXT record, any appearances other than the first are silently ignored.

## Interpreting DNS-SD TXT Records

When examining a TXT record for a given named attribute, there are four types of results:

- The attribute is not present. For an attribute that takes a Boolean value, this would indicate that the value of the attribute is false.
- The key of an attribute is present but no equals sign or value appears. For an attribute that takes a Boolean value, this indicates that the value of the attribute is true.
- The attribute is present with an empty value (there's an equals sign, but nothing following).
- The attribute is present with a non-empty value (there's an equals sign, with one or more bytes following).

The specification for a given DNS-SD service specifies how these four states are to be interpreted. For example, for some keys, there may be a natural true/false Boolean interpretation:

- Present implies true.
- Absent implies false.

For other keys it may be sensible to define other semantics, such as value/no value/unknown.

Clients should ignore unknown keys they find in TXT records. This allows the protocol to be enhanced over time, adding new keys with new meanings, without breaking compatibility with older clients.

To further support possible changes to the specification of a particular service type, authors are encouraged to include a version attribute of the form txtvers=xxx. Even if you don't anticipate future versions of your specification, you may still find in the future that you need to make a correction or addition to fix a mistake, or to address an unanticipated condition in the use of your service. Version numbers allow a client to ignore TXT records with versions newer than the highest *txtvers* number that the client knows how to interpret. The initial value of *txtvers* should be 1. Then, at a later time, if changes have to be made that result in a TXT record that is fundamentally incompatible with older clients, which they have no hope of reading correctly, then incrementing the *txtvers* to the next number signals to those older clients that they shouldn't even bother trying to parse this TXT record data. Such incompatible changes are best avoided if at all possible, but it is still good to have a mechanism available so that if incompatible changes are unavoidable, it is at least possible to make the change safely, without confusing old clients or causing them to behave incorrectly.

## Summary

DNS Service Discovery using Multicast DNS provides a simple, efficient, lightweight way to discover what services of a given type are available to you on the local network. Next, Chapter 5 shows how DNS Service Discovery using Unicast DNS takes the same elegant, simple concepts and scales literally to the entire planet, using the existing hierarchy of DNS servers that's already in place and well understood at just about all large companies, universities, and other similar organizations around the world.

# CHAPTER 5
# Service Discovery Beyond the Local Link

Zeroconf is designed to make it easy for you to discover services that are close to you. The word *close* can be ambiguous. You go to your neighborhood coffee shop and the people drinking their cappuccinos at the next table are *physically close* to you. You may be able to use a Zeroconf-enabled chat client, text editor, or audio application to interact with them, to collaborate on a document, or to listen to their music library. In the preceding three chapters, you have been introduced to the components of Zeroconf that are designed to allow you to painlessly discover and offer services to devices that are close to yours—where *close* implies proximity in a network sense. Devices on the same link can use IP to communicate with one another and can present a list of available services in a user-friendly format.

As you drink your morning coffee, the person at the next table may be just a couple of feet away, but you may have never met them. They are not what you would describe as close in the sense of someone who is personally close, they just happen to be near you. There are many people who you might describe as being *personally close*: friends, family members, coworkers, and people you interact with on a regular basis.

If you are a Mac OS X user who uses iChat as your chat client, the differences in these two notions of close are reflected in the two windows you can use to find people to chat with. The Bonjour window shows you names of people on your local link who are available to chat. You may never have met these people and may not know their email addresses or chat usernames. If they have authorized the Bonjour connection, they just automatically appear in your Bonjour window. All that is required is that they have advertised a service of type _presence._tcp. Contrast this with your Buddy window. This only includes people who you have designated as buddies. These people may not be nearby, but they are people you are most interested in interacting with on a regular basis.

Chapter 4 described how DNS Service Discovery (DNS-SD) allows you to discover and to advertise services using PTR, SRV, and TXT records. In Chapter 4, we conveniently avoided the question of whether we were talking about Unicast or Multicast DNS. This was intentional, because it really doesn't matter. DNS-SD was created to work with both Unicast and Multicast DNS. Multicast DNS is perfect for small networks because of its zero-configuration nature. Instead of trying to predict where each query and announcement needs to go, it just sends them all to every peer on the network and lets the peers sort what they need. Clearly, this can't work on a global scale. If every machine on the Internet were busy sending packets that were replicated and delivered to every other machine on the Internet, every machine would be buried under an avalanche of unwanted traffic. Clearly, at a certain stage, we have to move out of the zero-configuration world and into the world of configuration and infrastructure. By building DNS-SD on top of Multicast DNS on the local network, that gives us a natural candidate for what configuration and infrastructure we should use when operating on larger networks: Unicast DNS. In most respects, the DNS-SD part of the protocol works just the same, regardless of whether it's running over Multicast DNS or Unicast DNS. The difference is that Multicast DNS is configuration-free and infrastructure-free, whereas Unicast DNS is more efficient on large networks but requires some configuration and infrastructure.

One configuration detail that needs to be worked out when using Unicast DNS is which domain(s) to use. When you browse on the local network, it's clear that the domain you want is *local*. When you browse on the global Internet, there are millions of domains to choose from. How does the computer know which to use? The answer to that question is Domain Enumeration, covered in this chapter. This chapter also covers how computers make service information available to other computers that may be thousands of miles away. It covers how computers get timely updates when that service information changes. Finally, whenever we talk about global networking in today's world, NAT (Network Address Translation) rears its ugly head. In the 1970s and 1980s, TCP/IP programmers never had to worry about NAT. Perhaps in the future, using IPv6, network programmers will again not have to worry about NAT. But, in today's world, NAT is a problem we can't ignore, and this chapter explains how wide-area service advertising deals with NAT.

# Domain Enumeration

When you browse on the local network, it's clear that the domain you want is *local*. When you browse on the Internet, you can ask DNS-SD to browse in any valid DNS domain, like *apple.com* or *oreilly.com*. Whether you get any results will depend on whether the domain is advertising any services. Clearly, one way to decide which domain(s) to browse is to have the user type them in. However, the spirit of Zeroconf is *zero configuration*, so we don't want to make the user start manually configuring things now. The computer should automatically learn from its environment about interesting domains to browse. The way DNS-SD does this is with Domain Enumeration queries. DNS-SD performs five Domain Enumeration queries:

- Where are interesting domains to browse for services?

  The Domain Enumeration query string for this is b._dns-sd._udp.

- Of that list, what is the recommended default domain to browse?

  The Domain Enumeration query string for this is db._dns-sd._udp.

- Where are recommended places I might want to register to advertise my services?

  The Domain Enumeration query string for this is r._dns-sd._udp. (Advertising services may require authorization and credentials, so just because a given domain is recommended to people on this network doesn't necessarily mean that you have permission to advertise services there.)

- Of that list, what is the recommended default domain to register services?

  The Domain Enumeration query string for this is dr._dns-sd._udp.

- For legacy client applications that don't specify any particular domain when browsing for services, are there any additional domains that we should browse in addition to the usual *local* domain?

  The Domain Enumeration query string for this is lb._dns-sd._udp.

When your laptop finds itself on a new network, it typically learns certain information from the DHCP server, including the address it's been assigned, the netmask for that network, the address(es) of one or more DNS services, and the default DNS search domain recommended for users on that network.

DNS-SD uses this information to construct its Domain Enumeration queries in two ways: domain- and address-based.

The first way is a domain-based query. DNS-SD takes each of the five Domain Enumeration query strings above, appends the default DNS search domain, and does a PTR query. For example, at Apple, the DHCP server informs clients that the domain is *apple.com*, so DNS-SD will do a PTR query for lb._dns-sd._udp.apple.com. to determine if browse operations done by legacy clients should browse any other domain in addition to *local*.

The second way is an address-based query, which allows more fine-grained, location-specific defaults to be fed to clients based on which network segment they are on. DNS-SD does address-based queries by taking the client's IP address and performing a logical AND operation with the netmask to get the *base address* for the subnet. This address is then reversed in the manner of a normal *in-addr.arpa* reverse lookup, and this name is then appended to each of the Domain Enumeration query strings. For example, if the client's IP address is 192.168.1.2 and the netmask is 255.255.0.0, then the base address for the subnet is determined to be 192.168.0.0, and DNS-SD will do a PTR query for `lb._dns-sd._udp.0.0.168.192.in-addr.arpa.` to determine if there's a recommended legacy browse domain for that particular network.

# Advertising Static Services

If you run your own DNS server, or are friendly with the network administrator who does, then you can create magical results just by adding a few lines to your DNS zone file to create the right records to support the domain-based or address-based Domain Enumeration queries. You just need to add a couple of lines to answer those queries and then add three records for each static service you want to advertise. At Apple, various interesting web pages are statically advertised, so that they magically show up in Safari's Bonjour Bookmarks list. For example, the web page of information for new employees is advertised. You can imagine a scenario that used to happen quite frequently: on a new employee's third day, she would want to find out some information that's available on the New Employees page, but she couldn't remember the URL. She'd ask coworkers around her, but they'd all been at Apple for years and hadn't looked at the New Employees page for a long time, so they couldn't remember the URL either. Thus, a hunt for the New Employees page would begin. That scenario doesn't happen anymore. Now, the page appears in Safari's Bonjour Bookmarks list and any employee, new or old, can find it easily, even if she doesn't remember the URL.

Any organization can easily advertise services this way. A hotel offering network access in its rooms can just add a few lines to their DNS server and have the hotel's web page magically show up in clients' web browser's list of discovered pages. An airport offering 802.11 wireless service can have airport information pages and flight departure times magically appear in passengers' web browsers. A school or university can advertise pages of information relevant to students and visitors. An ISP can advertise pages of information relevant to its customers. A café or coffee shop can advertise pages with menus and price lists.

Example 5-1 shows a very simple example of the lines to add to a DNS zone file to answer Domain Enumeration queries and advertise a single web page in that domain.

*Example 5-1. Statically advertising a web page*

```
; Invite clients to browse this domain ("@" means "this domain")
b._dns-sd._udp              PTR     @
lb._dns-sd._udp             PTR     @

; Advertise our web page ("www.<this domain>" in this example)
_http._tcp                  PTR     Our\ Web\ Page._http._tcp
Our\ Web\ Page._http._tcp   SRV     0 0 80 www
                            TXT     path=/
```

For more information on setting up your own DNS server, see *DNS and BIND* by Paul Albitz and Cricket Liu (O'Reilly).

## Wide-Area Preference Settings

As provided by Apple in Mac OS X 10.4 Tiger and in Bonjour for Windows 1.0, Wide-Area service discovery is a behind-the-scenes technology. The APIs are there for developers to use, but until developers start using those APIs or DNS administrators start advertising the automatic legacy browse domains described above, end users will see no difference. However, if you look in Apple's Darwin open source repository, you'll find source code for user-interface control panels for Mac OS X and for Windows, to allow developers (and adventurous end users) to experiment with the technology. Also, at time of writing, precompiled binaries of those control panels are available with instructions at *http://www.dns-sd.org/ClientSetup.html*. These control panels allow you to set system-wide defaults that will cause standard, unmodified Zeroconf applications to browse for and/or register network services in wide-area domains, rather than only on the local link.

Figure 5-1 shows the Bonjour Preference Pane as it appears when installed on Mac OS X.

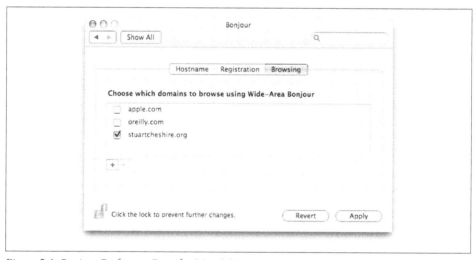

*Figure 5-1. Bonjour Preference Pane for Mac OS X*

Figure 5-2 shows the Bonjour Control Panel as it appears when installed on Microsoft Windows.

On both Windows and Macintosh, the Bonjour Control Panel has three tabs: Hostname, Registration, and Browsing.

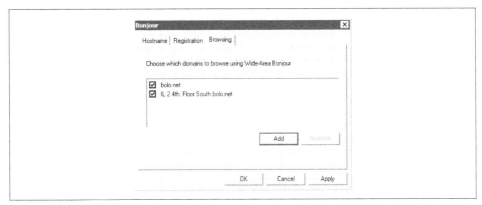

*Figure 5-2. Bonjour Control Panel for Windows*

## Hostname

If you have a Dynamic DNS hostname assigned to you by your DNS server admin, who ensures that everyone's hostname is unique, (or if you run your own DNS server with Dynamic Update), you can enter it here and click Apply. The hostname must be fully qualified, so don't enter a hostname like *steve*, enter a hostname like *steve. bonjour.example.com*. The yellow dot will turn green to confirm a successful registration with the DNS server, or red if a permanent error occurs, such as trying to update a name that you're not authorized to update. If the dot remains yellow, that indicates lack of network connectivity; for example, your Ethernet cable may not be plugged in. Connect the cable or otherwise establish connectivity, and the dot should turn green or red as appropriate. Note that hostname registrations will not work if your computer is behind a NAT gateway, unless that NAT gateway supports a NAT port mapping protocol. If you have an Apple AirPort Extreme or AirPort Express base station, you can turn on NAT-PMP, described below, using the AirPort Admin Utility. Certain NAT gateways that support the UPnP Home Gateway Protocol may also work.

If the DNS server requires credentials to authenticate secure updates, click Password… and enter the key name and key data given to you by the DNS operator. The key name is most often the name of your DNS domain, for example, *bonjour.example.com*. The key data or "password" is most often a random-looking string of characters—for example, CnMMp/xdDomQZ4TelKIHeQ==.

## Registration

If you'd like to advertise services on your machine that are discoverable anywhere on the Internet (or anywhere behind your firewall), click the checkbox and enter an appropriate DNS domain in the Registration panel. DNS-SD-advertised services such as Personal File Sharing, Personal Web Sharing, Remote Login, FTP Sharing, SubEthaEdit shared documents, iPhoto sharing, etc., will be visible from anywhere in the world. As with Dynamic DNS hostnames, if your computer is behind a NAT gateway, wide-area service registrations will only work if the NAT gateway supports NAT-PMP or the UPnP Home Gateway Protocol.

Just like your hostname registration, the DNS server for your DNS-SD domains may require you to enter a key name and password before it will accept service registrations. Simply click Password… and enter the key name and key data given to you by the DNS server operator.

## Browsing

If you don't want to advertise services on your machine but do want to discover services advertised by others, enter a default browse domain in the Browsing panel.

For fun, try this on Mac OS X 10.4 Tiger or the equivalent steps on Windows using the Bonjour plug-in for Internet Explorer:

1. Open a Safari window.
2. Press Cmd-Opt-B to bring up the bookmarks list.
3. Click on the Bonjour icon.
4. Now, with the Safari window still visible, go to the Bonjour Preference Page in System Preferences.
5. Click + and enter *dns-sd.org* as a browse domain.
6. Click Apply and watch a bunch of new stuff instantly appear in the Safari Bonjour Bookmarks list.
7. Uncheck *dns-sd.org* and click Apply again, and the new stuff instantly vanishes.

## Dynamic DNS Updates

Think back to the days before mobile phones. If you wanted to remain in contact while you traveled around, you had to leave detailed directions on how you could be reached. Someone might say, "I have a 10 o'clock meeting with Stan, so you can call me over on the main campus between 9 and 11 at xxx-xxxx. Then, I have lunch with Betty, so you can call me at Sushi Sally's from around noon to 1 at yyy-yyyy. Then, I need to head in to the city. I should be at Dana's around 3, so call me at zzz-zzzz if you need me." Now you just say, "I'll be running around all day, just call me on my mobile." One number follows you around all day, one number that can be used to access the device you carry all day long as you move from one local cell area to another. The person trying to reach you does not need to be aware of your physical location.

Consider the same fun-packed day, but this time you are taking your laptop with you from place to place. If, at each location, you are able to connect to the Internet, then, in the absence of firewalls, you can check your email and use instant messaging with your usual group of friends. For email, you are logging in to a mail server somewhere and initiating a request that conveys your current location. No one sending you email has to track where you are. They sent the mail to an address that is handled by a mail server, and you connect to that same server to download your mail. Similarly, with the chat program, you log in to a server at a well-known DNS name or address to announce your availability and to determine which of your other friends are currently available. No one needs to know the physical location of your laptop. While these solutions work, they are heavyweight and awkward. People don't need to know your location to send you email, but you need to keep polling the mail server to find out if new mail has arrived. The mail server can't tell you when mail arrives if it doesn't know where you are or how to reach you. Instant messaging gives the illusion of direct peer-to-peer communication but requires some organization to run the big "server in the sky" that's actually the intermediary for all communication. The need for a big, expensive server in the sky can be a serious impediment to the creation of new network applications and new uses for the Internet.

Dynamic DNS Update provides part of the answer to this problem. By having a fixed DNS name and using Dynamic DNS Update to update your DNS address record every time your IP address changes, people can now find your current IP address at any time by looking up the current DNS address record for your fixed DNS name.

Wide-area DNS-SD builds on standard Secure DNS Dynamic Update as defined in RFC 2136 "Dynamic Updates in the Domain Name System (DNS UPDATE)" (*http://www.ietf.org/rfc/rfc2136.txt*) and RFC 3007 "Secure Domain Name System (DNS) Dynamic Update" (*http://www.ietf.org/rfc/rfc3007.txt*).

The abstract for RFC 3007 explained the need for Dynamic DNS Update as follows.

> The Domain Name System was originally designed to support queries of a statically configured database. While the data was expected to change, the frequency of those changes was expected to be fairly low, and all updates were made as external edits to a zone's Master File.
>
> Using this specification of the UPDATE opcode, it is possible to add or delete RRs or RRsets from a specified zone.

## Dynamic DNS Update Leases (DNS-UL)

Secure DNS Dynamic Update provides almost all the solution we need, but not quite. It allows a client to create and update records on a DNS server but makes no provision for garbage-collecting stale records. When your laptop arrives on a new network, it can create or update its address records, but what happens if your laptop crashes, or runs out of battery power, or you unceremoniously disconnect its Ethernet cable or shut off the wireless interface without giving it a chance to delete the address record? The IP address you got from the DHCP server has a lease time associated with it, and if the laptop fails to renew the lease, when the time expires the

DHCP server will reclaim that address. RFC 2136 provides no such lease time on DNS record creation. Once created, a DNS record remains valid until someone comes along and decides to delete it.

Dynamic DNS Update Leases (see *http://files.dns-sd.org/draft-sekar-dns-ul.txt*) remedies this omission.

### Changes to the message format

The requests and responses for DNS-UL use the same format as those described in RFC 2136 for Dynamic DNS Update, with the addition of a single OPT-RR as the last record in the Additionals section. The new EDNS0 Option Code, UPDATE-LEASE, has been assigned the number 2. The advantages of using an OPT-RR to encode the update lease are that (1) minimal modifications to a name server's frontend are required and (2) servers that do not implement this extension will automatically return NOTIMPL.

The fixed part of the OPT-RR is described in RFC 2671 (*http://www.ietf.org/rfc/rfc2671.txt*), and is shown in Table 5-1.

*Table 5-1. The fixed part of the OPT-RR*

| Field name | Field type | Description |
| --- | --- | --- |
| NAME | Domain name | Empty (root domain) |
| TYPE | u_int16_t | OPT |
| CLASS | u_int16_t | Sender's UDP payload size |
| TTL | u_int32_t | Extended RCODE and flags |
| RDLEN | u_int16_t | Describes RDATA |
| RDATA | Octet stream | {attribute, value} pairs |

The variable part of the data is contained in the RDATA and consists of one or more sets of the three fields OPTION-CODE, OPTION-LENGTH, and OPTION-DATA. In the DNS-UL requests and responses, there will be one set of these fields, and the OPTION-CODE will have the value UPDATE-LEASE (i.e., 2), the OPTION-LENGTH will indicate the size in octets of the OPTION-DATA (i.e., 4), and the OPTION-DATA will have desired lease (request) or granted lease (response), in seconds.

In the request, the value of the lease is a signed 32-bit number with the requested lease life in seconds. This value must be chosen to balance between the desire to have accurate information and the need to not burden the network or the server. The current recommended minimum lease is 1,800 seconds, which is 30 minutes. In the response, the value of the lease is the time granted by the server. This value is not restricted to be less than or equal to the value requested and could also be greater.

### Refresh messages

In order to keep resource records from being deleted by the server, clients should send a refresh message when 75% of the current lease has elapsed. If the client uses UDP and does not receive a response from the server within two seconds, the client can either retry with TCP or continue to retry with UDP, doubling the length of time between successive attempts. If, for any reason, the lease of a resource record expires without being refreshed, the server must not respond to queries with this record and is allowed to delete the record from its database.

Refresh messages are nearly identical to those used for DNS-UL requests. The change is that the resource records to be refreshed are contained in the Update section and in the Prerequisites section as an "RRSet exists (value dependent)" pre-requisite. The requested and granted lease times do not need to be the same as in the original request. If a client has sent more than one update to a single server, the client may coalesce the refresh messages into a single message. The client can include all existing updates to the server as long as at least one of the included resource records has elapsed at least 75% of its original lease.

A server sends an acknowledgment to a valid refresh request. This response is identical to the previously described DNS-UL response and contains the new lease of those records being refreshed. If no records in the refresh request have completed 75% of their leases, the updates are not refreshed and the response will contain the smallest remaining lease of all the records in the refresh message.

# DNS Long-Lived Queries (DNS-LLQ)

Software development teams that are collocated experience synergies that are harder to replicate in teams working remotely. You may be working in one area of the code and overhear two people discussing another area of the code that you have quite a lot of experience with. You can easily jump in and join the conversation. There are also benefits of working remotely. Once you take the time for commuting, the time taken on incidental conversation with colleagues, and the time spent trying to block out the noise of others working, you find many more hours in the day to get work done. How, in this setting, do you make yourself available to exchange ideas with your colleagues? Email, Net meetings, instant messaging, and IRC chat rooms all contribute to the virtual work environment—but it is not the same as being there.

The same synergies exist for DNS-SD in a Multicast DNS environment. When you're on the local network, you hear announcements when new services arrive. You hear goodbye packets with services go away. If a service goes away without sending its goodbye packet, and later, another client attempts (unsuccessfully) to contact it, you hear that too. What we want to do is provide similar timeliness for remote clients that may be far removed from the local network.

A standard DNS query gives you the answer that's true at that moment in time. If you want to find out later what's changed, you have to do another query. Querying very frequently puts a large load on the network and on the DNS server. Querying only occasionally imposes lower load, but your information may become out of date. When using polling, there is no good answer.

Instead of polling, DNS-SD extends DNS to support long-lived queries (LLQ). In addition to asking a question of the server, it uses an EDNS0 extension to say, in effect, "…and tell me in the future if the answer to this question changes." DNS long-lived queries are described at *http://files.dns-sd.org/draft-sekar-dns-llq.txt*.

## LLQ Message Format

LLQ messages extend the standard DNS message format described in RFC 1035 (*http://www.ietf.org/rfc/rfc1035.txt*) with a new OPT-RR and RDATA format, similar to the way that Dynamic DNS Update was extended as described earlier. This time, the RDATA triples are of the form OPTION-CODE, OPTION-LENGTH, and LLQ-Metadata. The OPTION-CODE is filled with the value of the EDNS0 Option Code for LLQ, which is 1.

The LLQ-Metadata consists of a VERSION field used to identify the version of the LLQ protocol implemented and an LLQ Opcode field that consists of one of the following codes: LLQ-SETUP (1), LLQ-Refresh (2), or LLQ-EVENT (3). The ERROR field is next and contains one of the following error codes: NO-ERROR (0), SERV-FULL (1), STATIC (2), FORMAT-ERR (3), NO-SUCH-LLQ (4), BAD-VERS (5), and UNKNOWN-ERR (6). The remaining two fields are LLQ-ID, which is a unique identifier for a particular LLQ, and LEASE-LIFE, which indicates how long the LLQ will remain in effect.

## LLQ Setup Four-way Handshake

The setup of long-lived queries is a four-way handshake consisting of the following steps.

### Step 1: initial request

The initial request is sent by the client to the server. The format for this request is an extension of a standard DNS query using an OPT-RR containing LLQ metadata in its Additionals section. The RDATA triple consists of an OPTION-CODE, OPTION-LENGTH, and LLQ-Metadata. This triple may appear one or more times. Values should be as follows:

- The OPTION-CODE should be set to LLQ (1).
- The LLQ-Metadata section consists of fields for the LLQ-OPCODE, ERROR, LLQ-ID, and LEASE-LIFE.

- In an initial setup request, the LLQ-OPCODE is set to LLQ-SETUP and the LLQ-ID is set to 0.
- In requests the ERROR field should be set to NOERROR and the LEASE-LIFE should contain the desired life of the LLQ request in seconds.

## Step 2: challenge

In response to an LLQ setup request, a server will send a setup challenge to the requestor. The reason for the challenge is to prevent abuse of the LLQ feature by rogue machines that might otherwise use spoof source addresses to set up LLQs on behalf of some other unsuspecting machine. The challenge packet contains a large number selected at random by the DNS server. A legitimate client setting up an LLQ receives the challenge and answers it correctly. An impostor generating fake packets with spoof source addresses will not receive the challenge packet and will be unable to fake a correct response to the challenge it never received.

This challenge is a DNS Response, with the DNS message ID matching that of the request and with all questions contained in the request present in the questions section of the response. The challenge contains one OPT-RR with an LLQ metadata section for each LLQ request, which will indicate the success or failure of each request.

The LLQ-Metadata section consists of a field VERSION, which indicates the version of the LLQ protocol implemented in the server, and an LLQ-OPCODE field with value LLQ-SETUP. The remaining fields are ERROR, LLQ-ID, and LEASE-LIFE. Possible values for the ERROR-CODE include the following:

- NO-ERROR
- FORMAT-ERR, which indicates the LLQ was improperly formatted
- SERV-FULL, which indicates the server is overloaded by the number of LLQs being managed or by the rate at which the requests are being received
- STATIC, which indicates the data for this name and type is not expected to change frequently, so the server does not consider LLQ the appropriate mechanism for this service
- BAD-VERS, which indicates the protocol version in the client request is not supported on the server
- UNKOWN-ERR

On error, LLQ-ID is set to 0.

On success, a large random number generated by the server that is unique for the requested name, type, and class is created and stored as the LLQ-ID. The LEASE-LIFE is set to the actual life of the LLQ in seconds. This value may be less than, equal to, or greater than the LLQ requested.

In the case of a SERV-FULL error, the LEASE-LIFE is used for a different purpose. It is set to the time in seconds after which the client may retry the LLQ Setup. For all other errors, the LEASE-LIFE is set to 0.

### Step 3: challenge response

The client has been listening for a response to the original setup request. If no response was received, then up to three requests are transmitted with two seconds between the first two and four seconds between the second and third. Another eight seconds after transmitting the third request, the server should be assumed to be down or unreachable and the client should begin the process again no more than once per hour.

When the client receives a successful setup challenge, it sends a challenge response, which is a DNS request with questions from the request and challenge, and a single OPT-RR in the Additionals section with the RDATA that echoes the random LLQ-ID and granted LEASE-LIFE for each set of fields in the order that the questions were issued.

If the client receives a challenge with an error, it responds as follows:

- For a STATIC error, the client honors the resource record TTLs in the response and does not poll the server.
- In the case of a SERV-FULL error, the client may retry the LLQ Setup Request after an interval equal to that contained in the LEASE-LIFE field.
- If there is another type of error or the server is determined not to support LLQ, the client may resort to polling the server not more than once every 30 minutes for a given query.

### Step 4: ACK and answers

The final step of the handshake is the acknowledgment that the server sends when it receives a successful challenge response. A successful challenge response is one in which the LLQ-ID and LEASE-LIFE echoed by the client match the values issued by the server. The server sends a DNS response containing all available answers to the questions contained in the original setup request, additional resource records for those answers in the Additionals section, and, finally, an OPT-RR with the RDATA format as follows:

- An OPTION-CODE with value LLQ, followed by an OPTION-LENGTH field.
- The LLQ-Metadata portion is the now familiar VERSION and LLQ-OPCODE, which is set to LLQ-SETUP.
- The ERROR field should be set to NO-ERROR.
- The LLQ-ID is the originally granted long identification number.
- The LEASE-LIFE is the remaining life of LLQ in seconds.

The reason for the challenge/response precaution at steps 3 and 4 is to prevent a kind of network attack called a *byte-multiplication attack*. Suppose you were a mischievous individual with a desire to cause trouble for bigcompany.com. You might decide to try to flood their network with traffic. You send nonsense data to their web server as fast as you can over your DSL line at home, but you find two things: your DSL line is so slow compared to their connection that they don't even notice you, and when they do notice you, they can easily trace the packet stream back to the source, and you go to jail. Imagine how much better your attack could be if you could convince other machines, with much fatter network pipes, to flood the victim's machine on your behalf. This is the essence of a byte-multiplication attack. You send request packets to well-connected machines, using the IP address of your intended victim as the fake source address in your packets, so that all the replies go to the victim's machine instead of yours. If a reply packet is 100 times bigger than the request packet, then 1 Mbps of requests can generate 100 Mbps of responses directed at the victim's machine. The challenge/response phase prevents DNS LLQ from being abused in this way. Before it begins sending answers, the DNS server sends the challenge to the target machine, requesting positive confirmation that it truly requested that stream of answer packets. Because the challenge packet is about the same size as the initial request packet, this phase of the protocol itself can't be used to mount a very effective byte-multiplication attack—it only multiplies the attack size by one! Given that existing conventional DNS queries can already be crafted to result in a multiplier ratio larger than this, this means that DNS LLQ doesn't add any new byte-multiplication potential to the DNS protocol.

## Refreshes and Expiration

In order to extend the LLQ beyond the granted LEASE-LIFE, the client sends a Refresh request when 80% of its lease life has elapsed. This request is identical to the LLQ Challenge Response, with the exception that the LLQ-OPCODE is set to LLQ-REFRESH instead of LLQ-SETUP. The client should coalesce refresh methods for all LLQs established with a given server as long as one of them has elapsed at least 80% of its LEASE-LIFE. If including all of the LLQs causes the message to no longer fit in a single packet, the client should include all that will fit, preferring those closest to expiration. The requested LEASE-LIFE for a single LLQ should equal the original granted LEASE-LIFE. For multiple LLQs, the client should request the same LEASE-LIFE for all of them as the one granted for the soonest to expire.

The server responds to an LLQ refresh message with a response similar to the ACK described in step 4 above with the LLQ-OPCODE set to LLQ-REFRESH. If the client attempts to refresh an expired or nonexistent LLQ, the server returns an ERROR value of NO-SUCH-LLQ. If the client fails to extend the LLQ beyond the granted LEASE-LIFE, or if the client terminates a lease by sending a request with LEASE-LIFE equal to 0, the lease expires.

## Event Responses

Once the LLQ has been successfully set up, the server delivers change notifications to the client. There are two kinds of change notification that can occur and require action:

*Add Events*

These occur when a new resource record appears that answers an LLQ. Often, these are the result of a dynamic DNS update. This added record is sent in the Answer section of the event to the client.

*Remove Events*

These occur when a resource record becomes invalid. The deleted resource record is sent in the Answer section of the event to the client, with the TTL of the resource record set to -1 to indicate the record has been removed.

The format of the OPT-RR RDATA begins with the OPTION-CODE with value LLQ and the OPTION-LENGTH field. The VERSION is the version of the LLQ protocol implemented in the server, and the LLQ-OPCODE is set to LLQ-EVENT. The ERROR field has value 0, the LLQ-ID is as above, and the LEASE-LIFE is set to 0.

Upon receiving a change notification from the server, the client sends an acknowledgment back to the server. This acknowledgment is a DNS response echoing the OPT-RR contained in the change notification, with the message ID of the notification echoed in the message header.

## Identifying Whether the Local DNS Cache Supports LLQ

A client can first try to issue its LLQ request to the local DNS caching server, just like normal DNS queries. However, most DNS caches today don't implement LLQ and will return a NOTIMPL or FORMERR error.

In this case, the client should contact the authoritative server directly to issue its LLQ request. The client first uses an SOA query to determine the zone and authoritative server responsible for the name it's querying. It then does an SRV query for the name _dns-llq._udp.*zone* to find the target host and port number where LLQ service is offered for this zone. Usually, it will be the same host as the master DNS server but on a port number other than the normal DNS port 53. If the client receives an NXDOMAIN response to its SRV query, the client concludes that the zone does not support LLQs and instead resorts to low-rate polling to keep its data reasonably up to date.

# NAT Port Mapping Protocol (NAT-PMP)

The politics and economics of Internet access have made Internet addresses a rationed resource. Originally, Internet Service Providers (ISPs) sought to charge customers

---

varying amounts depending on how many computers, printers, and other network devices they had. The logic was that anyone who had more than one computer, or owned a network printer, must be a business, and therefore should be charged a lot more for the exact same speed of network connectivity. Customers, naturally, were not enthusiastic about the idea of paying a printer tax to their ISP. NAT was invented and allowed customers to have any number of computers and other devices appear to their ISP as just a single device with a single IP address. ISPs countered by checking that the Ethernet address of the visible device matched the Ethernet address of the single computer the customer had signed up for. NAT vendors countered by adding configuration options to allow customers to set their NAT gateway to present a spoof Ethernet address matching the one the ISP was looking for. Around this time, the ISPs gave up the arms race, leaving us with today's situation: most people get just a single IP address from their ISP, and if they want to use more than one computer, they have to use NAT to share that one IP address.

One thing that NAT vendors initially were not keen to point out is that NAT's address sharing only half worked—it worked for outgoing connections but not for incoming ones. However, since at the time all that most Internet users knew about was the Web and email, they never noticed. Later, when security problems on the Internet became rife, some smart marketing people did what smart marketing people do—they recast NAT's *deficiency* as a *feature*. It was *good*, they said, that NAT didn't work for incoming connections, because that protected you from all the bad people out there. (Similar to how a telephone that was unable to receive incoming calls would protect you from receiving telemarketing calls.)

This is the world we find ourselves in today. What makes this a little sad is that the Internet is capable of much more than just the Web and email, but the prevalence of NAT makes many of those new uses difficult or impossible. Expert users may know how to set up manual port mappings for inbound connections, but the other 99% of users don't. If you want to make a new product that communicates peer-to-peer or otherwise receives inbound connections, then requiring your customers to set up manual port mappings is a recipe for bankruptcy. iChat AV on the Macintosh, for example, has to go to great lengths and perform fancy tricks to get peer-to-peer audio and video to work without manual port mappings and requires a special server on the public Internet to facilitate this; even then, it still doesn't work with all NAT gateways.

NAT Port Mapping Protocol (NAT-PMP) allows client software that needs inbound port mappings to request them, and, furthermore, if the client crashes or is disconnected or otherwise goes away, those port mappings are automatically tidied up. Of course, existing software that doesn't need or want inbound port mappings doesn't request them and doesn't get them.

NAT-PMP is described at *http://files.dns-sd.org/draft-cheshire-nat-pmp.txt*.

# Network Address Translation

The success of web browsing, email, and instant messaging is due, in large part, to the extent to which the end user has been shielded from the underlying protocols. When casual users click on a link in a web browser, they probably do not stop to consider that they have just issued a request and that the server responding to that request must know where to send the response. They almost certainly don't consider how this works when they have a private IP address, and all the packets are being modified by the NAT gateway before being sent out to the rest of the Internet.

Figure 5-3 shows the configuration page for a typical NAT gateway. Its real public Internet IP address is 69.3.204.77, but on the local network it uses the private address 192.168.1.1. The public IP address 69.3.204.77 is globally unique—at any moment in time, only one computer on the Internet on the entire planet has that address. On the other hand, at any moment in time, there are thousands, maybe millions, of devices all thinking they have the IP address 192.168.1.1.

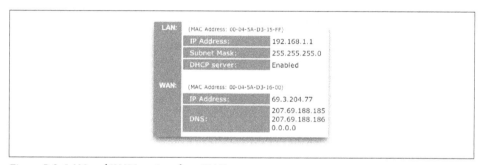

*Figure 5-3. LAN and WAN settings for a NAT gateway*

A computer on the local area network (LAN) connected to this NAT gateway may have an IP address such as 192.168.1.151. As with the address 192.168.1.1, there are probably thousands of computers around the world using the address 192.168.1.151 on their own LANs. If you or I were to send a packet addressed to 192.168.1.151, it would certainly not arrive at any machine outside of the LAN we were currently connected to.

When computer 192.168.1.151 sends out an outgoing TCP request to some machine on the Internet, the NAT gateway rewrites the source address in the packet from private address 192.168.1.151 to public address 69.3.204.77 (which is the IP address of the NAT gateway in this example). So that it can make sense of the replies that come back, it also rewrites the port number to a unique one that it's not already using. Now, the outgoing packet has a globally meaningful source address, and when the machine on the Internet replies, the replies will successfully make it back to the NAT gateway. When the NAT gateway gets the reply, it looks up the destination port number in its table to see which LAN client this packet belongs to. It then rewrites the destination address and port number back to what the local client is expecting, corrects the packet checksum, and forwards it on.

The reason this works is because when a local client contacts an external server, it sends out an outgoing TCP connection request. The NAT gateway gets to see that outgoing TCP packet, and from the data in the packet header, the NAT gateway can glean the information it needs to make an entry in its mapping table.

In contrast, when a local machine listens for incoming connections, it is a passive operation. It doesn't generate any packets or otherwise cause any activity that could allow the NAT gateway to work out what it was required to do. Even supposing the NAT gateway was able somehow to make the required mapping, external clients still couldn't connect to that service without knowing the correct public IP address and port number to use.

Accordingly, we have two problems to solve. The local machine has to inform the NAT gateway of its desire to receive incoming connections, and then, having made a port mapping, it has to place that information somewhere external clients can get at it, so that they know which address and port number they should use to access the service.

The public place to store the service information, you should not be surprised to hear, is the global DNS system, using DNS-UL. The public address is stored in an address record, and the port number is stored in an SRV record describing the service.

## Obtaining the Public Address

Before the local machine can perform a Secure DNS Dynamic Update to update its address record to give the NAT's public IP address, it first has to find out what that address is. It does this by—simply enough—asking the NAT gateway. The local machine sends a UDP request packet to port 5351 of its default gateway address. This protocol is *only* designed for the usual case where the NAT gateway is the one-and-only gateway on a small, single-subnet home network. The UDP packet contains two bytes of data. The first byte is the protocol version (currently 0) and the second byte is the opcode. Opcode 0 requests the public IP address.

Every packet used in the NAT Port Mapping Protocol starts with an eight-bit version followed by an eight-bit operation code. Opcodes 0–127 are used for client requests and opcodes 128–255 are used for the respective corresponding responses from the gateway. Responses also always contain two additional fields: a 16-bit result code in network byte order with success represented by a response code of 0, and a "seconds since reboot" field. Clients use the "seconds since reboot" field to detect if the gateway crashes, is power-cycled, or otherwise restarted. If this happens, your typical NAT gateway will completely forget any mappings it may have created (yet another of the many shortcomings of NAT gateways), so this is a valuable hint to tell clients that they should reissue all their mapping requests to recreate their mappings.

If, after 250 ms, the client has not received a response from the gateway device, it should reissue its request. In the absence of a response, this process is repeated, with the interval doubling each time until either a response is received or two minutes have passed. If two minutes passes without a response, then the client can conclude that this gateway does not support NAT port mapping protocol.

The first byte of the response is again 0 for the version and, this time, the second byte is 128, the response code corresponding to request code 0. The next two bytes contain the result code and the final four bytes contain the public IP address. The possible result codes are:

0   Success

1   Unsupported Version

2   Not Authorized/Refused (supported but disabled)

3   Network Failure

4   Out of resources (e.g., no more mappings currently available)

5   Unsupported opcode

If the result code is nonzero, the value stored in the public IP address field is undefined and must be disregarded by the client. In the future, other error codes may be added; any unknown nonzero result must be treated by the client as a permanent error.

NAT gateways often obtain their public IP address through DHCP or some other method that does not guarantee it will remain the same. If the public IP address changes, local machines will need to know to update their DNS records to show the new address. To let them know this, when its public IP address changes, the NAT gateway alerts devices on the local network by sending a series of gratuitous opcode 128 response packets to the all-hosts link-local multicast address 224.0.0.1 on port 5351, giving the new public IP address. This notification is sent 10 times, with an interval between the first two notifications of 250 ms and, as before, the interval between subsequent notifications doubling.

 NAT-PMP is *only* designed for the common simple case of a single NAT gateway serving a small, single-subnet home network. NAT-PMP is not intended to solve the problems of:

- Nested NAT (NAT behind another NAT).
- A NAT gateway serving a large multi-subnet routed private network, where the NAT gateway may not be the local default gateway for all hosts, and where all-hosts link-local multicast announcements from the NAT gateway may not reach all hosts.
- A NAT offering to receive inbound connections on more than one IP address at once. When a NAT has more than one public IP address, one must be selected as the single designated address for receiving and forwarding inbound connections.
- Transport traffic other than UDP- or TCP-based protocols.

# Creating and Destroying a Mapping

Once the client has determined its public IP address, the next step is to request a public port number at this public address, to be used to receive inbound connection requests. The client initiates a request for a mapping by sending a UDP request packet to port 5351 on the default gateway, with the following format:

- The first field is an eight-bit version code, currently set to 0.
- The second field is an eight-bit opcode that is set to 1 if the client is requesting a map to a UDP port and set to 2 if the client is requesting a map to a TCP port. A NAT device that implements this protocol must be able to create TCP-only and UDP-only port mappings. If a device can only create these port mappings in pairs, it should not implement this protocol.
- The third field is a 16-bit reserved field that must be set to 0.
- The fourth field is 16 bits and contains the number of the private port that the device currently uses for the service.
- The fifth field is 16 bits and is used for the number of the requested public port that will be mapped to the private port. Often, this requested port is the same value as the private port. If there is no preference, then this field should be set to 0.
- The sixth field is 32 bits and contains the requested lifetime in seconds. The recommended value for this field is 3,600 seconds (one hour).

As before, the client sends the request and waits for a response. If no response is received within 250 ms, the request is sent again. The client repeats this process with the interval between attempts doubling each time until either a response is received or until two minutes after the first request was sent. If no response is received in two minutes, an error message should be logged and the client should stop issuing requests.

---

## Scope and Applicability

The assumption is that this protocol will be used on small networks such as you might find in a home, small office, or coffee shop. The key is that there is a single logical link and that the default gateway is also the NAT translator for the network. This is used to ensure that stale mappings issued by the NAT translator do not persist when DHCP leases have expired. The NAT Port Mapping Protocol is explicitly not designed for more complicated networks.

NAT is a solution for extending the use of the limited number of IPv4 addresses. Any client using NAT Port Mapping should also implement IPv6 support as a preferred long-term solution. As IPv6 is more widely deployed, devices that need to use NAT for a public IPv4 address may have a public IPv6 address. Preference should be given to the IPv6 address, when available.

---

The response from the NAT device looks very similar to the request sent by the client behind the NAT.

- The first field is the eight-bit version code that is still set to 0.

- The second field is an eight-bit opcode that should be 128 greater than the opcode sent by the client. In other words, the value should be 129 for a UDP port and 130 for a TCP port.

- The third field is a 16-bit result code. As before, success is indicated by a 0 in this field. The values of the result code are listed in the preceding section.

- The fourth field repeats the private port sent in the request.

- The fifth field is 16 bits and contains the number of the mapped port. This is the value that the service will use together with the public IP address to advertise the service. If no public ports are available then the result code of 4 will indicate a lack of resources.

- The sixth field is 13 bits and is used to convey the actual lifetime of the mapping. This value is allowed to be equal to or less than the value requested by the client. It is not recommended that a lease be granted that is greater than that requested by the client.

The client should begin trying to renew the mapping halfway through the actual lifetime. The renewal packet is identical to the initial request packet, except that the fifth field, which contains the requested public port, is set to the actual port number that was allocated, rather than the port number the client may have originally requested (if different). Making the renewal packet identical to a request packet has a couple of useful properties. If the NAT gateway response to the first request packet is lost, then the client's retransmission of the request packet looks, to the NAT gateway, just like a renewal and is handled correctly. Conversely, if the NAT gateway crashes or is rebooted, then the client's renewal packet looks, to the NAT gateway, just like a brand new request. Since the client is requesting the same previously assigned public port number, the NAT gateway ends up re-creating the lost mapping. This makes the protocol self-healing in the face of packet loss and gateway reboots.

- If a client is unsuccessful in renewing a mapping before its lifetime expires, then the mapping is deleted.

- If a client's DHCP lease times out, the gateway device should also delete any mappings belonging to that client. Stale mappings pointing to a private IP address could potentially direct traffic to a new device that is assigned that IP address by the DHCP server. Since the NAT gateway and DHCP server are normally the same box, this is often easy to do.

- A client can request explicit deletion of a mapping by sending a request to the NAT device identical to the initial request, except that the requested lifetime in seconds is set to 0.

If the request to destroy a mapping is unsuccessful, the result code in the response is not zero. One example might be that the client attempts to delete a permanent port mapping manually configured by the human operator. In this case, the response code is 2 to indicate the request is not authorized.

If a mapping is successfully destroyed, the response packet has a result code of 0, contains the private and public ports of the destroyed mapping, and has a lifetime of 0. In the event that a NAT device receives a request to destroy a mapping that does not exist, it issues a response as if an actual mapping were successfully destroyed. This also is to guard against packet loss. For example, suppose the NAT gateway receives a mapping deletion request and successfully deletes the mapping, but the response packet is lost. When the client retransmits its request, not knowing the mapping was actually successfully deleted already, the NAT gateway needs to send it a "no error" successful response to assure it that the mapping was, as it requested, successfully deleted.

# Summary

Chapter 4 showed how DNS Service Discovery using Multicast DNS provides a simple, efficient, lightweight way to discover what services of a given type are available to you on the local network. DNS-SD using Unicast DNS takes the same elegant simple concepts and scales literally to the entire planet, using the existing hierarchy of DNS servers that's already in place and well understood at just about all large companies, universities, and other similar organizations around the world.

Dynamic DNS Update Leases provide for automatic garbage collection of stale records. DNS Long-Lived Queries give clients timely notification of information they're interested in. NAT Port Mapping Protocol lets clients behind NAT gateways receive incoming connections. Put these three technologies together with wide-area DNS Service Discovery, and computers at home behind NAT gateways can begin to function like computers connected to the "real" Internet.

# CHAPTER 6

# Getting Started with Bonjour/Zeroconf

The previous chapters presented an overview of how the Zeroconf infrastructure works. The remainder of the book contains information on creating Zeroconf applications in a variety of settings. This chapter introduces the *dns-sd* command-line test tool, which lets you, the human user, perform common DNS-SD operations such as advertising services, browsing, and resolving. The *dns-sd* tool is not something you'd ever use in a shipping product, and it's not intended to be used from shell scripts; it's provided as a testing, development, and troubleshooting tool. It serves three main purposes.

First, if you're a developer toying with the idea of adding Zeroconf to your product, the *dns-sd* tool allows you to experiment with "what if" scenarios, without writing a single line of code. If your product is a network camera that already supports RTSP and RTP video streaming, then the *dns-sd* tool lets you create a proxy advertisement for that camera, so that you can make it appear in the Open URL… menu in Quick-Time Player 7, so you can get a feel for how the user experience could be for end users if the product had native Zeroconf support. When making a project proposal to management, being able to show a demo like this, interoperating with existing real-world software, is very compelling.

Second, when you're ready to add Zeroconf to your product, the source code for the *dns-sd* tool (available from the Darwin open source repository) provides useful sample code to cut and paste into your application. The source code is approximately 700 lines of C, and it's basically a big switch statement with one case for each of the common DNS-SD operations. After prototyping by running the *dns-sd* tool with the appropriate command-line option for the operation your application needs to do, you can then find that particular case in the switch statement and copy that chunk of example code into your application.

Third, after you've added Zeroconf to your product, if you're troubleshooting problems, the *dns-sd* tool can provide a useful independent verification of whether your software is working correctly. If your product is one that advertises a service, then you can use dns-sd -B to verify that the service appears. If your product is one that browses for services, then you can use dns-sd -R to create advertisements and verify that they appear in your application when you run the command and then disappear when you stop it with Ctrl-C. If your product is one that browses for services, but it's not discovering what you think it should, you can use dns-sd -B for independent verification. If dns-sd -B shows the service but your application doesn't, then that suggests a bug in your application. If neither sees the service, that suggests a problem elsewhere.

# Working with Bonjour/Zeroconf

Before getting started, you will need to ensure that you have Bonjour/Zeroconf and the SDK installed on your machine. This section also contains a brief discussion of the different tasks involved in writing and running a Zeroconf application.

## Installing Bonjour

A useful page to bookmark is the Apple Developer Connection page for Bonjour, *http://developer.apple.com/bonjour/*. This page contains links to software, documentation, sample code, and other useful resources.

### Macintosh

Bonjour has been part of Mac OS X since the 10.2 Jaguar release. The portable, cross-platform "dns_sd.h" API was added in the 10.3 Panther release. The Java API was added in Panther Version 10.3.9 and is also available in 10.4 Tiger and later. The command-line tool described in this chapter is available in 10.4 and later and can be invoked from a terminal window using the command *dns-sd*. If you're running 10.3.x, you can use the substantially similar *mDNS* command, or you can build the *dns-sd* utility for yourself from the Darwin open source code and place it in */usr/bin*. The developer tools for Mac OS X include the C, Carbon, Cocoa, and Java APIs for DNS-SD.

### Windows

If your Windows machine didn't come from the manufacturer with Bonjour already installed, you can install it yourself. You can determine whether Bonjour is installed by running Internet Explorer and verifying whether the three-lobed, orange and gray Bonjour icon appears in the toolbar. If it does not, you can obtain the Bonjour for Windows installer from *http://www.apple.com/bonjour/*. If you're planning to write Bonjour software on Windows, you should also download the Bonjour SDK for Windows, containing header files, libraries, and sample code, from *http://developer.apple.com/bonjour/*.

### Linux/Unix

Some Linux distributions already include some variant of Zeroconf. You can also download Apple's Darwin open source code for the mdnsd daemon, providing Multicast DNS and DNS Service Discovery (but not link-local addressing, which is a lower-level OS function), and build and install it yourself. This daemon will run on Linux, FreeBSD, NetBSD, OpenBSD, Solaris, and other POSIX-compatible platforms.

### Other platforms

The Darwin open source repository for mDNSResponder also includes code for other platforms, such as Windows Mobile and the VxWorks embedded operating system used in specialized network devices such as printers and network cameras. On a simple, dedicated, single-function device, instead of having the mdnsd daemon running in the background serving multiple local clients, you would typically just run a single monolithic executable, mDNSResponderPosix, which directly advertises the services that the device provides. This code is licensed under the Apple Public Source License, and many hardware vendors include it in their products.

## Understanding Zeroconf

When creating a Zeroconf-enabled application, it is important to understand what Zeroconf does and does not do. As an analogy, consider a GUI application for guessing a number between 1 and 100. The user enters a guess and is told whether the guess is correct, too high, or too low. The number of guesses is incremented and the user can guess again. The interface might look something like that shown in Figure 6-1.

*Figure 6-1. Interface for the guessing game*

It helps to separate the code into three pieces.

*The GUI code*
> The developer does not have to write the code for a button, window, or text area. These are part of whatever framework is being used.

*The hooks in and out of the GUI code*
> The developer has to customize the button to display the appropriate text. The developer also has to provide a hook between the button and something that

handles the button being pressed. The developer has to provide some hook to the text area so that the application can retrieve its contents.

*The application logic*
> The developer must decide what action is taken when a button is pressed and provide the implementation for the method that was wired up in the previous step. This implementation has little to do with the GUI itself.

There is an analogous separation in a Zeroconf application. In this case, it is important and helpful to think of the code in the following three pieces:

*The provided Zeroconf infrastructure*
> This is the functionality that was described in Chapters 1–5. An application developer does not need to write the code to choose and claim an IP address in the local link.

*The hooks in and out of the Zeroconf infrastructure*
> The developer needs to announce services, browse for available services, resolve discovered services, and so on, using the language-specific APIs described in the chapters that follow. Throughout these APIs, the application specifies the DNS-SD name identifying the protocol and/or service in question. This is the code that serves as a bridge between the application and the underlying Zeroconf network infrastructure.

*The application logic*
> DNS-SD might advertise a service of a given name and type available at a given host and port, but the developer providing the service must write the application logic that starts with a connection to the port and determines what is done with incoming data, what actions will be taken, and what data will be sent back. In other words, DNS-SD helps your client discover your server, but it doesn't implement your client or server application logic for you.

The strength and power of Zeroconf is that it performs a specific task and no more. The only design constraint imposed by DNS-SD is that it is for advertising services that run over IP; aside from that, you are free to design your protocol however you see fit. It can be text-based or binary. It can encode data by using XDR, ASN.1, XML, or any other encoding method. It can be client-server or peer-to-peer. It can be RPC- or message-oriented. DNS-SD can advertise and discover IP protocols as ancient as FTP, Telnet, and LPR printing; protocols as recent as iChat, SubEthaEdit, and AirTunes; and future protocols not yet conceived.

The remainder of this chapter explores how to use the *dns-sd* command-line tool to experiment with DNS-SD yourself.

# The Command-Line Tool

The *dns-sd* tool can be run with a number of command-line options that allow you to specify the task the tool should perform. Figure 6-2 shows the available options.

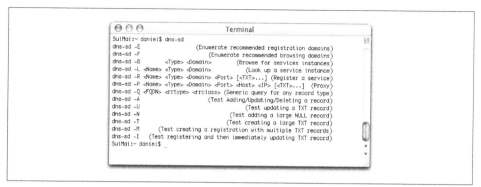

*Figure 6-2. Options for the command-line tool*

The first two options, -E and -F, return a list of the domains recommended for registering and browsing services, respectively. Normally, on your home network, the only domain you're likely to see is *local*. However, if your network administrator has created the Domain Enumeration records described in Chapter 5, then you may also see other recommended domains. These recommended domains are not an exhaustive list. You are free to browse any domain you wish and to register services in any domain for which you have the proper credentials. The domain enumeration functions are simply provided so that software can present a useful list of recommended defaults to users, instead of the users always having to know the domains in advance and manually type them in. The goal of Zeroconf software is zero configuration networking; DNS-SD lets the user discover services, so it should likewise let the user discover the domains where those services can be discovered.

The third option, -B, browses for all instances of a given type in a specified domain. Having discovered a list of service instances, you may then want to know more about one of them, and this is done by resolving it with the -L (lookup) option.

The fifth option, -R, allows you to register (advertise) a service. If you have some service running on your machine that is not yet Zeroconf-enabled, you can manually advertise on its behalf using the -R option. You should use this option responsibly. You can easily create a service advertisement for a service that doesn't really exist, which is fine for testing but could be very confusing for other users on your network.

The sixth option, -P, lets you create a proxy advertisement for a service running on some *other* machine.

The seventh option, -Q, is for testing arbitrary queries for *any* DNS name, resource record type, and resource record class, not necessarily DNS-SD names and record types.

The remaining options are specialized automated testing routines that most developers should never need to use. They're used by developers working on the Darwin open source project, for testing and verifying changes to the mDNSResponder daemon code itself.

# Browsing

There is a bit of a chicken-and-egg decision of whether to start by presenting browsing for services or registering services. If no services are registered, there is nothing to browse for. On the other hand, without a browser present, it is difficult to confirm that a service has been registered. Fortunately, today there are many existing applications and devices that advertise services with DNS-SD, so we'll start by browsing to discover some of those services.

The general form for the browse command is:

```
dns-sd -B <Type> <Domain>
```

*Type* should be of the form discussed in Chapter 4. In other words, an application protocol name followed by either ._tcp or ._udp. To browse for advertised web pages suitable for viewing in a web browser, enter _http._tcp for *Type*. This is exactly what Safari does to discover the list of advertised web pages, and you should see the same list that Safari displays. If you have a reasonably modern network printer, network camera, or even a TiVo on your network, you should see it appear in the list. If you have a Mac with Personal Web Sharing turned on and the user's web page content modified from the out-of-the-box default, you should see that too appear as an advertised page.

Omitting the *Domain* argument or giving the empty string means to use the default domain, which usually means just *local*, unless you are on a network that is advertising a legacy browse domain (see Chapter 5).

For another example, if there are one or more Macintosh or Windows machines on your local link sharing music via iTunes, you can browse for them. If you are using either operating system, you can share music yourself by starting iTunes and configuring Sharing from the preferences window, as shown in Figure 6-3.

The protocol iTunes uses to share music is the Digital Audio Access Protocol (DAAP). Browse to discover instances of this service type using the command:

```
dns-sd -B _daap._tcp
```

Depending on what is currently running, the results should look something like this:

```
% dns-sd -B _daap._tcp
Browsing for _daap._tcp
Timestamp     A/R Flags if Domain     Service Type       Instance Name
11:31:40.084  Add    2  5 local.      _daap._tcp.        Martian NetDrive Music
11:32:07.105  Add    2  5 local.      _daap._tcp.        Dim Sum Music
11:32:56.211  Add    2  5 local.      _daap._tcp.        Mu Shu's Music
11:33:13.785  Add    2  5 local.      _daap._tcp.        Session Casts
11:33:40.186  Rmv    0  5 local.      _daap._tcp.        Mu Shu's Music
```

You can browse for other service types, such as _ftp._tcp, _telnet._tcp, and _ssh._tcp. You can find the list of registered service types at *http://www.dns-sd.org/ServiceTypes. html*.

*Figure 6-3. Sharing music with iTunes*

Remember that this is still part of the "interface with Zeroconf" part of the process. DNS-SD will discover the service for you, but to use it you still need a client that implements that protocol.

## Registering (Advertising) a Service

Here is the template for the service registration command:

```
dns-sd -R <Name> <Type> <Domain> <Port> [<TXT>...]
```

*Name* is the user-friendly name of the service instance, such as "Dan's music." You can also just use the empty string "" for the name, and the registration will automatically use the system-wide default name, as set in Sharing Preferences on Mac OS X.

*Type* is the service type, just as with browsing.

*Domain* can be *local*, or any other domain where you have the credentials and authority to perform Dynamic DNS updates. If the Dynamic DNS server for that domain requires cryptographic authentication, then your cryptographic credentials need to be stored in the Mac OS X System Keychain (or equivalent on other platforms) for the mDNSResponder daemon to access them. As with browsing, the domain parameter can be the empty string, meaning "pick a sensible default for me," which is usually *local* unless you've used the Bonjour Preference Pane or similar tool to set a default registration domain.

*Port* is used to specify the TCP or UDP port number where the service can be reached. After the port number, you can give optional key/value pairs that are stored in the service's TXT record and delivered to clients when they resolve the service. This section contains several examples of registering services.

 If clients seem unable to connect to a service, check your firewall settings. You can have a service correctly listening on a port, advertise it with DNS-SD, and discover it with clients, but all that will be in vain if the firewall then blocks all the incoming connection requests. This is, after all, the purpose of a firewall—to prevent services running on your machine from receiving inbound connection requests directed to them. If you want services running on your machine to be able to receive inbound connection requests, you need to either turn off the firewall or at least add a rule allowing inbound connections to that specific port number.

Returning to our iTunes music example introduced in the previous section, we can now register a "fake" DAAP service that iTunes will discover and display in its sidebar list. Of course, if there is no real DAAP service running at the address you specify, there will be nothing there for iTunes to actually connect to, but the purpose of this example is to demonstrate how you can use the *dns-sd* tool to test your application's browsing code, possibly before you've even implemented the server part of the protocol. Register an instance named Mu Shu's Music like this:

```
% dns-sd -R "Mu Shu's Music" _daap._tcp "" 9904
Registering Service Mu Shu's Music._daap._tcp port 9904
Got a reply for Mu Shu's Music._daap._tcp.local.: Name now registered and active
```

Because the name of the service instance contained spaces, the string "Mu Shu's Music" is enclosed in double quotes. When you enter:

```
dns-sd -R "Mu Shu's Music" _daap._tcp local 9904
```

you will immediately see the second line indicating that the request to register the service has been initiated. There will be a short pause while the system probes the network to ensure that your chosen name is not already in use, and then you will see the confirmation that the name is registered and active. This is typical of the way in which you will programmatically work with the DNS-SD APIs as well. You will send a request and wait for a callback. The APIs in each language have been implemented so as not to lock the application while it waits for a response.

If you have iTunes installed and have configured the preferences to view shared music, Mu Shu's Music will now appear in your Shared Music folder. (See Figure 6-4.)

Of course, as there's no real service there, attempts to connect will fail and display an error message like the one shown in Figure 6-5.

You can also confirm that Mu Shu's Music has been successfully registered without using iTunes, by opening a second terminal window and browsing for services of type _daap._tcp using the command:

```
dns-sd -B _daap._tcp
```

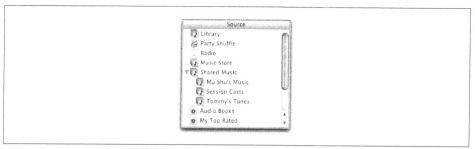

*Figure 6-4. Registered music appears in iTunes*

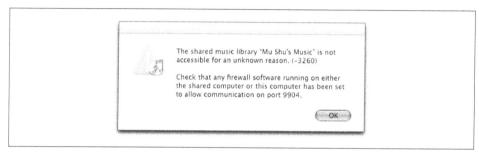

*Figure 6-5. Error when no implementation is present*

One of the entries should include a timestamp, Add, and the text Mu Shu's Music. Terminate the process that you used to register Mu Shu's Music by selecting that window and pressing Ctrl-C. Your browser window should now display a line with a timestamp, Rmv (meaning *remove*), and the text Mu Shu's Music. Start up the process again and the service instance should once again appear in the browser list as having been added.

Using the *dns-sd* command in this way, you can, with just a single one-line command, create advertisements for (possibly nonexistent) services that will be discovered and show up in your application's browsing user interface. This can be a great debugging aid while developing Zeroconf applications, because with minimal effort, you can get quick feedback on the effects of your actions.

 You should use care when creating fake service advertisements. Doing it on your own private closed network for testing is one thing, but doing it on a network with other users is likely to make you unpopular. The novelty of seeing fake services that don't really work wears off very quickly.

As a second example, suppose you are hosting a wiki on your computer. A wiki is a web site in which every web page is editable by anyone with access. Users can add and modify pages using a standard web browser. You could define and register a new protocol named *wiki*, but the existing HTTP protocol already supports wikis and requires nothing out of the ordinary to display and modify pages. Wikis come in many flavors and are implemented in Perl, Python, Java, Smalltalk, and many other languages. None of this matters to end users who will be exclusively interacting with the wiki using a web browser. Accordingly, the right protocol type to advertise is _http._tcp. This protocol type says, "This resource is an HTML page, fetched via HTTP, suitable for viewing in a conventional web browser." Since a wiki page fits that description, _http._tcp is the right service type to advertise.

Start up your wiki. This example uses the FitNesse wiki available at *http://www. fitnesse.org*. To start this particular wiki running on port 9097, type the following command in the directory that contains the wiki code:

```
sh run.sh -p 9097
```

Now, anyone can connect to the wiki if they know the name of the host on which it is running or the IP address, as well as the port that has been selected, but even in a small group of people, publicizing this information can be a hassle. You can tell people, but they forget. You can email the information, but emails get deleted or filed away in folders. You can write it on a Post-It note and stick it on the wall, but that rapidly becomes an untidy mess. DNS-SD lets you advertise it so that a descriptive name appears right in the user's web browser. Since the FitNesse wiki does not yet advertise itself via DNS-SD, you can manually advertise on its behalf using the *dns-sd* command:

```
dns-sd -R "Bonjour Wiki" _http._tcp "" 9097
```

Anyone using a Zeroconf-enabled web browser will now see a link to "Bonjour Wiki" appear in their server list. This is especially helpful in settings where you cannot be certain that the machine hosting the wiki will necessarily retain the same IP address, for example, because it is using DHCP. Collaborators can just discover the wiki by name and be connected, as shown in Figure 6-6.

*Figure 6-6. Advertising a web server as a DNS-SD service of type _http._tcp*

Figure 6-6 shows that when a user selects "Bonjour Wiki" from the drop-down list, it is resolved to the domain *hargau.local.* along with the registered port number 9097. This name resolution is the topic of the next section.

There are some limitations to advertising on behalf of the FitNesse wiki server using the *dns-sd* command. For instance, we have two processes running instead of one, and we have to take care to make sure that when the server is running, the *dns-sd* command is running, and when the server is stopped, the *dns-sd* command is stopped too. It is much better, in the long term, if the DNS-SD registration call is integrated into the FitNesse wiki server itself. What the *dns-sd* command gives us is the ability, with just a simple one-line command, to evaluate the user experience of seeing the server automatically appear in the web browser and then to evaluate, based on that, whether it's worth taking the next step and doing the work to integrate the registration code into the software in question.

## Resolving

Browsing gives you the name of nearby services of a specified service type, but before you can attempt to connect to a service, you need to know at least the address and port number to connect to. You may also want to know the hostname and other miscellaneous attributes that are stored in the service's TXT record. Every time you connect to a service in Safari's Bonjour list, Safari is resolving the service and then connecting to it. Using the command line, the general form of the command is this:

```
dns-sd -L <Name> <Type> <Domain>
```

*Name*, *Type*, and *Domain* are the same name, type, and domain as discovered in the browsing step. Note that you should not necessarily assume that the discovered type and domain will be the type and domain you originally browsed for. Usually they will be, but not always. For example, it's possible in certain cases to browse one domain (e.g., *local*) and discover advertisements for services that exist in another domain (e.g., *apple.com.*). By taking care to store the name, type, and domain reported in the browse result, and passing all three back to the resolve call, you can ensure that your application will work correctly in these cases.

We can resolve an instance of HTTP service in the "local" domain called "Bonjour Wiki" using the following command:

```
dns-sd -L "Bonjour Wiki" _http._tcp local
```

The response looks like this:

```
13:17:52.498 Bonjour\032Wiki._http._tcp.local. can be reached at HarGau.local.:9097
```

Because this is a text-oriented command-line interface, spaces are escaped as \032, following the standard DNS escaping convention. In a GUI, escaping is not needed and all punctuation characters and spaces are displayed just as themselves, the way they should be.

If you resolve an iTunes music service, in addition to the name, service type, host, and port on which the service is running, the TXT record is also returned:

```
% dns-sd -L "Dim Sum Music" _daap._tcp local
Lookup Dim Sum Music._daap._tcp.local
11:43:11.063  Dim\032Sum\032Music._daap._tcp.local. can be reached at
SuiMai.local.:3689
              TXT \0x09txtvers=1\0x0EVersion=196608\0x13iTSh Version=131073\0x17M...
```

The key/value pairs in this example show that txtvers=1, Version=196608, and iTSh Version=131073. When one copy of iTunes connects to another, these values let it determine, before it even attempts to open the TCP connection, if the other speaks a compatible version of DAAP.

The TXT record keys in Apple's iChat application are a little more self-explanatory. The service type for iChat AV's Bonjour advertisements is _presence._tcp. We can simulate an iChat Bonjour advertisement for someone named "Sam Jones" with status "away," as shown here:

```
% dns-sd -R "Sam Jones" _presence._tcp "" 9092 txtvers=1 status=dnd
Registering Service Sam Jones._presence._tcp port 9092
txtvers=1
status=dnd
Got a reply for Sam Jones._presence._tcp.local.: Name now registered and active
```

In addition to passing in the service name, type, domain, and port, we have provided two key/value pairs that are stored in the service's TXT record. Here, txtvers has been set to 1 and status has been set to dnd (do not disturb). Similarly, we can simulate an iChat Bonjour advertisement for someone named "Jack Smith" with status "available," like this:

```
% dns-sd -R "Jack Smith" _presence._tcp "" 9093 txtvers=1 status=avail
Registering Service Jack Smith._presence._tcp port 9093
txtvers=1
status=avail
Got a reply for Jack Smith._presence._tcp.local.: Name now registered and active
```

You can use the command-line tool to look up Jack Smith:

```
% dns-sd -L "Jack Smith" _presence._tcp local
Lookup Jack Smith._presence._tcp.local
12:01:07.062  Jack\032Smith._presence._tcp.local. can be reached at
HarGau.local.:9093
              TXT \0x09txtvers=1\0x0Cstatus=avail
```

Note that when you register a service, you pass the key/value as individual command-line arguments, and the tool builds the correct TXT record for you in the proper DNS TXT record format, with each component prefixed with a length byte. When you resolve a service with dns-sd -L, you see the TXT record in its raw form, with the length byte before each component key/value pair. In this case, you see that the length of the string "txtvers=1" is 9 characters and the length of the string "status=avail" is 12 characters (0x0C in hexadecimal).

Now that we've created our two simulated iChat Bonjour advertisements, we can see what iChat itself makes of them, as shown in Figure 6-7. Jack Smith is shown as available (green circle) and Sam Jones is shown as busy (red square).

*Figure 6-7. iChat's browser for local chat service*

## Proxying

Suppose you'd like to quickly and easily simulate the user experience customers might get with your product if it advertised with DNS-SD, but your product is a hardware device, not a piece of software running on a general-purpose Mac, Linux, or Windows computer. This is where the –P option comes into play. This allows your general-purpose Mac, Linux, or Windows computer to advertise a service that's actually being offered *by some other piece of hardware*. The proxy advertising command takes this general form:

    dns-sd –P <Name> <Type> <Domain> <Port> <Host> <IP> [<TXT>...]

*Name*, *Type*, *Domain*, *Port*, and *TXT* are just the same as when advertising with the -R option.

The two new options are *IP*, the address of the device, and *Host*, a name for it. Generally speaking, any old name (usually a dot-local name) will do, as long as it is unique. Obviously, you wouldn't ship a product this way, because to use the proxy advertising command you need to know the device's address, and the whole point of Zeroconf is that you shouldn't have to know or care what a device's address is. Nonetheless, this can be an easy way to do a quick demo if you need to convince management why the product should use Zeroconf. Usually, the hardest part of doing this demo is finding the device's IP address to advertise, which sort of makes the point of why you want it to use Zeroconf!

There are some interesting tricks you can play with proxy advertising. For example, the service for which you create a proxy advertisement doesn't even need to be on your local network. You can set up a local proxy for a distant web site somewhere out on the Internet: use the *host* command to discover the IP address of the public web site. Now, advertise this by registering a service of type _http._tcp with a name of your choosing. The host is a locally unique name that will be set to resolve to the given IP address. In the example shown here, the *www.apple.com* web page is advertised as a service called "apple," running on a target host called *apple.local*, which resolves to 17.254.3.183.

```
% host apple.com
apple.com has address 17.254.3.183
% dns-sd -P apple _http._tcp "" 80 apple.local 17.254.3.183
Registering Service apple._http._tcplocal host apple.local port 80
Got a reply for apple._http._tcp.local.: Name now registered and active
Got a reply for apple.local: Name now registered and active
```

Now "apple" will show up in your Bonjour menu in the Safari web browser, as shown in Figure 6-8. You can also reach the same IP address by entering the URL *apple.local* in the web browser. In either case, the request will be resolved to the IP address and the browser will show the contents associated with *www.apple.com*.

*Figure 6-8. The proxy service appears in the Bonjour list*

## Monitoring

The remaining command-line options test some of the more arcane areas of DNS-SD functionality, such as the little-known event-notification functionality. For example, if a client wants to be informed of changes in server state, it can initiate a query for the service's TXT record, leave the query running indefinitely, and then the client is notified every time the server's TXT record changes. iChat uses this capability to provide timely updates to Bonjour buddies availability, status messages, and icons, without having to resort to polling to keep this information up to date.

You can witness this by using dns-sd -B _presence._tcp to find the list of iChat users advertised on the network, and then use dns-sd -Q to monitor one of them, like this:

```
dns-sd -Q cheshire@chesh7._presence._tcp.local txt
```

Every time the status for that user changes, you'll see a new TXT record result reported.

## Summary

The *dns-sd* command is not something you'd use in a real product, but it's a great way of experimenting with the technology, a great way of prototyping and simulating potential user experience in just a few minutes, and a useful test tool if your application isn't working quite right and you need a quick and easy diagnostic tool to help you find out why.

# CHAPTER 7

# Using the C APIs

In Chapter 6, you experimented with advertising, browsing for, and looking up Zero-conf services from the command line. In this chapter, you will learn how to perform those same operations programmatically, using the C APIs. The remaining chapters in the book address other APIs and languages. In each of the APIs, the general concepts are the same—you perform one of the basic DNS-SD operations and then receive results asynchronously. In C, this means you initiate a DNS-SD action such as browsing and provide the address of a callback function. When there is a response, the callback function is called and the appropriate information is passed to it. By the end of this chapter, you could write your own version of the *dns-sd* command-line tool.

If you skipped the preceding chapter, you may want to go back and read it, since the *dns-sd* command-line tool is a good learning tool for exploring the concepts, and it's a good debugging aid if your code is not working as expected. If you are creating a program that registers a service, then you can browse with the command-line tool to verify that the service is being advertised. As you run and quit your growing application during development, you can leave the command-line browser running in a terminal window to confirm when you have successfully registered your service. Similarly, if you are building an application that needs to browse for services of a particular type, and you don't have any real instances of that service handy, then you can use the command-line tool to register pretend instances for your application to discover.

## Asynchronous Programming Model

Before diving into the details of Zeroconf programming, there's one important high-level issue to understand—DNS-SD operations are asynchronous. That means that when you initiate some DNS-SD operation, the results of that operation may happen immediately, half a second later, a minute later, or even days later. Consider one real-world example, iTunes. When you run iTunes, it browses for other music sources on the local network. If you launch iTunes at home, there may be no other music sources, so nothing appears. A few days later, a friend may come to visit with a laptop offering shared iTunes music. Your friend connects his laptop to your network and, instantly, he appears in your iTunes list. That browse operation initiated by iTunes several days ago has just yielded its first result!

To create a good user experience, it's essential to understand and embrace this asynchronous programming philosophy. We've all seen, at some time or another, bad user interfaces where you get to watch some cute animation for 15 seconds while the computer "searches" the network, and then it stops "searching" and shows you what it's found. If the thing you're looking for isn't there, you have to try to fix what's wrong, then click some refresh button and watch the cute animation for another 15 seconds before you find out whether it worked this time.

For the programmer, there's no right answer for a fixed search time. If you set the search time too short, you risk giving up before all devices have responded, particularly on slow or busy networks. If you set the search time too long, you frustrate the user. A 15-second wait may be tolerable just once, but when the user is trying to troubleshoot a problem and she has to suffer that 15-second wait *over and over and over*, she gets very frustrated. DNS-SD solves this dilemma by simply not having a fixed search time. DNS-SD operations run for an indeterminate length of time, until you stop them. Results are delivered as they come, not all at the end after some fixed timeout. You can expect the first browsing results to show up in as little as a few milliseconds. Slower devices may take a second or two to respond. Devices not yet connected to the network will, of course, only show up once they are connected, which could be hours, days, or weeks later.

Don't be tempted to make a Zeroconf application that starts a browse operation, lets it run for some fixed time, and then stops it and presents the results to the user. Zeroconf applications don't work this way, and yours will look crude and amateurish if you make this mistake. In particular, you should never have a Refresh button in Zeroconf UI—as long as a DNS-SD browsing list is on the screen, it should be fresh all the time, so the user never needs to refresh it. DNS-SD uses a range of techniques to make long-lived operations efficient on the network. Writing code that once a minute does a DNS-SD browse for five seconds to see what's there and then stops it would actually be a lot less efficient on the network than just leaving a browse operation running continuously.

To support this asynchronous programming philosophy, DNS-SD needs a way to deliver these asynchronous events to your application as they happen. There is no one universal mechanism for delivering asynchronous events that's common among all programming languages, programming models, and operating systems. Some programming models are built around a single main event loop that receives an event notification, handles it, receives another event notification, handles it, and so on. Other programmers prefer to write multithreaded code, where each thread blocks and waits for a particular event of interest. Still other models use concepts like signal handlers or interrupt routines, where, when an event happens, the main thread is interrupted and suspended wherever it happens to be, the event handler routine is run, and then, afterward, control returns to the main thread.

Rather than try to dictate a particular programming model to use, the DNS-SD C API instead provides the necessary primitives so you can integrate its event delivery into whatever event-handling model you've chosen for your program. If you're using a main event loop, there are two things you need to do: you need to tell your main event loop to pay attention to DNS-SD event sources and, when one of those events happens, you need to ask DNS-SD what to do about it.

In this chapter, you'll see how to use DNS-SD C API with the various commonly used main event loop models: the Unix select( ) call, the Cocoa RunLoop, the Core Foundation CFRunLoop, and the Microsoft Windows GetMessage( ) Message Loop. You'll also see how to use DNS-SD C API by creating a separate independent thread for each active DNS-SD operation, if that's your preferred way of working.

We'll start by showing how to do each of the common DNS-SD operations using a Unix select( ) loop and then, later in the chapter, cover just the differences when using other event-handling models.

# Event Handling with a select( ) Loop

It is important to understand the structure for working with the socket-based DNS-ServiceDiscovery APIs. First, you call a function that might, for example, initiate browsing for a service or register a service. Along with the other parameters, you pass in the address of an uninitialized DNSServiceRef (which the call initializes) and also pass in the address of the function that should be called back when interesting events happen.

You then call DNSServiceRefSockFD( ), passing in the newly initialized DNSServiceRef, to extract the file descriptor for the Unix Domain Socket connection to the mdnsd daemon running in the background, and add this file descriptor to your select( ) loop. When the mdnsd daemon sends a message over the Unix Domain Socket connection to your process, your select( ) call will wake up, indicating that there is data waiting to be read on the file descriptor. You then call DNSServiceProcessResult( ); the DNS-SD code decodes the message and calls the appropriate callback function you previously specified when starting the operation.

This section covers the three functions used to access sockets and to perform the callback: DNSServiceRefSockFD( ), DNSServiceProcessResult( ), and DNSServiceRef-Deallocate( ). A listing of the DNSServiceDiscovery Error Codes is also provided.

# Event Callbacks

The use of asynchronous callbacks is essential for DNS-SD. Recall from your experience with the command-line tool that there was often a delay in discovering or registering services. You don't want to block the application while waiting for a reply to the function call. In addition, there may be more than one reply to a particular query. If you are browsing for services of a given type, there may be multiple instances of that type of service on the local network. Finally, you may wish to leave a service browser running so that you can track service instances as they come and go on the network.

The skeleton code in Example 7-1 provides an overview of the process. (As you will see later in this chapter, you follow each call to a core DNSServiceDiscovery function, such as DNSServiceBrowse( ), with some code that enables the asynchronous callback.)

*Example 7-1. Skeleton of select() loop*

```
void HandleEvents(DNSServiceRef serviceRef)
    {
    int dns_sd_fd = DNSServiceRefSockFD(serviceRef);
    // . . .
    while (!stopNow)
        {
        FD_ZERO(&readfds);
        FD_SET(dns_sd_fd, &readfds);
        // . . .
        tv.tv_sec = timeOut;
        tv.tv_usec = 0;
        int result = select(nfds, &readfds, (fd_set*)NULL, (fd_set*)NULL, &tv);
        if (result > 0)
            {
            // . . .
            if (FD_ISSET(dns_sd_fd, &readfds))
                err = DNSServiceProcessResult(serviceRef);
            if (err) stopNow = 1;
            }
        }
    }
```

You can see the basic structure in the HandleEvents( ) example function shown in Example 7-1. First, you pass the initialized service discovery reference to DNSService-RefSockFD( ), to get the file descriptor for the Unix Domain Socket that's being used to communicate with the mdnsd daemon running in the background. The file descriptor is added to the set of file descriptors the process is watching. After the select( ) call returns, if the bit is set to indicate that the DNSServiceDiscovery file descriptor has data available for reading, then you call DNSServiceProcessResult( ), which reads the message from the file descriptor, decodes it, and calls the appropriate callback function.

Note that a real networking program would probably be watching more file descriptors than just the DNS-SD one(s) and may also have time-based operations it's performing, too.

Example 7-2 shows a complete working example of a simple single-purpose HandleEvents( ) function. It runs until the user presses Ctrl-C to terminate the program, or one of the callback functions sets the stopNow variable. (If you're adding DNS-SD functionality to an existing select( )-based application, you'd probably add the DNS-SD file descriptors to your existing select( ) loop rather than changing your existing code to use the example select( ) loop shown here.)

*Example 7-2. HandleEvents using select()*

```
#include <dns_sd.h>
#include <stdio.h>           // For stdout, stderr
#include <string.h>           // For strlen(), strcpy(), bzero()
#include <errno.h>           // For errno, EINTR
#include <time.h>

#ifdef _WIN32
#include <process.h>
typedef    int    pid_t;
#define    getpid    _getpid
#define    strcasecmp    _stricmp
#define snprintf _snprintf
#else
#include <sys/time.h>        // For struct timeval
#include <unistd.h>           // For getopt() and optind
#include <arpa/inet.h>        // For inet_addr()
#endif

// Note: the select() implementation on Windows (Winsock2)
//fails with any timeout much larger than this
#define LONG_TIME 100000000

static volatile int stopNow = 0;
static volatile int timeOut = LONG_TIME;

void
HandleEvents(DNSServiceRef serviceRef)
    {
    int dns_sd_fd = DNSServiceRefSockFD(serviceRef);
    int nfds = dns_sd_fd + 1;
    fd_set readfds;
    struct timeval tv;
    int result;

    while (!stopNow)
        {
        FD_ZERO(&readfds);
        FD_SET(dns_sd_fd, &readfds);
        tv.tv_sec = timeOut;
        tv.tv_usec = 0;
```

*Example 7-2. HandleEvents using select() (continued)*

```
    result = select(nfds, &readfds, (fd_set*)NULL, (fd_set*)NULL, &tv);
    if (result > 0)
        {
        DNSServiceErrorType err = kDNSServiceErr_NoError;
        if (FD_ISSET(dns_sd_fd, &readfds))
            err = DNSServiceProcessResult(serviceRef);
        if (err) stopNow = 1;
        }
    else
        {
        printf("select() returned %d errno %d %s\n",
            result, errno, strerror(errno));
        if (errno != EINTR) stopNow = 1;
        }
    }
}
```

# Accessing the Underlying Unix Domain Sockets

Your code interacts only indirectly with the Unix Domain Socket connection. DNSServiceRefSockFD( ) lets you get the raw file descriptor so you can add it to the set of file descriptors your select( ) loop is watching. When data arrives on this socket, you call DNSServiceProcessResult( ) to let the DNS-SD code decode the message and call your callback function. When you've finished what you're doing (say the user closes the browsing window), you call DNSServiceRefDeallocate( ) to stop the operation, close the Unix Domain Socket connection to the daemon, and free the resources and memory used to perform the operation.

### DNSServiceRefSockFD( )

In Example 7-2, the DNSServiceRefSockFD( ) function was called like this:

```
    int dns_sd_fd = DNSServiceRefSockFD(serviceRef);
```

dns_sd_fd is given the value returned by DNSServiceRefSockFD( ). This value is the underlying file descriptor of the service discovery reference specified by serviceRef. The signature of DNSServiceRefSockFD( ) is:

```
    int DNSServiceRefSockFD (DNSServiceRef serviceRef);
```

### DNSServiceProcessResult( )

The function DNSServiceProcessResult( ) is used to call the appropriate callback function when there is a response from the mdnsd daemon running in the background. Its signature is deceptively simple:

```
    DNSServiceErrorType DNSServiceProcessResult(DNSServiceRef serviceRef);
```

For proper use, start by referring again to Example 7-2, where a call to DNSServiceProcessResult( ) was made like this:

```
result = select(nfds, &readfds, (fd_set*)NULL, (fd_set*)NULL, &tv);
if (result > 0)
    {
    DNSServiceErrorType err = kDNSServiceErr_NoError;
    if (FD_ISSET(dns_sd_fd, &readfds))
        err = DNSServiceProcessResult(serviceRef);
    if (err) stopNow = 1;
    }
```

One important thing to note in this small snippet is that you only want to call DNSServiceProcessResult( ) if select( ), or some similar system call, tells you data is ready. If you call DNSServiceProcessResult( ) when there is no data waiting to be read, it will block and wait until there is.

### DNS Service Discovery error codes

Table 7-1 contains a listing of the possible error codes that arise when calling functions in the DNSServiceDiscovery APIs. Some errors, like kDNSServiceErr_BadParam, may be returned as an immediate result if you pass invalid parameters to a function. Others, like kDNSServiceErr_NameConflict, may be passed asynchronously to your callback function if an error condition occurs later.

The DNSServiceDiscovery error names are all of the form kDNSServiceErr_NoErr, kDNSServiceErr_Unknown, and so on. In Table 7-1, the initial kDNSServiceErr_ part of each error name is omitted.

*Table 7-1. Error codes*

| Error: kDNSServiceErr_... | Code | Description |
| --- | --- | --- |
| NoErr | 0 | No error |
| Unknown | −65537 | Unexpected error condition (should not happen) |
| NoSuchName | −65538 | Given name does not exist |
| NoMemory | −65539 | Out of memory (should not happen, except on devices with very limited memory) |
| BadParam | −65540 | Parameter contains invalid data |
| BadReference | −65541 | Reference being passed is invalid |
| BadState | −65542 | Internal error (should not happen) |
| BadFlags | −65543 | Invalid values for flags |
| Unsupported | −65544 | Operation not supported |
| NotInitialized | −65545 | Reference not initialized |
| AlreadyRegistered | −65547 | Attempt to register a service that is registered |
| NameConflict | −65548 | Attempt to register a service with an already used name |

*Table 7-1. Error codes (continued)*

| Error: kDNSServiceErr_... | Code | Description |
|---|---|---|
| Invalid | −65549 | Certain invalid parameter data, such as domain name more than 255 bytes long |
| Incompatible | −65551 | Client library incompatible with daemon (should never happen, unless installed daemon and client library are not the same version) |
| BadInterfaceIndex | −65552 | Specified interface does not exist |

### DNSServiceRefDeallocate( )

In Example 7-2, the DNSServiceRef was created elsewhere and passed into the HandleEvents routine. You get a DNSServiceRef when you call one of the core DNS-Service functions:

- DNSServiceRegister( )
- DNSServiceBrowse( )
- DNSServiceResolve( )
- DNSServiceEnumerateDomains( )
- DNSServiceCreateConnection( )
- DNSServiceQueryRecord( )

When this reference is no longer needed, it should be deallocated using:

```
void DNSServiceRefDeallocate(DNSServiceRef serviceRef);
```

When you call DNSServiceRefDeallocate( ), the associated operation is stopped, the application's connection with the mdnsd daemon is terminated, the connecting socket is closed, and the memory associated with the reference is released. Before calling DNSServiceRefDeallocate( ), make sure you've removed the socket from your select( ) loop, or you'll have a select( ) loop with a dead socket in it, which can cause confusing results, especially in multithreaded programs.

# Using the DNSServiceDiscovery APIs

This section covers browsing for services, resolving services, registering services, and some of the less common operations, such as enumerating domains. In each case, there are three basic tasks to be performed: you initiate the operation, add the event source to your event loop, and provide the associated callback function. In the case of browsing, you call DNSServiceBrowse( ). In the examples that use the code shown in Example 7-2, you will next call HandleEvents( ) and pass in the now initialized service discovery reference. Finally, you will implement a callback function, which will be called when the mdnsd daemon has a relevant reply. The form of the callback function is specified. So, for example, when browsing for services, the callback function must have the same signature as specified by the typedef DNSServiceBrowseReply( ).

---

The number and type of the parameters passed to the callback function will be as indicated in the typedef. The process and the description of the parameters will quickly become familiar. After we finish describing browsing in detail, any repeated information will be summarized or omitted when describing resolving services, registering services, and enumerating domains.

## Browsing for Services

To browse for available services, you need to call the DNSServiceBrowse() function and specify the type of service you are searching for and the domain in which to search. You also pass in the address of your callback function and the address of an uninitialized DNSServiceRef. After the DNSServiceBrowse() call has started the operation and initialized the DNSServiceRef, you can extract the underlying file descriptor to add it to your select() loop. Each time the mdnsd daemon responds, your select() loop will wake up, you call DNSServiceProcessResult(), and that calls your callback function for you. This section provides details for the DNSServiceBrowse() and DNSServiceBrowseReply() functions, along with a table listing possible flag values and an example of how you might browse for a specific type of service.

### DNSServiceBrowse( )

You initiate browsing for a service by calling DNSServiceBrowse():

```
DNSServiceRef DNSServiceBrowse(
    DNSServiceRef *sdRef,
    DNSServiceFlags flags,
    uinte32_t interfaceIndex,
    const char *regtype,
    const char *domain,
    DNSServiceBrowseReply callBack,
    void *context);
```

The first parameter is the address of your uninitialized service discovery reference.

The flags parameter is used for specifying optional settings that apply to some of the DNSServiceDiscovery routines. Currently, no optional settings are defined for the DNSServiceBrowse() call, so you should pass zero for this parameter.

Normally, applications pass 0 for interfaceIndex, and DNS-SD browses on all available interfaces. However, should you wish to restrict browsing to one specific interface, such as Ethernet or wireless, you can specify that interface by giving its interface index, as used in the if_nametoindex() family of functions. You can see each interface's index value by using the *ifconfig* command and looking for the IPv6 scopeid values. Interface indexes are typically small integers. For example, on Mac OS X machines, the Ethernet interface is often index 4, and AirPort is often index 5. The other novel value you can pass for this parameter is kDNSServiceInterfaceIndexLocalOnly. This restricts DNS-SD to only finding other services that were registered on the same machine (though the service itself is not necessarily *running* on the same machine, because there can be proxies for services running on other machines). The applications that currently use this option are certain parallel processing products that have two versions at different prices—the single machine version and the network version. If the customer has only paid for the single machine version, the application only wants to find instances of the server process that are registered on the same machine, so it uses kDNSServiceInterfaceIndexLocalOnly.

The regtype is the same service type as entered when using the command-line tool in Chapter 6. It is the protocol followed by either ._tcp or by ._udp. For example, the regtype might have the value _http._tcp. The valid service names can be found at *http://www.dns-sd.org/ServiceTypes.html*.

The domain variable can have a specific value, such as local, or it can be NULL to indicate that the system should choose the appropriate list of domains to search. Generally, that list of domains to search will always include local, plus any additional unicast domains added explicitly by the user, plus any "legacy browse" domains automatically learned from the network.

The callBack is the address of your callback function to be called when an instance of the specified service is found. Details on the callback function are contained in the next section. The callback function is also called in the event of asynchronous errors.

The context parameter is also passed to the callback function. This allows you to write a single callback function, which is used by several different browse operations, because the context parameter allows you to tell which particular DNSServiceBrowse() operation this event pertains to. Typically, the context parameter will be the address of some structure or object holding your state pertaining to that operation. C may not be an object-oriented language, but the context parameter here has an equivalent role to the "self" variable in an object-oriented language. You are free to use any value you wish for the context parameter, including NULL, and it will be passed unchanged to your callback function.

### DNSServiceBrowseReply( )

The callback function passed in as a parameter for the DNSServiceBrowse() function will have the following form:

```
void MyBrowseReply
    (
    DNSServiceRef sdRef,
    DNSServiceFlags flags,
    uint32_t interfaceIndex,
    DNSServiceErrorType errorCode,
    const char *serviceName,
    const char *regtype,
    const char *replyDomain,
    void *context
    );
```

The most interesting parameters here are errorCode, serviceName, regtype, and replyDomain. If errorCode is nonzero, then an error has occurred, as listed in Table 7-1. If errorCode is zero (kDNSServiceErr_NoError), then serviceName, regtype, and replyDomain tell you the name, type, and domain for the newly discovered (or removed) service.

The sdRef is the DNSServiceRef of the operation to which this callback relates. If you have multiple browse operations running at once, being handled by the same callback function, the callback function can use the sdRef, or the context parameter, to help it locate whatever private internal state is necessary for it to make sense of the result.

The flags parameter tells the callback function two interesting things. First, if the kDNSServiceFlagsAdd bit is set, then a new service has been discovered. If this bit is not set, then the named service, previously discovered, has gone away and should be removed from your onscreen display. Second, if the kDNSServiceFlagsMoreComing bit is set, the callback function should not bother updating its UI and repainting the screen right away, because more results are coming immediately after this one. Suppose you discover 100 service instances on the network—adding each one to the onscreen list individually and redrawing the window for every one will make a slow and flickery display. If, instead, you wait until all 100 are in your list in memory before updating the screen, then the entire service list appears virtually instantaneously, fully formed on the screen, instead of building up one line at a time.

Note that if the kDNSServiceFlagsMoreComing bit is not set, that does not mean that there are no more answers coming *ever*. What it means is that there are no more answers coming *right now*, so you should go ahead and update the screen display and perform any other relevant processing you may have deferred. Even after you get a callback with the kDNSServiceFlagsMoreComing bit not set, you could easily get another one just a millisecond later giving data newly discovered from the network, and, in fact, you should expect this to happen quite frequently. Don't make the mistake of canceling your browse operation because you got a callback with the kDNSServiceFlagsMoreComing bit not set, and you thought that meant that was the last answer you'd ever get.

The interfaceIndex tells you on which interface the service was discovered, particularly useful if you passed 0 for the interfaceIndex when calling DNSServiceBrowse( ). Note that if your machine has both Ethernet and wireless, and there's some other machine connected via both Ethernet and wireless, then you will discover that machine's services twice, once via the Ethernet interface and once via the wireless interface. If one interface is turned off or disconnected, then you'll get remove events for only the service(s) discovered on the interface that went away. You therefore need to keep track of the interface indexes along with the name, type, and domain of each discovered service, so that when you receive remove events, you know which one to remove. If you're particularly ambitious, you could also make your UI display include an icon indicating on which interface each service was discovered.

### DNSServiceDiscovery flags

Table 7-2 contains a list of flags that are currently available to be used in the DNSServiceDiscovery APIs. The flags follow the format kDNSServiceFlags*xxx*, where *xxx* represents one of the flags listed in the table. For the sake of brevity in the table, the kDNSServiceFlags portion is not written.

*Table 7-2. DNSServiceDiscovery flags*

| Name kDNSServiceFlags... | Value | Description |
| --- | --- | --- |
| MoreComing | 1 | Don't update UI; the callback will be called immediately with more results. If this bit is not set, it's time to update your UI now. |
| Add | 2 | Add service, domain, or record to list. If this bit is not set, then remove the service, domain, or record. |
| Default | 4 | Enumerated domain is default domain. |
| NoAutoRename | 8 | Prevents auto-renaming in case of name conflict. |
| Shared | 16 | Allows multiple records with same full domain name. |
| Unique | 32 | Specifies resource record name must be unique on the network. |
| BrowseDomains | 64 | Domains recommended for browsing are to be enumerated. |
| RegistrationDomains | 128 | Domains recommended for registration are to be enumerated. |
| LongLivedQuery | 256 | When using DNSServiceQueryRecord with unicast names, tells daemon to set up long-lived query with the server. |

### Browsing example

The example will have two functions. You will start browsing using the function MyDNSServiceBrowse(). In it, you declare a DNSServiceErrorType and DNSServiceRef variables. You then call DNSServiceBrowse() and specify that you are browsing for services of type _http._tcp on the local network and pass in the function named MyBrowseCallBack as the callback function. Pass the service discovery reference to the HandleEvents() function in Example 7-2. If there is an error reported, then use DNSServiceRefDeallocate() to clean up. In summary, MyDNSServiceBrowse() has the following outline:

```
static DNSServiceErrorType MyDNSServiceBrowse()
    {
    DNSServiceErrorType error;
    DNSServiceRef serviceRef;
    error = DNSServiceBrowse(&serviceRef, /* parameters as described above */);
    if (!error)
        {
        HandleEvents(serviceRef);
```

```
        DNSServiceRefDeallocate(serviceRef);
        }
    return error;
    }
```

The second function is the callback function MyBrowseCallBack( ). If no error is reported, the flags are checked to see if the kDNSServiceFlagsMoreComing and kDNSServiceFlagsAdd flags are set. In this example code, a message is then printed to the screen that indicates whether the service is being added or removed, along with the service's name, type, and domain. If the kDNSServiceFlagsMoreComing flag is not set, then standard out is flushed to ensure that the information appears promptly on the user's screen. Both functions, along with main( ), are in Example 7-3.

*Example 7-3. DNSServiceBrowse example*

```
#include <dns_sd.h>
#include <stdio.h>      // For stdout, stderr
#include <string.h>     // For strlen(), strcpy(), bzero()

extern void HandleEvents(DNSServiceRef);

static void
MyBrowseCallBack(DNSServiceRef service,
                DNSServiceFlags flags,
                uint32_t interfaceIndex,
                DNSServiceErrorType errorCode,
                const char * name,
                const char * type,
                const char * domain,
                void * context)
    {
    #pragma unused(context)
    if (errorCode != kDNSServiceErr_NoError)
        fprintf(stderr, "MyBrowseCallBack returned %d\n", errorCode);
    else
        {
        char *addString  = (flags & kDNSServiceFlagsAdd) ? "ADD" : "REMOVE";
        char *moreString = (flags & kDNSServiceFlagsMoreComing) ? "MORE" : "    ";
        printf("%-7s%-5s %d%s.%s%s\n",
            addString, moreString, interfaceIndex, name, type, domain);
        }
    if (!(flags & kDNSServiceFlagsMoreComing)) fflush(stdout);
    }

static DNSServiceErrorType
MyDNSServiceBrowse( )
    {
    DNSServiceErrorType error;
    DNSServiceRef  serviceRef;
```

*Example 7-3. DNSServiceBrowse example (continued)*

```
    error = DNSServiceBrowse(&serviceRef,
                            0,              // no flags
                            0,              // all network interfaces
                            "_http._tcp",   // service type
                            "",             // default domains
                            MyBrowseCallBack, // call back function
                            NULL);          // no context
    if (error == kDNSServiceErr_NoError)
        {
        HandleEvents(serviceRef); // Add service to runloop to get callbacks
        DNSServiceRefDeallocate(serviceRef);
        }

    return error;
    }

int main (int argc, const char * argv[])
    {
    DNSServiceErrorType error = MyDNSServiceBrowse();
    if (error) fprintf(stderr, "DNSServiceDiscovery returned %d\n", error);
    return 0;
    }
```

Save the code in Example 7-3 as *MyDNSSDBrowser.c* and the code in Example 7-2 as *DNSServiceCallbackSelect.c*, then compile and run them. If there are no services of type _http._tcp running on your local network, you can always follow the instructions in Chapter 6 to register a pretend one using the command-line tool. You can also use the example included in the section "Registering a Service," later in this chapter.

# Resolving a Service

The pattern for resolving is identical to that for browsing. To resolve, you call DNSServiceResolve() and then add the event source to your select() loop. When a result or results become available, your callback function will be called. This section details both functions and provides an example of resolving a registered service to determine its host and port.

## DNSServiceResolve

To resolve a service, call DNSServiceResolve():

```
    DNSServiceErrorType DNSServiceResolve(
        DNSServiceRef *sdRef,
        DNSServiceFlags flags,
        uint32_t interfaceIndex,
        const char *name,
        const char *regtype,
```

```
    const char *domain,
    DNSServiceResolveReply callBack,
    void *context);
```

Pass name, regtype, and domain exactly as you received them in the DNSServiceBrowse()
callback. If you are resolving a service that you discovered in a still-active browse call,
then pass the discovered interfaceIndex to ensure that you resolve it on the specific
interface on which is was discovered. If you are resolving a service that you discovered some time ago (perhaps saving its name, regtype, and domain in a preference file
on disk), then you should set interfaceIndex to zero, because that service may now be
available via a different interface. For example, the user could have originally discovered the service via Ethernet but now wants to use that same service via wireless.

When the daemon has the service information for you, it will call your callback
function.

## DNSServiceResolveReply

Your DNSServiceResolve() callback function needs to have the following form:

```
void MyDNSServiceResolveReply
    (
    DNSServiceRef sdRef,
    DNSServiceFlags flags,
    uint32_t interfaceIndex,
    DNSServiceErrorType errorCode,
    const char *fullname,
    const char *hosttarget,
    uint16_t port,
    uint16_t txtLen,
    const char *txtRecord,
    void *context
    );
```

As before, errorCode tells you if the operation was successful, and sdRef and context
are provided to help your callback easily locate any state it needs. If you resolved
without specifying a particular interface, then interfaceIndex tells you on which
interface the answer was found.

The parameters hosttarget and port tell you where the service can be reached, today.
Note that this can change over time. A given named service can be moved to a different machine. This is why it is important to store only the name, type, and domain in
preference files on disk and resolve on demand when needed. If you store the hostname, port number, or even worse, the IP address, these could all be out of date when
the user comes to access the service at a later date. The port is given in network byte
order, exactly as needed for use in the sin_port field of a struct sockaddr_in you'd
pass to connect().

The fullname parameter gives you the fully qualified DNS name for the service, with
all necessary escaping of dots, spaces, backslashes, and nonprinting characters,

making the name safe to pass to DNSServiceQueryRecord( ) or the standard Unix function res_query( ). Most applications will never need to use this, but the fullname parameter is provided as a convenience for those that do. One example is iChat, which stores the user's picture as another DNS record with the same name as the service (SRV) record. Providing the properly escaped, fully qualified DNS name makes it easy for iChat to retrieve the image record using either res_query( ) or DNSServiceQueryRecord( ).

The txtLen and txtRecord parameters give you additional optional information about the service, if present. The data is presented in raw DNS TXT record format. To help you decode this format, the *dns_sd.h* header file provides helper functions TXTRecordContainsKey( ) and TXTRecordGetValuePtr( ), available in Mac OS X 10.4 and, later, Bonjour for Windows, Bonjour for Linux, etc.

```
int DNSSD_API TXTRecordContainsKey(uint16_t txtLen, const void *txtRecord,
    const char *key);

const void * DNSSD_API TXTRecordGetValuePtr(uint16_t txtLen, const void *txtRecord,
    const char *key, uint8_t *valueLen );
```

TXTRecordContainsKey( ) returns a Boolean true/false result indicating whether the named key appears in the text record.

TXTRecordGetValuePtr( ) returns a pointer to the value data for the named key. If the returned pointer is NULL, the named key did not appear in the text record or appeared with no = to indicate an associated value. If the returned pointer is non-NULL, then the named key appeared with an =. The valueLen indicates the length of the value data, which may be zero in the case of an empty value (i.e., "key=").

### Resolution example

In Example 7-4, the service with the name Not a real page of type _http._tcp is resolved using DNSServiceResolve( ). When MyResolveCallBack( ) is called, if there has been no error, then the name of the service being resolved is displayed along with the hostname and port number.

*Example 7-4. DNSServiceResolve Example*

```
#include <dns_sd.h>
#include <stdio.h>          // For stdout, stderr
#include <string.h>          // For strlen(), strcpy(), bzero()

extern void HandleEvents(DNSServiceRef);

static void
MyResolveCallBack(DNSServiceRef serviceRef,
                DNSServiceFlags flags,
                uint32_t interface,
                DNSServiceErrorType errorCode,
                const char *fullname,
```

*Example 7-4. DNSServiceResolve Example (continued)*

```
                    const char *hosttarget,
                    uint16_t port,
                    uint16_t txtLen,
                    const char *txtRecord,
                    void *context)
    {
    #pragma unused(flags)
    #pragma unused(fullname)

    if (errorCode != kDNSServiceErr_NoError)
        fprintf(stderr, "MyResolveCallBack returned %d\n", errorCode);
    else
        printf("RESOLVE: %s is at %s:%d\n", fullname, hosttarget, ntohs(port));
    if (!(flags & kDNSServiceFlagsMoreComing)) fflush(stdout);
    }


static DNSServiceErrorType
MyDNSServiceResolve( )
    {
    DNSServiceErrorType error;
    DNSServiceRef  serviceRef;

    error = DNSServiceResolve(&serviceRef,
                              0,  // no flags
                              0,  // all network interfaces
                              "Not a real page", //name
                              "_http._tcp", // service type
                              "local", //domain
                              MyResolveCallBack,
                              NULL);    // no context

    if (error == kDNSServiceErr_NoError)
        {
        HandleEvents(serviceRef);  // Add service to runloop to get callbacks
        DNSServiceRefDeallocate(serviceRef);
        }
    return error;
    }

int
main (int argc, const char * argv[])
    {
    DNSServiceErrorType error = MyDNSServiceResolve( );
    fprintf(stderr, "DNSServiceDiscovery returned %d\n", error);
                              //if function returns print error
    return 0;
    }
```

Run this example by compiling it and running it with *DNSServiceCallbackSelect.c*. If you have a real _http._tcp service available, you can substitute its name in place of Not a real page. Alternatively, you can follow the instructions in Chapter 6 to register a pretend _http._tcp service called Not a real page using the command-line tool, or you can proceed to the example in the section "Registering a Service" to write code to register your own pretend service with that name.

When you successfully resolve, you should see something like this:

```
RESOLVE: Not\032a\032real\032page._http._tcp.local is at SuiMai.local.:9092
```

Notice how the spaces in the fully qualified DNS name are replaced with \032 as part of the escaping process to make the name safe to use with Unix routines such as res_query( ).

## Registering a Service

To register a service, you call the DNSServiceRegister( ) function and specify the name and the type of the service you are registering, as well as details about the interface, host, domain, and port. As with browsing, you pass in the address of the callback function, a context pointer, and an uninitialized DNSServiceRef, and then add the event source to your select( ) loop. Each time the mdnsd daemon responds, you call DNSServiceProcessResult and the callback function will be invoked. This section provides details for the DNSServiceRegister( ) and DNSServiceRegisterReply( ) functions, along with details of how to add, update, or remove a resource record using DNSServiceAddRecord( ), DNSServiceUpdateRecord( ), and DNSServiceRemoveRecord( ). The section concludes with an example of how you might register a service.

### DNSServiceRegister

To register a service, call the DNSServiceRegister( ) function:

```
DNSServiceErrorType DNSServiceRegister(
    DNSServiceRef *sdRef,
    DNSServiceFlags flags,
    uint32_t interfaceIndex,
    const char *name,
    const char *regtype,
    const char *domain,
    const char *host,
    uint16_t port,
    uint16_t txtLen,
    const void *txtRecord,
    DNSServiceRegisterReply callBack,
    void *context);
```

The parameters should seem familiar from the discussion of resolving services using DNSServiceResolve( ). The difference is that now, instead of learning the host, port, and DNS TXT record data, you're providing it.

The interfaceIndex parameter allows you to advertise your service on only one specific interface, if desired. Most applications use zero for interfaceIndex. The other novel value you can pass for this parameter is kDNSServiceInterfaceIndexLocalOnly, which means that your service will not actually be advertised on the network but only made visible to other browsing clients on the same machine. One use of this is for background processes that provide a web-based user interface for configuration but (perhaps for security reasons) only allow configuration from the local machine, not remotely over the network. By advertising their service using kDNSServiceInterfaceIndexLocalOnly, their configuration page will appear in the Bonjour list in web browsers running on the local machine only, not on other machines on the network.

The name parameter is optional. If you pass NULL or an empty string, a system-wide default name is used for your service. For many services, when there is only usually one instance of that service on a given machine, using a system-wide default name is a sensible choice. Whether you specify an explicit name or use the system-wide default, Multicast DNS will ensure that it is unique on the local network. For example, if you advertise an HTTP server with the name "Web Server" and there is already a different HTTP service on the network with the same name, then yours will be automatically renamed to "Web Server (2)." If there's already a "Web Server (2)," then yours will be automatically renamed to "Web Server (3)," and so on. If you don't want this auto-rename behavior, then use the flag kDNSServiceFlagsNoAutoRename, and instead of renaming automatically, DNS-SD will call your callback function with a kDNSServiceErr_NameConflict error result so you can pick a new name for yourself. When this happens, your service registration will have been terminated. You will need to remove it from your select() loop, destroy the DNSServiceRef using DNSServiceRefDeallocate( ), and then try again with a new name.

The domain parameter is optional. If you pass NULL or an empty string, it means "pick a sensible default for me," which is what most applications do. Usually the sensible default will be local, possibly plus one wide-area domain as selected by the user.

The hostname parameter is optional. If you pass NULL or an empty string, it means the current host, which is what most applications do. You only need to specify a hostname when creating proxy registrations for services running on some other machine.

The port number is in network byte order. If you're using a fixed port number, then this is exactly as you would have used in the sin_port field of your struct sockaddr_in in your bind( ) call. If you're using a dynamic port number, this is exactly as you would have received it in the sin_port field of your struct sockaddr_in in your getsockname( ) call.

Some service types have extra data stored in the TXT record. For example, with HTTP services, the path to the page in question can be stored in the TXT record, e.g., path=/index.html. You need to provide a pointer to a properly formatted DNS TXT record. To help in the creation of properly formatted DNS TXT records, you can use the TXTRecordCreate( ) family of helper functions from the *dns_sd.h* header file, available in Mac OS X 10.4 and, later, Bonjour for Windows, Bonjour for Linux, etc.

## DNSServiceRegisterReply

The following is the prototype for the callback function used when registering a service:

```
void MyRegisterReply
    (
    DNSServiceRef sdRef,
    DNSServiceFlags flags,
    DNSServiceErrorType errorCode,
    const char *name,
    const char *regtype,
    const char *domain,
    void *context
    );
```

The parameters are similar to those for DNSServiceBrowseReply( ). Of particular interest is the name parameter. When auto-renaming is in effect, the name parameter tells you what name Multicast DNS finally picked for you. In some kinds of application, knowing your own name is important. For example, iChat kind of acts as both a client and a server on the same machine. When the client side of iChat browses, it finds all service instances, including its own. By knowing its own name, it can filter itself out of the list it presents to the user.

## DNSServiceAddRecord

Having registered a service, DNSServiceAddRecord( ) lets you add additional records with the same name as the service (SRV) record. This is rare, and most applications never need to do this. One example of an application that uses this is iChat. iChat uses this to add a separate record containing the user's picture. When you add a record using DNSServiceAddRecord( ), you get a DNSRecordRef, which you can subsequently use in DNSServiceUpdateRecord( ) to update the record's data and in DNSServiceRemoveRecord( ) to remove the record from the service registration.

Here is the signature of DNSServiceAddRecord( ):

```
int DNSServiceAddRecord(
    DNSServiceRef sdRef,
    DNSRecordRef *RecordRef,
    DNSServiceFlags *flags,
    uint16_t rrtype,
    uint16_t rdlen,
    const void *rdata,
    uint32_t ttl
    );
```

The sdRef parameter specifies the service you're adding the record to, and the specified DNSRecordRef is initialized as a result of this call.

The last four parameters are used to describe the record being added. The rrtype is the numerical value of the resource record type. The list of these numbers can be found at *http://www.iana.org/assignments/dns-parameters* and in the *dns_sd.h* header file. The rdlen is the length in bytes of rdata, which is (in theory) up to 64 KB of opaque binary data that is to be stored in the resource record being added. In practice, 100 bytes or 200 bytes is a reasonable size, and anything above 1,000 bytes can be inefficient on the network. Finally, ttl is a 32-bit signed value indicating the record's requested time to live in seconds.

## DNSServiceUpdateRecord

Use DNSServiceUpdateRecord( ) to request an update to a DNS record.

```
DNSServiceErrorType DNSServiceUpdateRecord(
DNSServiceRef sdRef,
DNSRecordRef RecordRef,
DNSServiceFlags flags,
uint16_t rdlen,
const void *rdata,
uint32_t ttl
);
```

RecordRef identifies the record to be updated. Either it is a DNSRecordRef created by DNSServiceAddRecord( ), DNSServiceRegisterRecord( ), or NULL, which means "Update the service's primary TXT record." Most services never update their TXT records. Again, the exception is iChat, which uses its TXT record to show the user's available/idle/away state, and consequently updates it all the time.

The rdlen, rdata, and ttl have the same meanings that were described for DNSServiceAddRecord( ).

## DNSServiceRemoveRecord

To request the removal of a resource record from a service's registration information, call DNSServiceRemoveRecord( ).

```
DNSServiceErrorType DNSServiceRemoveRecord(
DNSServiceRef sdRef,
DNSRecordRef RecordRef,
DNSServiceFlags flags
);
```

## Registration example

The registration example shown in Example 7-5 is similar to the browse example shown in Example 7-3. The function MyDNSServiceRegister( ) has roughly the same format as MyDNSServiceBrowse( ). The callback function, MyRegisterCallBack( ), reports that the service has been registered if no errors are reported and reports the errors if any exist. Here is the entire listing.

*Example 7-5. DNSServiceRegister example*

```
#include <dns_sd.h>
#include <stdio.h>            // For stdout, stderr
#include <string.h>            // For strlen(), strcpy(), bzero()
```

*Example 7-5. DNSServiceRegister example (continued)*

```c
extern void HandleEvents(DNSServiceRef);

static void
MyRegisterCallBack(DNSServiceRef service,
                   DNSServiceFlags flags,
                   DNSServiceErrorType errorCode,
                   const char * name,
                   const char * type,
                   const char * domain,
                   void * context)
    {
    #pragma unused(flags)
    #pragma unused(context)

    if (errorCode != kDNSServiceErr_NoError)
        fprintf(stderr, "MyRegisterCallBack returned %d\n", errorCode);
    else
        printf("%-15s %s.%s%s\n","REGISTER", name, type, domain);
    }

static DNSServiceErrorType MyDNSServiceRegister()
    {
    DNSServiceErrorType error;
    DNSServiceRef serviceRef;

    error = DNSServiceRegister(&serviceRef,
                               0,                    // no flags
                               0,                    // all network interfaces
                               "Not a real page",    // name
                               "_http._tcp",         // service type
                               "",                   // register in default domain(s)
                               NULL,                 // use default host name
                               htons(9092),          // port number
                               0,                    // length of TXT record
                               NULL,                 // no TXT record
                               MyRegisterCallBack,   // call back function
                               NULL);                // no context

    if (error == kDNSServiceErr_NoError)
        {
        HandleEvents(serviceRef);
        DNSServiceRefDeallocate(serviceRef);
        }

    return error;
    }

int main (int argc, const char * argv[])
    {
    DNSServiceErrorType error = MyDNSServiceRegister();
    fprintf(stderr, "DNSServiceDiscovery returned %d\n", error);
    return 0;
    }
```

Save the code in Example 7-5 as *MyDNSSDRegistrar.c* and compile it and run it along with *DNSServiceCallbackSelect.c*. Note that the port number for this service has been hardcoded to 9092. When you run this example, you should see the following message:

```
REGISTER    Not a real page._http._tcp.local.
```

You can verify that this service has been registered using the *dns-sd* command-line tool or by running the previous example of browsing. You should see this message:

```
ADD         Not a real page._http._tcp.local.
```

## Enumerating Domains

To date, most of the use of DNS-SD has been for link-local multicast discovery. It is natural that this is the area that would get the most interest, because this was the area of IP most desperately in need of improvement.

However, as link-local DNS-SD becomes mature, people begin to look outward to wide-area service discovery. When you begin to browse domains other than *local*, the question arises, "How does the machine know which domains to browse?" Forcing the user to configure this manually would not be in keeping with the spirit of Zero Configuration Networking. DNS-SD has mechanisms to learn this information from the local network, and the domain enumeration functions allow applications to access this information to present a good user interface. As with the other DNS-SD APIs, these interfaces are asynchronous and ongoing until cancelled, because information from the network can change at any time.

When an application wants to enable browsing in multiple domains, it asks for the list of recommended browsing domains. It should not automatically browse every domain it finds, because that would be extremely expensive on the network. Instead, it should present the list of domains to the user so he can pick. One domain will be delivered with the kDNSServiceFlagsDefault flag set, and that domain should be highlighted by default in the browser. It's the network equivalent of the "you are here" marker on a map. The list is purely advisory; users should still be allowed to manually enter additional domains to browse if they wish.

When an application wants to register its service in domains other than just *local*, it can ask for the list of recommended registration domains. As before, an application should not automatically register in every domain it finds. The list is intended to be shown to the user, so the user may pick one domain from the list. Also as before, the list is advisory, meaning users should be allowed to manually enter a different domain to register in if they wish. Most applications will not need to enumerate registration domains, because they will simply use the user's configured system-wide default by passing NULL for the domain when registering.

To enumerate domains, you need to call DNSServiceEnumerateDomain( ) and use a callback function built on the template provided by DNSServiceDomainEnumReply to collect the information. If the network administrator has not created the domain enumeration records described in Chapter 5, the only result you will get is *local*.

In this section, the signatures for DNSServiceEnumerateDomain( ) and DNSServiceDomainEnumReply( ) are provided along with an example of using this part of the API.

### DNSServiceEnumerateDomain

Begin searching for recommended browsing or registration domains using DNSServiceEnumerateDomain( ):

```
DNSServiceErrorType DNSServiceEnumerateDomains(
    DNSServiceRef *sdRef,
    DNSServiceFlags flags,
    uint32_t interfaceIndex,
    DNSServiceDomainEnumReply callBack,
    void *context);
```

Set the flag either using kDNSServiceFlagsBrowseDomains to return the domains recommended for browsing or using kDNSServicesFlagsRegistrationDomains to return the domains recommended for registering services. The sdRef is an uninitialized service discovery reference that will be initialized when DNSServiceEnumerateDomain( ) is called. The remaining variables are as they were for DNSServiceBrowse( ) and DNSServiceRegister( ).

### DNSServiceDomainEnumReply

The callback function for enumerating domains must be modeled on DNSServiceDomainEnumReply( ).

```
void MyDNSServiceDomainEnumReply
    (
    DNSServiceRef sdRef,
    DNSServiceFlags flags,
    uint32_t interfaceIndex,
    DNSServiceErrorType errorCode,
    const char *replyDomain,
    void *context
    );
```

The variables have been described previously for DNSServiceRegisterReply( ) and DNSServiceBrowseReply( ). Consult Table 7-2 for the flags that can be passed in. As before, kDNSServiceFlagsMoreComing indicates that you should wait to update your UI, as the callback function will be called again immediately. If kDNSServiceFlagsAdd is set, then the domain pointed to should be added to the list of domains, and if kDNSServiceFlagsAdd is not present, then the domain pointed to should be removed from the list. The kDNSServiceFlagsDefault flag is set if the domain is the domain that should be selected by default.

## Enumeration example

The enumeration example shown in Example 7-6 follows the same pattern as the previous examples. The call to DNSServiceEnumerateDomains( ) passes in the flag for browse domains. In the callback function, the discovered domains are displayed, along with an indication of whether there are kDNSServiceFlagsMoreComing and with a field showing whether the domain is being added or removed from the list and whether it is a default domain.

*Example 7-6. DNSServiceEnumerateDomains() example*

```
#include <dns_sd.h>
#include <stdio.h>              // For stdout, stderr
#include <string.h>            // For strlen(), strcpy( ), bzero( )

extern void HandleEvents(DNSServiceRef);

static void
MyEnumerateBrowseDomainsCallBack(DNSServiceRef sdRef,
                                 DNSServiceFlags flags,
                                 uint32_t interface,
                                 DNSServiceErrorType errorCode,
                                 const char *replyDomain,
                                 void *context)
    {
    #pragma unused(context)

    if (errorCode != kDNSServiceErr_NoError)
        fprintf(stderr, "EnumerateDomainsCallBack returned %d\n", errorCode);
    else
        {
        char *moreString = (flags & kDNSServiceFlagsMoreComing) ? "MORE" : "";
        char *addString  = "REMOVE";
        if (flags & kDNSServiceFlagsAdd)
            addString = (flags & kDNSServiceFlagsDefault) ? "DEFAULT" : "ADD";
        printf("%-8s%-5s%s\n", addString, moreString, replyDomain);
        }

    if (!(flags & kDNSServiceFlagsMoreComing)) fflush(stdout);
    }

static DNSServiceErrorType
MyDNSServiceEnumerateBrowse( )
    {
    DNSServiceErrorType error;
    DNSServiceRef  serviceRef;

    error = DNSServiceEnumerateDomains(
                &serviceRef,
                kDNSServiceFlagsBrowseDomains,  // browse domains
                0,  // all network interfaces
                MyEnumerateBrowseDomainsCallBack, //callback function
                NULL);    // no context
```

*Example 7-6. DNSServiceEnumerateDomains() example (continued)*

```
    if (error == kDNSServiceErr_NoError)
        {
        HandleEvents(serviceRef);  // Add service to runloop to get callbacks
        DNSServiceRefDeallocate(serviceRef);
        }
    return error;
    }

int
main (int argc, const char * argv[])
    {
    DNSServiceErrorType error = MyDNSServiceEnumerateBrowse();
    if (error) fprintf(stderr, "DNSServiceDiscovery returned %d\n", error);
    return 0;
    }
```

You can run this example by compiling it and running it with *DNSServiceCallback-Select.c*. As mentioned before, if your network administrator has not created any domain enumeration records, the only result you will get is local.

```
    ADD             local.
```

## Other Operations

This section outlines some of the other lesser-used functions from *dns_sd.h*.

DNSServiceCreateConnection( ) and DNSServiceRegisterRecord( ) are used by applications that need to create a large number of records. A single DNSServiceRef is created using DNSServiceCreateConnection( ), and then multiple records are registered on that single connection.

DNSServiceQueryRecord( ) allows the client to query for any arbitrary DNS record, with any name, type, or class, unicast or multicast. It is, in many ways, similar to the standard Unix res_query( ) function, except that it operates asynchronously with a callback function.

DNSServiceReconfirmRecord( ) is used for cache management. Multicast DNS caches data for efficiency, but anytime data is cached, it can become out of date. If a client believes that data is out of date, it can call DNSServiceReconfirmRecord( ) to provide a hint to the cache management algorithm. For example, suppose a client gets a host's address record using DNSServiceQueryRecord( ), but the host does not respond. If the client calls DNSServiceReconfirmRecord( ), then Multicast DNS will requery for the record, and if no response is received, then the record will be deleted from the cache. In addition, any SRV records referencing that target host will automatically be considered potentially suspect and will, in turn, be reconfirmed. If the SRV records are not confirmed, then they too will be deleted from the cache, and any PTR records referencing the now-departed SRV records will also be considered potentially suspect. After a short time, if these records are not confirmed, they will also be deleted from the cache. The end result of this is that services being advertised from the departed host will disappear from browsing lists soon, instead of waiting a full hour for the record's TTL to expire. This call is highly specialized, and most applications will never have to use it, because in normal cases cache reconfirmation is handled automatically. In normal cases, if a host crashes, then the DNSServiceQueryRecord( ) call to look up its IP address will fail, and that will automatically kick off the chain of reconfirmations that purges the stale SRV and PTR records, too.

# Event Handling with Cocoa RunLoop or Core Foundation CFRunLoop

So far in this chapter, you have used the select( ) loop to receive the asynchronous event notifications central to DNS-SD. In this last section, you will see alternative event delivery solutions. First, without any changes to the code presented in Examples 7-3 through 7-6, you can swap out the cross-platform code presented in Example 7-2 for a Mac OS X specific run loop that uses Core Foundation classes. Second, you will see how to alter the code to take advantage of the Windows-specific event loop.

If you're writing a Cocoa or Core Foundation application, you'll probably be using a Cocoa RunLoop or Core Foundation CFRunLoop (which are actually the same thing under the covers). You'll want to add a Cocoa- or Core Foundation–compatible event-generating object to your RunLoop. To do that, you extract the Unix Domain Socket from the DNSServiceRef, construct a CFSocket from that, and then construct a CFRunLoopSourceRef from that. The rough outline is shown in Example 7-7.

*Example 7-7. Skeleton of CFRunLoop*

```
typedef struct MyDNSServiceState
    {
    DNSServiceRef      service;
    CFSocketRef        socket;
    CFRunLoopSourceRef    source;
    } MyDNSServiceState;

void
HandleEvents(DNSServiceRef serviceRef)
    {
    // . . .
    // Access the underlying Unix domain socket and create a CFSocket
    sock = DNSServiceRefSockFD(ref->service);
    ref->socket = CFSocketCreateWithNative(NULL, sock,
            kCFSocketReadCallBack, MySocketCallBack, &context);
    // . . .
    // Create a CFRunLoopSource from the CFSocket, add to run loop and start.
    ref->source = CFSocketCreateRunLoopSource(NULL, ref->socket, 0);
    CFRunLoopAddSource(CFRunLoopGetCurrent( ), ref->source, kCFRunLoopCommonModes);
```

*Example 7-7. Skeleton of CFRunLoop (continued)*

```
    // . . .

    CFRunLoopRun( );
    }
```

DNSServiceRefSockFD( ) extracts the Unix Domain Socket from the DNSServiceRef.

CFSocketCreateWithNative( ) makes a CFSocket from a native Unix socket.

CFSocketCreateRunLoopSource( ) makes a CFRunLoopSource from the CFSocket.

Once added to the RunLoop, MySocketCallBack( ) will be called every time there is data waiting to be read. You can use a single MySocketCallBack( ) routine for all of your DNS-SD operations. All it has to do is call DNSServiceProcessResult( ) on the right DNSServiceRef, and DNS-SD will do the rest to invoke the right callbacks.

```
    static void
    MySocketCallBack(CFSocketRef s, CFSocketCallBackType type,
                     CFDataRef address, const void * data, void * info)
        {
        //. . . cast the context info to initialize ref
        MyDNSServiceState * ref = (MyDNSServiceState *)info;
        // . . . use the service discovery reference for callback
        err = DNSServiceProcessResult(ref->service);
        // handle error . . .
        }
```

Example 7-8 shows the full listing with all of the details.

*Example 7-8. Core Foundation RunLoop example*

```
// Simple example of how to handle DNSServiceDiscovery events using a CFRunLoop

#include <dns_sd.h>
#include <CoreFoundation/CoreFoundation.h>


// Structure to hold CFRunLoop-related state

typedef struct MyDNSServiceState
    {
    DNSServiceRef       service;    // Active DNSServiceDiscovery operation
    CFSocketRef         cfsocket;   // CFSocket for this operation
    CFRunLoopSourceRef  source;     // RunLoopSource for this CFSocket
    } MyDNSServiceState;


// Remove a DNSServiceDiscovery operation from a CFRunLoop's
// set of active event sources

static void DNSServiceRemoveSource(CFRunLoopRef rl, MyDNSServiceState *ref)
    {
    assert(rl != NULL);
    assert(ref != NULL);
```

*Example 7-8. Core Foundation RunLoop example (continued)*

```
        // Remove the CFRunLoopSource from the current run loop.
        CFRunLoopRemoveSource(rl, ref->source, kCFRunLoopCommonModes);
        CFRelease(ref->source);

        // Invalidate the CFSocket.
        CFSocketInvalidate(ref->cfsocket);
        CFRelease(ref->cfsocket);

        // Workaround to give time to CFSocket's select() thread
        // so it can remove the socket from its FD set before we
        // close the socket by calling DNSServiceRefDeallocate.
        usleep(1000);

        // Terminate the connection with the daemon, which cancels the operation.
        DNSServiceRefDeallocate(ref->service);
        free(ref);
    }


// Helper function: When CFRunLoop indicates an interesting event,
// this function calls DNSServiceProcessResult() to handle it

static void MySocketCallBack(CFSocketRef s, CFSocketCallBackType type,
                CFDataRef address, const void *data, void *info)
    {
    #pragma unused(s)
    #pragma unused(type)
    #pragma unused(address)
    #pragma unused(data)

    DNSServiceErrorType err;
    MyDNSServiceState *ref = (MyDNSServiceState *)info;
    assert(ref != NULL);

    // Read a reply from the daemon, which will call the appropriate callback.
    err= DNSServiceProcessResult(ref->service);
    if (err != kDNSServiceErr_NoError)
        {
        fprintf(stderr, "DNSServiceProcessResult returned %d\n", err);
        // Terminate the discovery operation and release everything.
        DNSServiceRemoveSource(CFRunLoopGetCurrent(), ref);
        }
    }


// Add a DNSServiceDiscovery operation to a CFRunLoop's
// set of active event sources

static void DNSServiceAddSource(CFRunLoopRef rl, MyDNSServiceState *ref)
    {
    CFSocketContext context = { 0, ref, NULL, NULL, NULL };
    CFSocketNativeHandle sock = DNSServiceRefSockFD(ref->service);
    assert(sock != -1);
```

*Example 7-8. Core Foundation RunLoop example (continued)*

```
    // Create a CFSocket from the underlying Unix Domain socket.
    ref->cfsocket = CFSocketCreateWithNative(NULL, sock,
                    kCFSocketReadCallBack, MySocketCallBack, &context);

    // Prevent CFSocketInvalidate from closing DNSServiceRef's socket.
    CFOptionFlags f = CFSocketGetSocketFlags(ref->cfsocket);
    CFSocketSetSocketFlags(ref->cfsocket, f & ~kCFSocketCloseOnInvalidate);

    // Create a CFRunLoopSource from the CFSocket.
    ref->source = CFSocketCreateRunLoopSource(NULL, ref->cfsocket, 0);

    // Add the CFRunLoopSource to the current run loop.
    CFRunLoopAddSource(rl, ref->source, kCFRunLoopCommonModes);
    }


// Simple example: Here we just add a single DNSServiceDiscovery event source,
// and then call CFRunLoopRun() to handle the events. In a program that already
// has a main RunLoop, you'd just keep that as is, and use DNSServiceAddSource/
// DNSServiceRemoveSource to add and remove event sources from that RunLoop.

void HandleEvents(DNSServiceRef serviceRef)
    {
    MyDNSServiceState ref = { serviceRef };
    DNSServiceAddSource(CFRunLoopGetCurrent(), &ref);

    CFRunLoopRun();
    }
```

Save this as *DNSServiceCallbackCF.c*. Compile and run this with any of the files from Examples 7-3 to 7-6 in place of *DNSServiceCallbackSelect.c*. The results should be the same as before.

Note that because a Cocoa RunLoop and a Core Foundation CFRunLoop are actually the same thing (Cocoa and Core Foundation just provide their own APIs to access the same underlying object), the code shown above can also be used in an Objective-C program. It may not look much like Objective-C (no square brackets all over the place), but that's no problem. The Objective-C compiler also fully supports standard C, and the code will compile and do exactly what you need.

DNSServiceDiscovery's context parameter helps us interface with Objective-C's object-oriented paradigm. When calling one of the DNSServiceDiscovery API routines, pass in the address of your C-style callback function and, for the context parameter, pass a reference to the object (usually self) that you want to handle the events, like this:

```
    DNSServiceBrowse(&ref, 0, 0, srvtype, "", BrowseReplyFn, self);
```

Then, in your C-style callback function, you recover the object context by writing something like MyObjectType *self = (MyObjectType *)context, as shown here:

```
void BrowseReplyFn(DNSServiceRef sdRef, DNSServiceFlags flags,
    uint32_t interfaceIndex, DNSServiceErrorType errorCode,
    const char *serviceName, const char *regtype, const char *replyDomain,
    void *context)
    {
    MyObjectType *self = (MyObjectType *)context;
    [self doThis];
    [self doThat];
    [self addName: [NSString stringWithUTF8String:serviceName]];
    //... and so on
    }
```

# Event Handling with Microsoft Windows GetMessage( ) Message Loop

There are some differences in working with the Windows event loop. In this example, you will configure and create a window that is not displayed in the application. This gives you a template for developing GUI-based Zeroconf applications for Windows. The Zeroconf events are processed as messages to this window. Here is the outline of the HandleEvents( ) function for Windows:

```
void HandleEvents(DNSServiceRef inServiceRef)
    {
    //...   Configure and create a window that is not shown but that
    // is used to process DNS-SD events as messages to the window.

    wind = CreateWindow(wcex.lpszClassName, wcex.lpszClassName, 0,
                        CW_USEDEFAULT, 0, CW_USEDEFAULT, 0, NULL,
                        NULL, instance, NULL);

    // ... Associate the DNS-SD browser with our window

    err = WSAAsyncSelect((SOCKET) DNSServiceRefSockFD(gServiceRef), wind,
                        DNSSD_EVENT, FD_READ | FD_CLOSE);

    assert(err == kDNSServiceErr_NoError);

    // DNS-SD events are dispatched while in this loop.

    while(GetMessage(&msg, NULL, 0, 0))
        {
        TranslateMessage(&msg);
        DispatchMessage(&msg);
        }

    // Clean up.
```

```
        WSAAsyncSelect((SOCKET) DNSServiceRefSockFD(gServiceRef), wind,
                                    DNSSD_EVENT, 0);
    }
```

When a window event is received, it is processed in the callback function WndProc( ). If the event is a DNS-SD event, it is passed on to DNSServiceProcessResult( ) as before. Here is the sketch of WndProc( ):

```
    static LRESULT CALLBACK WndProc(HWND inWindow, UINT inMsg,
                                    WPARAM inWParam, LPARAM inLParam)
    {
    LRESULT result;
    switch(inMsg)
        {
        case DNSSD_EVENT:
            DNSServiceProcessResult(gServiceRef);
            result = 0;
            break; //...
        }
    return(result);
    }
```

All of the details are provided in the code listing in Example 7-9.

*Example 7-9. Windows event loop example*

```
#include     "stdafx.h"
#include     <assert.h>
#include     <stdio.h>
#include     <dns_sd.h>

// Constants

#define DNSSD_EVENT        (WM_USER + 0x100)
                    // Message sent to Window when a DNS-SD event occurs.
// Prototypes

void HandleEvents(DNSServiceRef inServiceRef);

static LRESULT CALLBACK WndProc(HWND inWindow,
                                UINT inMsg,
                                WPARAM inWParam,
                                LPARAM inLParam);

static void DNSSD_API
    BrowserCallBack(DNSServiceRef       inServiceRef,
                    DNSServiceFlags inFlags,
                    uint32_t inIFI,
                    DNSServiceErrorType       inError,
                    const char * inName,
                    const char * inType,
                    const char * inDomain,
                    void * inContext);
```

*Example 7-9. Windows event loop example (continued)*

```
// Globals

static DNSServiceRef        gServiceRef = NULL;

// Main entry point for application.

void HandleEvents(DNSServiceRef inServiceRef)

    {
    HINSTANCE       instance;
    WNDCLASSEX       wcex;
    HWND            wind;
    MSG             msg;
    int             err;

    gServiceRef = inServiceRef;

    // Create the window. This window won't actually be shown,
    // but it demonstrates how to use DNS-SD with Windows GUI
    // applications by having DNS-SD events processed as messages
    // to a Window.

    instance = GetModuleHandle(NULL);
    assert(instance);

    wcex.cbSize = sizeof(wcex);
    wcex.style      = 0;
    wcex.lpfnWndProc = (WNDPROC) WndProc;
    wcex.cbClsExtra     = 0;
    wcex.cbWndExtra     = 0;
    wcex.hInstance = instance;
    wcex.hIcon      = NULL;
    wcex.hCursor = NULL;
    wcex.hbrBackground = NULL;
    wcex.lpszMenuName = NULL;
    wcex.lpszClassName = TEXT("ZeroconfExample");
    wcex.hIconSm = NULL;
    RegisterClassEx(&wcex);

    wind = CreateWindow(wcex.lpszClassName, wcex.lpszClassName, 0,
                        CW_USEDEFAULT, 0, CW_USEDEFAULT, 0, NULL,
                        NULL, instance, NULL);

    assert(wind);

    // Associate the DNS-SD browser with our window
    // using the WSAAsyncSelect mechanism. Whenever something
    // related to the DNS-SD browser occurs, our private Windows message
    // will be sent to our window so we can give DNS-SD a
    // chance to process it. This allows DNS-SD to avoid using a
    // secondary thread (and all the issues with synchronization that
    // would introduce), but still process everything asynchronously.
```

*Example 7-9. Windows event loop example (continued)*

```
        // This also simplifies app code because DNS-SD will only run when we
        // explicitly call it.

        err = WSAAsyncSelect((SOCKET) DNSServiceRefSockFD(gServiceRef), wind,
                             DNSSD_EVENT, FD_READ | FD_CLOSE);

        assert(err == kDNSServiceErr_NoError);

        // Main event loop for the application. All DNS-SD events are
        // dispatched while in this loop.

        while(GetMessage(&msg, NULL, 0, 0))
            {
            TranslateMessage(&msg);
            DispatchMessage(&msg);
            }

        // Clean up. This is not strictly necessary since the normal
        // process cleanup will close DNS-SD socket(s) and release memory,
        // but it's here to demonstrate how to do it.

        WSAAsyncSelect((SOCKET) DNSServiceRefSockFD(gServiceRef), wind,
                       DNSSD_EVENT, 0);
    }

// Callback for the Window. DNS-SD events are delivered here.

static LRESULT CALLBACK WndProc(HWND inWindow, UINT inMsg,
                                WPARAM inWParam, LPARAM inLParam)
    {
    LRESULT result;

    switch(inMsg)
        {
        case DNSSD_EVENT:

            // Process the DNS-SD event. All DNS-SD callbacks occur from
            // within this function.

            if (DNSServiceProcessResult(gServiceRef) != kDNSServiceErr_NoError)
              result = -1;
            else
              result = 0;
            break;

        default:
          result = DefWindowProc(inWindow, inMsg, inWParam, inLParam);
          break;
        }

    return(result);
    }
```

# Event Handling with Microsoft Windows MFC

If you're programming using the Microsoft Windows MFC (Microsoft Foundation Classes) programming model, then you don't need your own event loop. You just declare the messages that your window accepts, and, as events happen, MFC sends the appropriate message to your window object. Example 7-10 shows an outline of what you need to do to integrate (in this example) DNS-SD browsing into an MFC application.

*Example 7-10. Windows MFC example*

```
#include "stdafx.h"
#include <dns_sd.h>
#include <winsock2.h>

#define WM_PRIVATE_SERVICE_EVENT            ( WM_USER + 0x100 )

class MyWindow
:
    public CWnd
{
public:

    MyWindow( );
    virtual ~MyWindow( void );

protected:

    // General

    afx_msg int     OnCreate( LPCREATESTRUCT inCreateStruct );
    afx_msg void    OnDestroy( void );
    afx_msg LONG    OnServiceEvent( WPARAM inWParam, LPARAM inLParam );

    // Browsing

    static void DNSSD_API
    BrowseReply(
            DNSServiceRef           inRef,
            DNSServiceFlags         inFlags,
            uint32_t                inInterfaceIndex,
            DNSServiceErrorType     inErrorCode,
            const char *            inName,
            const char *            inType,
            const char *            inDomain,
            void *                  inContext );

    DECLARE_MESSAGE_MAP( )

private:

    DNSServiceRef m_serviceRef;
};
```

*Example 7-10. Windows MFC example (continued)*

```
BEGIN_MESSAGE_MAP( MyWindow, CWnd )
    ON_WM_CREATE( )
    ON_WM_DESTROY( )
    ON_MESSAGE( WM_PRIVATE_SERVICE_EVENT, OnServiceEvent )
END_MESSAGE_MAP( )

int
MyWindow::OnCreate( LPCREATESTRUCT inCreateStruct )
    {
    DNSServiceErrorType err;

    err = CWnd::OnCreate( inCreateStruct );

    if ( err )
        goto exit;

    err = DNSServiceBrowse( &m_serviceRef, 0, 0, "_http._tcp", NULL, BrowseReply, this );

    if ( err )
        goto exit;

    err = WSAAsyncSelect( (SOCKET) DNSServiceRefSockFD(m_serviceRef), m_hWnd,
                          WM_PRIVATE_SERVICE_EVENT, FD_READ|FD_CLOSE);

exit:

    if ( err )
        {
        if ( m_serviceRef )
            {
            DNSServiceRefDeallocate( m_serviceRef );
            m_serviceRef = NULL;
            }
        }

    return( err );
    }

void MyWindow::OnDestroy( void )
    {
    // ...

    if ( m_serviceRef )
        {
        WSAAsyncSelect( ( SOCKET ) DNSServiceRefSockFD( m_serviceRef ), m_hWnd, 0, 0 );
        DNSServiceRefDeallocate( m_serviceRef );
        }

    // ...
    }
```

*Example 7-10. Windows MFC example (continued)*

```
LONG MyWindow::OnServiceEvent(WPARAM inWParam, LPARAM inLParam)
    {
    SOCKET              sock = (SOCKET) inWParam;
    DNSServiceErrorType err;

    if ( WSAGETSELECTERROR(inLParam) && !(HIWORD(inLParam)))
        goto exit;

    ASSERT( ( SOCKET ) DNSServiceRefSockFD( m_serviceRef ) == sock );
    err = DNSServiceProcessResult( m_serviceRef );
    ASSERT( !err );

exit:

    return ( 0 );
    }

void DNSSD_API MyWindow::BrowseReply(
        DNSServiceRef       inRef,
        DNSServiceFlags     inFlags,
        uint32_t            inInterfaceIndex,
        DNSServiceErrorType inErrorCode,
        const char *        inName,
        const char *        inType,
        const char *        inDomain,
        void *              inContext )
    {
    MyWindow * self = reinterpret_cast<MyWindow*>( inContext );
    ASSERT( self );

    // ...
    }
```

# Event Handling with Independent Threads

DNS-SD also accommodates programmers who prefer to use multiple threads rather than a single thread and an event loop. Because the DNSServiceProcessResult( ) blocks if no data is available, you can simply create a thread and have it spin calling DNSServiceProcessResult( ). When no data is available, the thread will sleep. When data arrives, the thread will wake up, handle it, and then go back to sleep again. Example 7-11 shows how to set up event handling using independent threads.

*Example 7-11. Event handling with independent threads*

```
void ThreadProc(DNSServiceRef ref)
    {
    while (DNSServiceProcessResult(ref) == kDNSServiceErr_NoError)
        continue;
    }
```

This has the advantage that your callback routines will get executed "by magic," without you having to take any special action aside from creating the thread and starting it running in the first place. Of course, magic comes at a price. When callback routines get executed by magic, you no longer have control over exactly when they will run and what else might be happening at the same time. As with all multi-threaded code, you need to take good care to use the proper locking to avoid race conditions and crashes.

## Summary

This chapter introduced the lowest level, cross-platform, C-programming API for Zeroconf's DNS Service Discovery. It also introduced the important DNS-SD concepts of asynchronous event handling and continuous live updating, which apply no matter which language or API you choose to use. The following chapters present other APIs and languages. In some, callbacks are scheduled preemptively using threads, and you need to take care to write thread-safe code. In others, callbacks are scheduled cooperatively out of a main event loop, and you don't have to worry about thread safety, reentry, and race conditions, but in your callback functions and methods you need to be careful to avoid doing time-consuming operations. If your callback function or method does anything that blocks for a long period of time, you'll cause your application's whole user interface to lock up while it waits for your callback to finish what it's doing.

# CHAPTER 8

# Using the Java APIs

Starting in Mac OS X 10.3.9, new APIs enable Java software to advertise and discover services on the network using Zeroconf's DNS Service Discovery. The same Java DNS-SD APIs are also available in Bonjour for Windows, Bonjour for Linux, Solaris, *BSD, etc., enabling Java software to make use of Zeroconf's DNS Service Discovery across a wide range of platforms, not just on Mac OS X. In this chapter, you will take a quick look through the APIs, see short examples of how to register, browse for, add TXT records to, and resolve services, and finally see a complete example of using Java DNS-SD in a tic-tac-toe game.

## Understanding the APIs

The `com.apple.dnssd` package exposes an abstract factory class, `DNSSD`, used to create the various types of `DNSSDService` objects, two classes used to manipulate DNS records, a collection of interfaces that are implemented as appropriate by client code to receive callback messages, and an exception:

- Factory Class:
  - — DNSSD
- References to ongoing asynchronous operations:
  - — DNSSDService
  - — DNSSDRegistration
- DNS Record Classes:
  - — DNSRecord
  - — TXTRecord
- Callback Interface Classes, implemented by client:
  - — BaseListener
  - — RegisterListener
  - — BrowseListener

— ResolveListener

— DomainListener

— QueryListener

- DNSSD Error Exception:

— DNSSDException

The pattern for using the APIs will most often consist of calling a static method from the DNSSD factory class, passing in an instance of a class that implements the appropriate interface to receive callback messages. For example, when calling DNSSD.browse( ) to initiate a browsing operation, the client must supply an object that implements the BrowseListener interface.

As with all the different flavors of DNS-SD API, the Java APIs are asynchronous—you start an operation and get callback messages when interesting events happen—and to make effective use of the API, it is helpful to understand the mechanism by which those callback messages are delivered. Recall that in the C API, since there is no single event-handling model universally adopted by all C programs, the API returns a socket file descriptor to the client, so that the client can integrate it into the client's chosen event-handling model, such as a select( ) loop or similar. In contrast, when using the Mac OS X Cocoa APIs, it is assumed that the client will be using a Cocoa RunLoop, so ongoing asynchronous operations are automatically added to the current RunLoop, and events are automatically delivered sequentially to the client, as with other RunLoop events.

Unlike C (and its standard libraries), Java was designed from the start with full support for multithreaded code, so just as it is reasonable to assume that Cocoa programs use a RunLoop, it is reasonable to assume that Java programs can take advantage of threads. For this reason, Java clients get a benefit not present in the C API: Java clients don't need to take any special scheduling action to receive the events generated by the DNS-SD APIs. As soon as an asynchronous operation is initiated, the listener object will immediately begin receiving events, delivered "by magic," as it were, on a different thread automatically created for this purpose. Of course, all magic comes at some cost, and the cost is that the client code needs to be thread-safe. The moment a client thread calls DNSSD.browse( ), the listener object may start receiving events, running on another thread, even before the DNSSD.browse( ) call has returned to the caller. For this reason, even though the DNSSDService object is returned as the result of the DNSSD.browse( ) call, it is also passed as the first parameter in listener object methods, so that those methods can get reliable access to that value if they need it (for example, to stop the operation once they've received the result they need). Don't make the mistake of writing client code that calls DNSSD.browse( ) and places the result into some global or class variable, and then writing listener object methods that make use of the value in that variable. Frequently, the listener object methods will be invoked so quickly that they will be running before the main thread has done its assignment, resulting in the listener object methods accessing the value of the variable before it has been set.

Another issue to be aware of is that some other Java APIs have multithreading restrictions. For example, if you're writing Swing/AWT GUI code, it's important to remember that Swing components can be accessed by only one thread at a time. Generally, this thread is the event-dispatching thread. If you don't heed this warning, and you make Swing calls from other threads, then your program will be unreliable and is likely to fail randomly in mysterious ways. Since the typical purpose of a BrowseListener object is to update the user interface in response to services coming and going on the network, and since BrowseListener events are delivered asynchronously as they happen, on their own thread, this presents a small dilemma. How can a BrowseListener method legally perform Swing/AWT user interface operations? The solution is that the BrowseListener should use SwingUtilities.invokeAndWait to cause the event to be handled synchronously on the AWT event dispatching thread, where it can safely make user interface calls. The tic-tac-toe programming example at the end of this chapter demonstrates how to do this. There is also some sample code in the Clients/Java folder of Apple's Darwin mDNSResponder project. That code defines helper classes with names like SwingBrowseListener, which act as intermediaries between the raw DNS-SD events, delivered on their own background threads, and your own listener routines, which need to run on the AWT event-dispatching thread if they're going to make user interface calls. These helper objects receive the raw DNS-SD events on your behalf and then schedule your listener method to be executed on the AWT event-dispatching thread. Similar techniques can be used to accommodate other packages that have their own multithreading restrictions.

In this section, you will survey the com.apple.dnssd package.

## The DNSSD Class

The factory class com.apple.dnssd.DNSSD is the workhorse of the Java DNS-SD API. You never instantiate objects of this class but instead call one of these public static methods:

- static DNSSDRegistration register(java.lang.String serviceName, java.lang. String regType, int port, com.apple.dnssd.RegisterListener listener)

- static DNSSDRegistration register(int flags, int ifIndex, java.lang.String serviceName, java.lang.String regType, java.lang.String domain, java.lang.String host, int port, com.apple.dnssd.TXTRecord txtRecord, com.apple.dnssd.Register-Listener listener)

- static DNSSDService browse(java.lang.String regType, com.apple.dnssd.Browse-Listener listener)

- static DNSSDService browse(int flags, int ifIndex, java.lang.String regType, java.lang.String domain, com.apple.dnssd.BrowseListener listener)
- static DNSSDService resolve(int flags, int ifIndex, java.lang.String serviceName, java.lang.String regType, java.lang.String domain, com.apple.dnssd.ResolveListener listener)

By now, with knowledge of the *dns-sd* command-line tool and the C API, the register/browse/resolve operations should be quite familiar. One difference to be aware of is that, whereas the DNSServiceDiscovery C API follows the established Berkeley Sockets convention that port numbers are always given in network byte order, the standard Java networking APIs use port numbers in host integer byte order, and the DNSServiceDiscovery Java API adheres to that established Java convention. Another difference you will notice is that the Java API has two register methods and two browse methods. Whereas the C API always requires you to pass the full set of parameters for any given call (passing zero or NULL to indicate default values), the Java API makes use of method overloading to provide variants. If you don't want to limit browsing to a particular interface, you're happy to let the system pick the domain(s) to browse, and you don't need to specify any special flags, then you can just leave out those parameters completely and use the simpler version of the browse( ) method.

- static DNSSDService enumerateDomains(int flags, int ifIndex, com.apple.dnssd.DomainListener listener)
- static DNSSDService queryRecord(int flags, int ifIndex, java.lang.String serviceName, int rrtype, int rrclass, com.apple.dnssd.QueryListener listener)
- static void reconfirmRecord(int flags, int ifIndex, java.lang.String fullName, int rrtype, int rrclass, byte[] rdata)

These three methods provide access to some of the more specialized DNS-SD functionality: enumerating the list of wide-area domains recommended for this network, querying for a specific individual named DNS Resource Record Set (RRSet), and signaling to the daemon that you believe a particular DNS Resource Record in its cache may be stale and out of date. The way they work is exactly equivalent to their counterparts in the C API.

As a simple example, you can browse for a service of type _example._tcp from the command line using:

```
dns-sd -B _example._tcp
```

In a Java program, you can accomplish the same task using a call to DNSSD.browse, as shown in the example below, where myBrowseListener is an instance of a class that implements the BrowseListener interface:

```
DNSSDService b = DNSSD.browse("_example._tcp", myBrowseListener);
```

The result of the DNSSD.browse() call is a reference to the newly created DNSSDService object, which you need to keep so that you can call b.stop() when it's time to stop the ongoing operation. If you never call b.stop(), then the asynchronous operation you've initiated will run forever, consuming network bandwidth, memory, and CPU time until your program eventually exits! Typically, a program would call DNSSD.browse() when a user brings up a window to browse the network, and call b.stop() when the user closes that window.

It is common for the object making the DNSSD.browse call to implement the BrowseListener interface itself, in which case, you would substitute this in place of myBrowseListener.

In addition to the classes detailed above, the DNSSD class contains the following utility methods:

- constructFullName(java.lang.String serviceName, java.lang.String regType, java.lang.String domain)
- getIfIndexForName(java.lang.String ifName)
- getNameForIfIndex(int ifIndex)

DNS-SD uses structured service names, containing an instance name, a service type, and a domain. In the on-the-wire format used in DNS packets, the three components are concatenated into a single, fully qualified DNS name. If you need to mix and match the service-oriented DNS-SD APIs with conventional low-level DNS APIs, you'll need to know the right fully qualified DNS name to use for a particular service. The constructFullName() call builds the correct fully qualified DNS name from DNS-SD's serviceName, regtype, and domain. The name is also properly escaped according to the standard DNS conventions; for example, if the instance name contains a dot (.), then it will appear as (\.) in the escaped DNS name, as required by the standard DNS APIs.

On machines with multiple physical interfaces, DNS-SD allows you to optionally restrict registering, browsing, and resolving to a single physical interface. To do this, you pass an interface index value when making the API calls. Because Java has historically not provided APIs for working with interface indexes, the Java DNS-SD API provides a couple of helper functions, getIfIndexForName() and getNameForIfIndex(), which convert from an interface name to its index value, and vice versa.

The DNSSD class also includes constants (of type public final static int) that are used in various places by the API. For example, when you register a service, if a different service of that type already exists with the same name, Multicast DNS will normally pick a new unique name for you automatically. If, instead, you would like the service registration to simply fail and signal an error so that you can write your own code to select a new name, then you would pass the flag value NO_AUTO_RENAME when calling DNSSD.register().

# The Listener Interfaces

With most DNS-SD operations, you don't want to block and wait for a response. You will generally issue a request and pass in a handle to an object that implements the appropriate listener interface. This listener will then be called when interesting events occur, such as discovery of an instance of the service type you're looking for.

## BaseListener

All of the interfaces in the `com.apple.dnssd` package extend `BaseListener`. As a result, every listener must implement the `operationFailed` method:

```
operationFailed(com.apple.dnssd.DNSSDService service, int errorCode)
```

If an asynchronous operation encounters a failure condition, then the listener's `operationFailed()` method is called. These kinds of failures are rare. For example, one contrived way you could deliberately cause the `operationFailed()` method to be called would be to start a DNS-SD operation and then kill the background daemon with a Unix `kill -9` command. Currently, under normal circumstances, the only asynchronous failure that applications may reasonably need to expect are name conflicts for service registrations. If a program registers a service using the `NO_AUTO_RENAME` flag, and the computer subsequently joins a network where a service of the same type with that name already exists, then the program will get informed via an `operationFailed()` callback that it's service registration had to be cancelled, and if it wants to continue advertising, then it should pick a new name and try again. (If the program didn't specify `NO_AUTO_RENAME`, then its service registration will be automatically renamed on its behalf, and it will be notified of the new name via a `serviceRegistered` callback instead.)

Each asynchronous operation (e.g., register, browse, resolve) has its corresponding Listener interface (e.g., `RegisterListener`, `BrowseListener`, `ResolveListener`).

# DNSSDException

The `DNSSDException` class is used to report DNS-SD error conditions. This exception generally indicates a programming error and is not expected to occur during normal program operation. (The only exceptional condition a program should be prepared to deal with during normal operation are name conflicts for advertised services, and those events are reported asynchronously via `operationFailed` or `serviceRegistered` callbacks.)

Just as with all Java exceptions, your exception handler can use `getMessage()` to get a string describing the nature of the error, and it can use `printStackTrace()` to show you where the error occurred. If you want to find the actual error code from the daemon, you can use the `DNSSDException` class's `getErrorCode()` method. Table 8-1 shows error codes returned by the mdnsd daemon.

*Table 8-1. Error codes returned by the Java DNS-SD API*

| Error | Code |
|---|---|
| NO_ERROR | 0 |
| UNKNOWN | -65537 |
| NO_SUCH_NAME | -65538 |
| NO_MEMORY | -65539 |
| BAD_PARAM | -65540 |
| BAD_REFERENCE | -65541 |
| BAD_STATE | -65542 |
| BAD_FLAGS | -65543 |
| UNSUPPORTED | -65544 |
| NOT_INITIALIZED | -65545 |
| ALREADY_REGISTERED | -65547 |
| NAME_CONFLICT | -65548 |
| INVALID | -65549 |
| INCOMPATIBLE | -65551 |
| BAD_INTERFACE_INDEX | -65552 |

# Using the APIs

In this section, you will see quick examples of performing specific tasks using the Java APIs. You will begin by registering a service and verifying that it is being advertised correctly by using the *dns-sd* command-line tool. Next, you will browse using Java code to discover the service you just registered, and resolve the service to get the target host and port number. The final example in this section revisits registering a service, but this time with attached attributes, stored in the service's TXT record.

## Registering a Service

There are two steps you must take to register a service:

1. Call DNSSD.register( ) using one of the two available signatures.
2. Provide a class that implements the RegisterListener interface.

### The DNSSD.register( ) call

The first step can be as simple as a single line of code:

```
DNSSDRegistration r = DNSSD.register("Moët & Chandon", "_example._tcp", 9099, this);
```

This advertises a service of type _example._tcp, which is listening on port 9099, with the instance name Moët & Chandon. Remember that instance names are not restricted like conventional DNS hostnames. Service instance names can contain uppercase, lowercase, spaces, punctuation, accented characters, and even non-roman characters like Kanji.

The return value from calling DNSSD.register() is a DNSSDRegistration object. DNSSDRegistration extends DNSSDService, so you can use the stop() method when it is time to stop advertising the service.

You can also add additional records to a registered service, and you can get a reference to the service's primary TXT record if you need to update that record to contain new data:

```
DNSRecord addRecord(int flags, int rrType, byte[] rData, int ttl)
DNSRecord getTXTRecord()
```

Most applications don't need to use the calls, but one well-known example that does is iChat, which adds the user's image icon as an additional record and updates the service's TXT record each time the user's status message changes.

The register() method might throw a DNSSDException, which must be caught. In our example program, the only reason you'd get an exception would be if you had an illegal parameter because of a typing mistake, say, "_txp" where it should say "_tcp." Using printStackTrace() in your exception handler can help you track down and debug this kind of mistake.

Before you compile this code, you first need to make sure that the calling object (this) implements the required RegisterListener interface.

### The RegisterListener

To fulfill the requirement for a RegisterListener, you could create a whole new class especially for this purpose, but usually that is not necessary. Usually, the object responsible for registering a service is also the natural place to handle events pertaining to that registration, so all you have to do is add serviceRegistered() and operationFailed() methods to that class and declare that it now implements the RegisterListener interface.

In this current example, name conflicts should be handled automatically for us because we don't use NO_AUTO_RENAME, so we don't expect the operationFailed() method to be called at all. If it is called, it just prints a message to the standard error output to help us debug the code and find out what went wrong.

The serviceRegistered() method in our example will print a message to standard output displaying the advertised service's name, type, and domain. Note that the service's name may *not* be the name we asked for, if that name is already in use. Indeed, many programs don't specify a name at all, just passing in an empty string for the name and letting DNS-SD automatically use the system-wide default name, handling name conflicts as necessary.

```
public void serviceRegistered(DNSSDRegistration registration, int flags,
    String serviceName, String regType, String domain)
```

```
{
    System.out.println("Registered Name  : " + serviceName);
    System.out.println("             Type  : " + regType);
    System.out.println("             Domain: " + domain);
}
```

It's important to understand that in the dynamic world of networking, success at one moment in time is not a guarantee of continued future success in perpetuity. The serviceRegistered callback indicates that, at this moment, the service is being advertised on the network under the indicated name. Over the lifetime of a long-running program, the program should expect that it is quite possible that the name may change, and the serviceRegistered( ) method may be called again with new data. After the initial probing and announcement of the chosen unique service name, that name may subsequently change as a result of both internal and external factors.

The internal factor is explicit user action. If you registered your service using an empty string for the name so that your service uses the system-wide default name, and the user subsequently decides to change the system-wide default name, then she doesn't need to quit and relaunch your server for it to get the new name. The name is updated live, and you will get a new serviceRegistered( ) callback telling you the new name.

The external factor that may cause your service name to change is connecting to a new network. If the user starts your server on his laptop when it's not connected to any network, and then (perhaps hours or days later) connects to a network where your chosen name is already in use, one of two things will happen. If you specified NO_AUTO_RENAME, then your operationFailed method will be called. If you did not specify NO_AUTO_RENAME, then Multicast DNS will automatically select a new unique name for you and notify you with a new serviceRegistered callback.

The importance of the instance name provided in the serviceRegistered( ) callback depends on what kind of program you're writing. For a background process like an FTP server with no user interface, the program itself may not care at all what name is being advertised, as long as users can find it and connect. For a server program with a user interface, it may want to find out its advertised name simply for cosmetic reasons, to display it in a status window.

The kind of program for which the reported instance name is most interesting is the kind that's both a client and a server. For example, iChat advertises its presence on the network using Bonjour and, at the same time, browses to find other iChat instances on the network. One of the instances it discovers will be itself, but naturally iChat wants its Bonjour window to show only other users on the network, not itself. By comparing discovered instances against its own name as reported in the serviceRegistered( ) callback, iChat can tell when it has discovered itself on the network and filter that particular discovered entity from the list displayed in its Bonjour window.

Some developers have asked why DNS-SD doesn't do this filtering automatically. The problem is that the definition of *self* is slippery. Does *self* mean the same machine? Same user ID? Same process? Same thread? Automatically preventing discovery of all services on the same machine would be wrong. Some background processes use a web-based configuration interface, which they advertise with DNS-SD. If DNS-SD couldn't discover services on the same machine, these local background processes wouldn't show up in Safari on that machine. This would create the non-sensical situation where you could configure the process from any machine on the network *except* the one where the process is actually running! Another problem scenario is multiuser Unix machines, which can have more than one user logged on at a time. If DNS-SD couldn't discover services on the same machine, two users logged onto the same Unix machine from different X Window terminals would be effectively invisible to each other. Preventing discovery of services that happen to be running with the same user ID causes a similar set of inadvertent problems.

Automatically filtering discovery of services advertised from the same Unix process ID also doesn't necessarily give the results you might want. Sometimes the entity doing the browsing and the entity doing the advertising aren't the same process, even though they are conceptually related. For example, in Mac OS X Printer Sharing, the UI code showing the list of network printers doesn't want to show local printers that are being shared on the network by this machine, but the code displaying the print dialog user interface is not the same Unix process as the background process advertising those printers. In this case, automatic filtering based on Unix process IDs would fail to provide the desired result.

Ultimately, the only way to meet the needs of all applications is to report the names of advertised services in the serviceRegistered( ) callback and let applications that require some kind of self-filtering implement that filtering, in the way that makes sense for that particular application.

For the most part, though, most applications don't need any kind of self-filtering. If you find yourself thinking that you don't want to discover entities on the same machine, the question to ask is, "Why?" Usually, the answer will be that there's a different way to discover and communicate with entities on the same machine. If that's the case, the question to ask is, "Why?" Why have two different ways of doing the same thing, one for local entities and a different one for remote entities? Sometimes there are valid performance arguments for making local entities a special case, but in most cases, it is just a historical design accident. In most cases, instead of having two different mechanisms for doing roughly the same thing, each with their own bugs, features, and idiosyncrasies, it is smarter to have one mechanism—built on IP—and concentrate on making that IP-based mechanism fully featured, reliable, and efficient.

## Complete TestRegister program listing

Example 8-1 shows a complete listing, which you can compile with *javac*, to advertise a named service using DNS-SD. This program uses new ServerSocket(0); to get a unique port number assigned by the system so that it can advertise it via DNS-SD, but it does not include code to actually provide any real service on this port. In this example, the program just waits for 30 seconds doing nothing, then calls b.stop( ) and exits.

*Example 8-1. Java program to advertise a named service using DNS-SD*

```
import java.net.*;
import com.apple.dnssd.*;

class TestRegister implements RegisterListener
  {
  // Display error message on failure
  public void operationFailed(DNSSDService service, int errorCode)
    {
    System.out.println("Registration failed " + errorCode);
    }

  // Display registered name on success
  public void serviceRegistered(DNSSDRegistration registration, int flags,
    String serviceName, String regType, String domain)
    {
    System.out.println("Registered Name  : " + serviceName);
    System.out.println("          Type   : " + regType);
    System.out.println("          Domain: " + domain);
    }

  // Do the registration
  public TestRegister(String name, int port)
    throws DNSSDException, InterruptedException
    {
    System.out.println("Registration Starting");
    System.out.println("Requested Name: " + name);
    System.out.println("          Port: " + port);
    DNSSDRegistration r = DNSSD.register(name, "_example._tcp", port, this);
    Thread.sleep(30000);  // Wait thirty seconds, then exit
    System.out.println("Registration Stopping");
    r.stop( );
    }

  public static void main(String[] args)
    {
    if (args.length > 1)
      {
      System.out.println("Usage: java TestRegister name");
      System.exit(-1);
      }
    else
      {
```

*Example 8-1. Java program to advertise a named service using DNS-SD (continued)*

```
    try
      {
      // If name specified, use it, else use default name
      String name = (args.length > 0) ? args[0] : null;
      // Let system allocate us an available port to listen on
      ServerSocket s = new ServerSocket(0);
      new TestRegister(name, s.getLocalPort( ));
      }
    catch(Exception e)
      {
      e.printStackTrace( );
      System.exit(-1);
      }
    }
  }
}
```

### Testing the registration program

The easiest way to verify that the program successfully registers a service is to start up *dns-sd* and start browsing for services of type _example._tcp using the command:

```
% dns-sd –B _example._tcp
Browsing for _example._tcp
```

Open a separate terminal window and compile *TestRegister.java*:

```
% javac TestRegister.java
```

Now you can run the TestRegister program by executing:

```
% java TestRegister "My Chosen Name"
Registration Starting
Requested Name: My Chosen Name
        Port: 51619
```

After a one-second pause, when it has confirmed that the name is indeed unique, it also prints:

```
Registered Name  : My Chosen Name
          Type  : _example._tcp.
          Domain: local.
```

In the first terminal window, where you are running *dns-sd*, you will now see that "My Chosen Name" appears. After 30 seconds, the program will display "Registration Stopping" and exit, and in the *dns-sd* window you should see a remove event as the named service goes away.

With our TestRegister program, we can also demonstrate name conflict detection and automatic renaming. Run the TestRegister program again in the second terminal window and, while it is still running, quickly open a third terminal window and run the same command again:

```
% java TestRegister "My Chosen Name"
Registration Starting
```

```
Requested Name: My Chosen Name
        Port: 51625
Registered Name  : My Chosen Name (2)
        Type  : _example._tcp.
        Domain: local.
```

This time you'll see that, because the name "My Chosen Name" was already in use for a different advertised service, the second instance was automatically renamed to "My Chosen Name (2)."

One detail worth noting here is that a conflict is detected because we have two different instances of our program running, listening on different ports. Two different instances of a service can't use the same name; when browsing, the user would see only one service instance instead of two, and one or the other service would be rendered inaccessible. However, if instead of having two different instances on different ports, we had just one service instance running, listening on one port, and we simply registered that service twice with the exact same parameters—same name, same type, same host, and same port—then no conflict would be reported. Registering the same service twice is arguably a programming error, but it's not a conflict because the two registrations are in complete agreement. The API permits duplicate registrations like this to allow for proxy servers where (perhaps for fault-tolerance reasons) a given service may be deliberately advertised by multiple proxies.

This simple example highlighted the code you need to write to register an instance of a service in a Java application. What you have done is advertised that a named service of a particular type is available on this machine at the specified port. You have not set up the code to listen on that port or to react when your service is contacted. The section "An Extended Example: Tic-Tac-Toe" at the end of this chapter will take you through this additional step.

## Browsing for Services

Browsing to discover our advertised service using the *dns-sd* tool is very easy, and doing so using Java code is barely any harder. To browse, you need to perform two steps similar to those you just used to register your service:

*   Call `DNSSD.browse()` using one of the two available signatures.
*   Provide a class that implements the `BrowseListener` interface.

As with the `DNSSD.register()` example, it is common for the object initiating the browse operation to be the one that wants to receive the results, so it implements the `BrowseListener` interface itself and specifies itself (`this`) as the listener object in the `DNSSD.browse()` call.

To function as a `BrowseListener`, a class must implement `operationFailed()`, `serviceFound()`, and `serviceLost()`. Under normal circumstances, the operation-Failed() method will never be invoked. In our example program, the `serviceFound()`

and serviceLost() methods just print out information to show the events they receive, very much like the output of *dns-sd*.

```
public void serviceFound(DNSSDService browser, int flags, int ifIndex,
        String name, String regType, String domain)
  {
  System.out.println("Add flags:" + flags + ", ifIndex:" + ifIndex +
    ", Name:" + name + ", Type:" + regType + ", Domain:" + domain);
  }
```

Whenever a new instance of a service is discovered, serviceFound() will be called and will write a line to standard out beginning with the word "Add," followed by the name, type, and domain.

The serviceLost() method takes the exact same parameter list as serviceFound(). The only difference in our example program is that instead of printing "Add" it prints "Rmv" (which stands for *remove*).

Example 8-2 shows a complete listing, which you can compile with *javac*, to browse for services using DNS-SD. In this example, the program just runs for 30 seconds, displaying add and remove events as they arrive, and then calls b.stop() and exits. Of course, in a real program, you wouldn't use a fixed timeout like 30 seconds. You'd start the browse operation running when the user brings up a browsing window, and stop it when they close the browsing window.

*Example 8-2. Java program to browse for services using DNS-SD*

```
import com.apple.dnssd.*;

class TestBrowse implements BrowseListener
  {
  // Display error message on failure
  public void operationFailed(DNSSDService service, int errorCode)
    {
    System.out.println("Browse failed " + errorCode);
    System.exit(-1);
    }

  // Display services we discover
  public void serviceFound(DNSSDService browser, int flags, int ifIndex,
          String name, String regType, String domain)
    {
    System.out.println("Add flags:" + flags + ", ifIndex:" + ifIndex +
      ", Name:" + name + ", Type:" + regType + ", Domain:" + domain);
    }

  // Print a line when services go away
  public void serviceLost(DNSSDService browser, int flags, int ifIndex,
          String name, String regType, String domain)
    {
    System.out.println("Rmv flags:" + flags + ", ifIndex:" + ifIndex +
      ", Name:" + name + ", Type:" + regType + ", Domain:" + domain);
    }
```

```
public TestBrowse( ) throws DNSSDException, InterruptedException
   {
   System.out.println("TestBrowse Starting");
   DNSSDService b = DNSSD.browse("_example._tcp", this);
   System.out.println("TestBrowse Running");
   Thread.sleep(30000);
   System.out.println("TestBrowse Stopping");
   b.stop( );
   }

public static void main(String[] args)
   {
   try { new TestBrowse( ); }
   catch(Exception e)
      {
      e.printStackTrace( );
      System.exit(-1);
      }
   }
}
```

After you've compiled the TestBrowse program, we'll demonstrate it using our TestRegister program. Open three terminal windows. In the first, run java TestRegister "My Chosen Name." In the second, run that same command a second time. In the third window, a second or two later, run java TestBrowse:

```
% java TestBrowse
TestBrowse Starting
Add flags:3 ifIndex:5 Name:My Chosen Name Type:_example._tcp. Domain:local.
Add flags:2 ifIndex:5 Name:My Chosen Name (2) Type:_example._tcp. Domain:local.
TestBrowse Running
Rmv flags:0 ifIndex:5 Name:My Chosen Name Type:_example._tcp. Domain:local.
Rmv flags:0 ifIndex:5 Name:My Chosen Name (2) Type:_example._tcp. Domain:local.
TestBrowse Stopping
```

You'll see that TestBrowse finds our two service instances, "My Chosen Name" and "My Chosen Name (2)."

Another thing to notice is that, even though TestBrowse prints out "TestBrowse Running" on the very next line of the program after the DNSSD.browse( ) call, the services are discovered so fast that they're printed even *before* that line gets to execute.

Each TestRegister process exits 30 seconds after it was started, and we see the "Rmv" line printed for each service as it goes away. Finally, after running for 30 seconds itself, TestBrowse calls b.stop( ) and exits.

You can now advertise a named service and discover a list of named services. The third step, to actually use a service, is to resolve its name to its current address and port number.

## Resolving a Service

With the *dns-sd* command-line tool, we use `dns-sd -L` to resolve a named service. DNS-SD deliberately separates browsing from resolving. When you browse, you get a list of names, not IP addresses. This is because, when using link-local addresses or DHCP, IP addresses can change from day to day. When using dynamically allocated ports and NAT gateways, TCP port numbers for a given service can change from day to day, too. A program that stores a service's IP address and port number in a preference file on disk may well find that tomorrow that address and port number no longer work. What remains stable for a given service instance is its name, and the Java DNS-SD API provides the `DNSSD.resolve()` call to translate—at time of use—from service instance name to the correct target host and port number for that service at that moment.

Resolving follows the same pattern as registering and browsing: first call `DNSSD.resolve()` and then provide a class that implements the `ResolveListener` interface. To function as a `ResolveListener`, a class must implement `operationFailed()` and `serviceResolved()`. Under normal circumstances, the `operationFailed()` method will never be invoked.

Our `serviceResolved()` example just prints out the information it's given. When you register a service using the *dns-sd* tool, you can specify a list of "key=value" attributes, which are stored in the service's DNS TXT record. Our `serviceResolved()` method prints out those, too:

```
for (int i = 0; i < txtRecord.size(); i++)
  {
  String key = txtRecord.getKey(i);
  String value = txtRecord.getValueAsString(i);
  if (key.length() > 0) System.out.println("\t" + key + "=" + value);
  }
```

This example, for illustrative purposes, iterates through the whole TXT record, printing out every key it finds. In a real program, you would write code to retrieve just the specific named keys that you care about, using `txtRecord.contains("key")` when you just want to know if a given key is present, and `txtRecord.getValue("key")` or `txtRecord.getValueAsString("key")` to retrieve the value associated with a given named key.

Example 8-3 shows a complete listing, which you can compile with *javac*, to resolve a named service using DNS-SD. In the case of a multi-homed host, you may receive more than one successful resolve event (e.g., if the same named service is reachable via both Ethernet and wireless). In this example, the program just runs for five seconds, displaying resolve events as they arrive, and then calls `r.stop()` and exits. Ideally, in a real program, instead of using a fixed timeout, you'd present some indication to the user that the program was attempting to connect and let the user decide how long to wait before clicking the Cancel button to give up.

*Example 8-3. Java program to resolve a named DNS-SD service*

```
import com.apple.dnssd.*;

class TestResolve implements ResolveListener
  {
  // Display error message on failure
  public void operationFailed(DNSSDService service, int errorCode)
    {
    System.out.println("Resolve failed " + errorCode);
    System.exit(-1);
    }

  // Display information when service is resolved
  public void serviceResolved(DNSSDService resolver, int flags, int ifIndex,
    String fullName, String hostName, int port, TXTRecord txtRecord)
    {
    System.out.println("Service Resolved: " + hostName + ":" + port);
    System.out.println("Flags: " + flags +
      ", ifIndex: " + ifIndex + ", FQDN: " + fullName);

    for (int i = 0; i < txtRecord.size(); i++)
      {
      String key = txtRecord.getKey(i);
      String value = txtRecord.getValueAsString(i);
      if (key.length() > 0) System.out.println("\t" + key + "=" + value);
      }
    }

  public TestResolve(String name, String domain)
    throws DNSSDException, InterruptedException
    {
    System.out.println("TestResolve Starting");
    DNSSDService r = DNSSD.resolve(0, DNSSD.ALL_INTERFACES,
      name, "_example._tcp", domain, this);
    System.out.println("TestResolve Running");
    Thread.sleep(5000);
    System.out.println("TestResolve Stopping");
    r.stop();
    }

  public static void main(String[] args)
    {
    if (args.length != 2)
      {
      System.out.println("Usage: java TestResolve name domain");
      System.exit(-1);
      }
    else
      {
      try
        {
        new TestResolve(args[0], args[1]);
        }
```

*Example 8-3. Java program to resolve a named DNS-SD service (continued)*

```
      catch(Exception e)
        {
        e.printStackTrace( );
        System.exit(-1);
        }
      }
    }
  }
```

After you've compiled TestResolve, we'll test it by registering a fake service using the *dns-sd* command:

```
% dns-sd -R "My Chosen Name" _example._tcp local 123 key=val anotherkey=anotherval
```

Now you can use your TestResolve program to look up that service:

```
% java TestResolve "My Chosen Name" local
TestResolve Starting
Service Resolved: mymac.local.:123
Flags: 0, ifIndex: 5, FQDN: My\032Chosen\032Name._example._tcp.local.
        key=val
        anotherkey=anotherval
TestResolve Running
TestResolve Stopping
```

As with the browsing example, it's common for the resolve to succeed so quickly that the program gets the result before it's even had time to print out its "TestResolve Running" line. The reason DNS-SD operations are asynchronous is not because they usually take a long time, but because occasionally they might, particularly when there's some kind of network problem; and it is precisely at those times—when struggling with other problems—that the user will be least forgiving toward your program if it decides to lock up and become unresponsive.

You'll see that TestResolve finds our registered service on this host, listening (we pretend) on port 123, with two TXT record attributes, key=val and anotherkey=anotherval.

Now that you know not only how to register, browse, and resolve, but also how to access named attributes in the TXT record, it's time to revisit our registration example and add a TXT record full of attributes to it.

## Registering a Service with DNS TXT Record Attributes

To register a service with DNS TXT record attributes, we first need to create the TXT record:

```
TXTRecord txtRecord = new TXTRecord( );
txtRecord.set("txtvers", "1");
txtRecord.set("status", "ready");
txtRecord.set("difficulty", "medium");
```

By convention, the first key in a TXT record should be a txtvers key, indicating the version that a client needs to have implemented in order to usefully understand the following keys in this TXT record. After the initial txtvers key, the rest of the keys are up to your protocol-creating imagination.

In this example, all the values we set are textual strings, but (despite the name) DNS TXT records are perfectly capable of holding raw binary data, too. If you have some binary data you wish to attach as an attribute, you can do so directly using the alternate form of the TXTRecord.set() method, which takes a raw byte array as the value:

```
TXTRecord.set(java.lang.String key, byte[] value)
```

You can store any binary data you wish, so you shouldn't feel compelled to use something like hexadecimal characters or Base-64 encoding to turn binary data into text before you store it as a key/value attribute. The only constraint is that key/value attributes are intended for storing *small* amounts of additional information about a service. The length of the key name, plus the length of the value data, cannot add up to more than 254 bytes—yet another reason not to double the size of your binary data by needlessly turning it into hexadecimal text.

As your program evolves over time, you may define new key names with new meanings. If you're careful, you can generally write code to be forward- and backward-compatible. If a client tries to fetch a given named key from a TXT record and finds it missing, it can conclude that it is talking to an older server that predates the invention of that key, and most of the time, it's possible to write a client to take the right steps to work with that older server. If a client communicates with a newer server that defines new key names that were invented after the client was written, the client will generally ignore those new keys—the client only calls getValue() for key names it knows about, and the rest simply go unnoticed. However, if you find in the future that you have no choice but to make a change to your TXT record keys that is so drastic that compatibility is simply not going to be possible, you should specify that these new TXT records have a new version number in their txtvers key. This way, as long as you had the foresight to write your first clients so they check the txtvers key and display an error message if it does not contain a version number they understand (i.e., 1 in the first clients), this can help make the upgrade transition to the newer version of the protocol easier. Instead of simply failing mysteriously, the client can at least tell the user that she should upgrade to a newer version. Most protocol designers hope they never have to make a change so drastic that it breaks compatibility, but should you find yourself in this situation, the txtvers key can help make the transition go a little more smoothly.

To register a service with TXT record attributes, you need to use the longer version of DNSSD.register() with the additional parameters:

```
DNSSDRegistration r = DNSSD.register(0, DNSSD.ALL_INTERFACES,
  name, "_example._tcp", null,  // Name, type, and domain
  null, port,                   // Target host and port
  txtRecord, this);             // TXT record and listener object
```

If you compare this new usage of register( ) with the one presented in the section "Registering a Service," you will note that there are several extra parameters, and that most of them have the value zero or NULL to signify that DNS-SD should use sensible default values.

Example 8-4 shows a complete listing for registering a service with added TXT record attributes. The change compared to Example 8-1 is indicated by the comment, "New code to register with TXT record begins here." In this example, as in Example 8-1, the program just waits for 30 seconds doing nothing, then calls b.stop( ) and exits.

*Example 8-4. Java program to advertise a service with TXT record attributes*

```
import java.net.*;
import com.apple.dnssd.*;

class TestRegisterWithAttributes implements RegisterListener
  {
  // Display error message on failure
  public void operationFailed(DNSSDService service, int errorCode)
    {
    System.out.println("Registration failed " + errorCode);
    }

  // Display registered name on success
  public void serviceRegistered(DNSSDRegistration registration, int flags,
    String serviceName, String regType, String domain)
    {
    System.out.println("Registered Name  : " + serviceName);
    System.out.println("          Type  : " + regType);
    System.out.println("          Domain: " + domain);
    }

  // Do the registration
  public TestRegisterWithAttributes(String name, int port)
    throws DNSSDException, InterruptedException
    {
    System.out.println("Registration Starting");
    System.out.println("Requested Name: " + name);
    System.out.println("          Port: " + port);

    // New code to register with TXT record begins here
    TXTRecord txtRecord = new TXTRecord( );
    txtRecord.set("txtvers", "1");
    txtRecord.set("status", "ready");
    txtRecord.set("difficulty", "medium");
    DNSSDRegistration r = DNSSD.register(0, DNSSD.ALL_INTERFACES,
      name, "_example._tcp", null,  // Name, type, and domain
      null, port,                    // Target host and port
      txtRecord, this);              // TXT record and listener object
    // New code to register with TXT record ends
```

```
    Thread.sleep(30000);  // Wait thirty seconds, then exit
    System.out.println("Registration Stopping");
    r.stop();
    }

  public static void main(String[] args)
    {
    if (args.length > 1)
      {
      System.out.println("Usage: java TestRegisterWithAttributes name");
      System.exit(-1);
      }
    else
      {
      try
        {
        // If name specified, use it, else use default name
        String name = (args.length > 0) ? args[0] : null;
        // Let system allocate us an available port to listen on
        ServerSocket s = new ServerSocket(0);
        new TestRegisterWithAttributes(name, s.getLocalPort());
        }
      catch(Exception e)
        {
        e.printStackTrace();
        System.exit(-1);
        }
      }
    }
  }
```

After you've compiled TestRegisterWithAttributes, we'll demonstrate it using our TestBrowse program. In one terminal window, run:

```
% java TestBrowse
```

While that's still running, in another terminal window, run:

```
% java TestRegisterWithAttributes "My Chosen Name"
```

In the TestBrowse window, you should see the service added. Now, while TestRegisterWithAttributes is still running, run TestResolve in a third terminal window:

```
% java TestResolve "My Chosen Name" local
TestResolve Starting
Service Resolved: mymac.local.:52658
Flags: 0, ifIndex: 5, FQDN: My\032Chosen\032Name._example._tcp.local.
        txtvers=1
        status=ready
        difficulty=medium
TestResolve Running
TestResolve Stopping
```

# Adding, Updating, and Removing Additional Records

A standard DNS-SD service is described by two DNS records: an SRV record, giving target host and port number, and a TXT record, containing zero or more key/value attributes. For almost all applications, advertising a service with these two records is all that's needed. However, there are certain applications—iChat being the prime example—that have extra requirements. For the benefit of applications like this, DNS-SD provides some additional specialized APIs to add, update, and remove additional records.

DNS-SD allows applications to add additional DNS records to an existing service registration using DNSSDRegistration's addRecord method. iChat attaches a small JPEG image to each advertised service, containing the user's icon or picture, and because this is too large to fit in a TXT record attribute, iChat attaches it as an additional record. Adding records like this is something that should not be done indiscriminately because of the cost in increased network traffic, but in the case of iChat, it is the most appropriate way to communicate a user's icon to all the other iChat clients on the local network.

Calling addRecord( ) returns a DNSRecord object, which supports two operations, update( ) and remove( ). If you need to change the data in the record (as iChat does when the user changes the icon), then you can use update( ) to provide new data to replace the old data in the record.

When adding a record, you need to specify the DNS type of the record. The original DNS types are listed in RFC 1035, and newer types are given in later RFCs. For example, the SRV record type (type 33) is specified in RFC 2782. You can also find the list of currently defined DNS types at *http://www.iana.org/assignments/dns-parameters*. On many systems, you can also find the defined types listed in one of the C header files, such as */usr/include/nameser.h* or */usr/include/dns_sd.h*. The current IANA list of DNS types is shown in Table 8-2.

*Table 8-2. DNS resource record types*

| TYPE | Value | Meaning | Reference |
|---|---|---|---|
| A | 1 | A host address | RFC1035 |
| NS | 2 | An authoritative name server | RFC1035 |
| MD | 3 | A mail destination (OBSOLETE; use MX) | RFC1035 |
| MF | 4 | A mail forwarder (OBSOLETE; use MX) | RFC1035 |
| CNAME | 5 | The canonical name for an alias | RFC1035 |
| SOA | 6 | Marks the start of a zone of authority | RFC1035 |
| MB | 7 | A mailbox domain name (EXPERIMENTAL) | RFC1035 |
| MG | 8 | A mail group member (EXPERIMENTAL) | RFC1035 |
| MR | 9 | A mail rename domain name (EXPERIMENTAL) | RFC1035 |

Table 8-2. DNS resource record types (continued)

| TYPE | Value | Meaning | Reference |
|------|-------|---------|-----------|
| NULL | 10 | A null RR (EXPERIMENTAL) | RFC1035 |
| WKS | 11 | A well-known service description | RFC1035 |
| PTR | 12 | A domain name pointer | RFC1035 |
| HINFO | 13 | Host information | RFC1035 |
| MINFO | 14 | Mailbox or mail list information | RFC1035 |
| MX | 15 | Mail exchange | RFC1035 |
| TXT | 16 | Text strings | RFC1035 |
| RP | 17 | For Responsible Person | RFC1183 |
| AFSDB | 18 | For AFS Data Base location | RFC1183 |
| X25 | 19 | For X.25 PSDN address | RFC1183 |
| ISDN | 20 | For ISDN address | RFC1183 |
| RT | 21 | For Route Through | RFC1183 |
| NSAP | 22 | For NSAP address, NSAP style A record | RFC1706 |
| NSAP-PTR | 23 | | |
| SIG | 24 | For security signature | RFC2535 RFC3755 RFC4034 |
| KEY | 25 | For security key | RFC2535 RFC3755 RFC4034 |
| PX | 26 | X.400 mail mapping information | RFC2163 |
| GPOS | 27 | Geographical Position | RFC1712 |
| AAAA | 28 | IP6 Address | Thomson |
| LOC | 29 | Location Information | Vixie |
| NXT | 30 | Next Domain (OBSOLETE) | RFC2535, RFC3755 |
| EID | 31 | Endpoint Identifier | Patton |
| NIMLOC | 32 | Nimrod Locator | Patton |
| SRV | 33 | Server Selection | RFC2782 |
| ATMA | 34 | ATM Address | Dobrowski |
| NAPTR | 35 | Naming Authority Pointer | RFC2168, RFC2915 |
| KX | 36 | Key Exchanger | RFC2230 |
| CERT | 37 | CERT | RFC2538 |
| A6 | 38 | A6 | RFC2874 |
| DNAME | 39 | DNAME | RFC2672 |
| SINK | 40 | SINK | Eastlake |
| OPT | 41 | OPT | RFC2671 |
| APL | 42 | APL | RFC3123 |

*Table 8-2. DNS resource record types (continued)*

| TYPE | Value | Meaning | Reference |
|------|-------|---------|-----------|
| DS | 43 | Delegation Signer | RFC3658 |
| SSHFP | 44 | SSH Key Fingerprint | *RFC-ietf-secsh-dns-05.txt* |
| IPSECKEY | 45 | IPSECKEY | RFC4025 |
| RRSIG | 46 | RRSIG | RFC3755 |
| NSEC | 47 | NSEC | RFC3755 |
| DNSKEY | 48 | DNSKEY | RFC3755 |
| UINFO | 100 | IANA-Reserved | |
| UID | 101 | IANA-Reserved | |
| GID | 102 | IANA-Reserved | |
| UNSPEC | 103 | IANA-Reserved | |
| TKEY | 249 | Transaction Key | RFC2930 |
| TSIG | 250 | Transaction Signature | RFC2845 |
| IXFR | 251 | Incremental transfer | RFC1995 |
| AXFR | 252 | Transfer of an entire zone | RFC1035 |
| MAILB | 253 | Mailbox-related RRs (MB, MG, or MR) | RFC1035 |
| MAILA | 254 | Mail agent RRs (OBSOLETE; see MX) | RFC1035 |
| ANY | 255 | A request for any record(s) | RFC1035 |

When adding or updating records, it is your responsibility to make sure that the byte array data you provide is properly formatted for the DNS record type in question. You can specify the DNS time to live (TTL), though for most applications, it's most sensible to simply pass zero and let DNS-SD use its default TTL.

On the receiving side, to read records other than the standard SRV and TXT pair (which are retrieved using the resolve call), clients use DNSSD's queryRecord( ) method, providing a QueryListener object to receive the asynchronous results. A QueryListener object needs to implement the queryAnswered( ) method:

```
queryAnswered(DNSSDService query, int flags, int ifIndex,
    String fullName, int rrtype, int rrclass, byte[] rdata, int ttl)
```

Whenever an answer becomes available, the queryAnswered( ) method is called. Due to a quirk of the API, the queryAnswered( ) method is also called if a previously valid answer expires. You can tell if the answer is coming or going by checking bit 1 (value 2) of the flags field (the kDNSServiceFlagsAdd flag of the C API). If (flags & 2) is non-zero, then a new answer is being added; if zero, then a previous answer is being removed.

The queryAnswered( ) method is given the raw bytes of the DNS resource record; it is the responsibility of the queryAnswered( ) method to know how to interpret the DNS record type it requested.

There is another style of update that iChat performs. Your status message is stored as a key/value attribute in the service's TXT record, and whenever you update your status message, iChat doesn't de-register its service and register a new one; instead, it just updates the TXT record to contain the new data. To perform this kind of update, you don't need to add another TXT record to the service. All services implicitly have a TXT record, even if you didn't specify one. If you don't specify a TXT record when registering a service, then the service automatically gets an empty TXT record containing no key/value attributes. (Strictly speaking, to comply with the DNS rules for the format of DNS TXT records, the service gets a TXT record containing a single empty string.)

Before you can use the update method to provide new data, you need an object upon which to invoke that method. To get the object representing the service's standard TXT record, upon which to perform updates, the Java DNS-SD API provides the DNSSDRegistration.getTXTRecord( ) method. The update method requires you to provide properly formatted DNS TXT record data, and this is where the TXTRecord's getRawBytes( ) method comes in handy:

```
DNSRecord record = registration.getTXTRecord( );
byte rawbytes[] = txtRecord.getRawBytes( );
record.update(0, rawbytes, 0);
```

As with other DNS-SD methods, passing zero for the flags and zero for the record TTL causes sensible default values to be used.

Example 8-5 shows a complete listing that you can compile with *javac*, which first registers a service with the default empty TXT record, then at ten-second intervals updates the TXT record to say status=ready, status=steady, and finally, status=go. The change compared to Example 8-1 is indicated by the comment, "New code to update TXT record begins here."

*Example 8-5. Java program to advertise a service and update its TXT record*

```
import java.net.*;
import com.apple.dnssd.*;

class TestRegisterWithUpdates implements RegisterListener
  {
  // Display error message on failure
  public void operationFailed(DNSSDService service, int errorCode)
    {
    System.out.println("Registration failed " + errorCode);
    }

  // Display registered name on success
  public void serviceRegistered(DNSSDRegistration registration, int flags,
    String serviceName, String regType, String domain)
    {
    System.out.println("Registered Name  : " + serviceName);
    System.out.println("            Type  : " + regType);
```

*Example 8-5. Java program to advertise a service and update its TXT record (continued)*

```
    System.out.println("           Domain: " + domain);
    }

  // Do the registration
  public TestRegisterWithUpdates(String name, int port)
    throws DNSSDException, InterruptedException
    {
    System.out.println("Registration Starting");
    System.out.println("Requested Name: " + name);
    System.out.println("          Port: " + port);

    DNSSDRegistration r = DNSSD.register(name, "_example._tcp", port, this);

    // New code to update TXT record begins here

    TXTRecord txtRecord = new TXTRecord( );
    txtRecord.set("txtvers", "1");

    Thread.sleep(10000);  // Wait ten seconds before updating TXT record
    txtRecord.set("status", "Ready");
    System.out.println("Ready");
    r.getTXTRecord( ).update(0, txtRecord.getRawBytes( ), 0);

    Thread.sleep(5000);
    txtRecord.set("status", "Steady");
    System.out.println("Steady");
    r.getTXTRecord( ).update(0, txtRecord.getRawBytes( ), 0);

    Thread.sleep(5000);
    txtRecord.set("status", "Go");
    System.out.println("Go");
    r.getTXTRecord( ).update(0, txtRecord.getRawBytes( ), 0);

    // New code to update TXT record ends

    Thread.sleep(30000);  // Wait thirty seconds, then exit
    System.out.println("Registration Stopping");
    r.stop( );
    }

  public static void main(String[] args)
    {
    if (args.length > 1)
      {
      System.out.println("Usage: java TestRegisterWithUpdates name");
      System.exit(-1);
      }
    else
      {
      try
        {
        // If name specified, use it, else use default name
```

```
        String name = (args.length > 0) ? args[0] : null;
        // Let system allocate us an available port to listen on
        ServerSocket s = new ServerSocket(0);
        new TestRegisterWithUpdates(name, s.getLocalPort());
        }
    catch (Exception e)
        {
        e.printStackTrace();
        System.exit(-1);
        }
      }
    }
  }
```

Example 8-6 shows a complete listing that you can compile with *javac*, which resolves the named service and then begins monitoring its TXT record for changes. The change compared to Example 8-1 is indicated by the comment, "New code to update TXT record begins here."

*Example 8-6. Java program to monitor a TXT record for changes*

```
import com.apple.dnssd.*;

class TestResolveWithMonitoring implements ResolveListener, QueryListener
  {
  private DNSSDService monitorQ = null;

  // Display error message on failure
  public void operationFailed(DNSSDService service, int errorCode)
    {
    System.out.println("Resolve failed " + errorCode);
    System.exit(-1);
    }

  public void queryAnswered(DNSSDService query, int flags, int ifIndex,
    String fullName, int rrtype, int rrclass, byte[] rdata, int ttl)
    {
    if ((flags & 2) != 0)
      {
      boolean blankPrinted = false;
      TXTRecord txtRecord = new TXTRecord(rdata);
      for (int i = 0; i < txtRecord.size(); i++)
        {
        String key = txtRecord.getKey(i);
        String value = txtRecord.getValueAsString(i);
        if (key.length() > 0)
          {
          if (!blankPrinted)
            {
            blankPrinted = true;
            System.out.println();
            }
```

```java
        System.out.println("\t" + key + "=" + value);
        }
      }
    }
  }

  // Display information when service is resolved
  public void serviceResolved(DNSSDService resolver, int flags, int ifIndex,
    String fullName, String hostName, int port, TXTRecord txtRecord)
    {
    System.out.println("Service Resolved: " + hostName + ":" + port);
    System.out.println("Flags: " + flags +
      ", ifIndex: " + ifIndex + ", FQDN: " + fullName);

    // Now that we've got a resolve result,
    // start monitoring the TXT record and stop the resolve call.
    try { monitorQ = DNSSD.queryRecord(0, ifIndex, fullName, 16, 1, this); }
    catch (Exception e) { e.printStackTrace( ); System.exit(-1); }
    resolver.stop( );
    Thread.sleep(1);
    }

  public TestResolveWithMonitoring(String name, String domain)
    throws DNSSDException, InterruptedException
    {
    System.out.println("TestResolveWithMonitoring Starting");
    DNSSDService r = DNSSD.resolve(0, DNSSD.ALL_INTERFACES,
      name, "_example._tcp", domain, this);
    System.out.println("TestResolveWithMonitoring Running");
    Thread.sleep(30000);
    System.out.println("TestResolveWithMonitoring Stopping");
    if (monitorQ == null) r.stop( );
    else monitorQ.stop( );
    try { Thread.sleep(1); }
    catch (Exception e) { e.printStackTrace( ); System.exit(-1); }
    }

  public static void main(String[] args)
    {
    if (args.length != 2)
      {
      System.out.println("Usage: java TestResolveWithMonitoring name dom");
      System.exit(-1);
      }
    else
      {
      try
        {
        new TestResolveWithMonitoring(args[0], args[1]);
        }
      catch (Exception e)
        {
```

*Example 8-6. Java program to monitor a TXT record for changes (continued)*

```
        e.printStackTrace( );
        System.exit(-1);
        }
    }
  }
}
```

After you've compiled `TestRegisterWithUpdates` and `TestResolveWithMonitoring`, we can test them. In one terminal window, run:

```
% java TestRegisterWithUpdates "My Chosen Name"
```

While that's still running, in another terminal window, run `TestResolveWithMonitoring`:

```
% java TestResolveWithMonitoring "My Chosen Name" local
TestResolveWithMonitoring Starting
Service Resolved: mymac.local.:54444
Flags: 0, ifIndex: 5, FQDN: My\032Chosen\032Name._example._tcp.local.
TestResolveWithMonitoring Running

        txtvers=1
        status=Ready

        txtvers=1
        status=Steady

        txtvers=1
        status=Go
TestResolveWithMonitoring Stopping
```

First, the `TestResolveWithMonitoring` client resolves the name. After it's discovered the target host and port, it starts a query for the TXT record and stops the resolve. Now, each time the TXT record is updated, the `queryAnswered` method gets called with the new data.

> In the first version of the Java DNS-SD API there was a bug that if you stopped one DNS-SD operation and then immediately started another, the new operation could begin reusing the same underlying file descriptor before the background thread had finished cleaning up. To avoid running into this bug there are a couple of precautions you can take:
>
> - Use a `Thread.sleep(1);` after stopping any operation, to allow the background thread to run and do its necessary cleanup.
> - If you have a sequence of code that starts and stops DNS-SD operations, particularly in a listener callback method, write your code to start all the new operations first, *before* it begins stopping old operations. That way the kernel won't be tempted to reuse the same file descriptors, because at the point that you start each new operation, the old operations haven't been stopped yet, so the file descriptors are still in use and aren't eligible to be recycled.

Now that we've built some toy one-page programs to demonstrate the concepts, it's time to write a real program that actually does something.

## An Extended Example: Tic-Tac-Toe

Tic-tac-toe is a game ordinarily played on paper by two people sitting near each other. The board is a three-by-three grid and usually one player marks squares using X's and the other using O's. The players alternate marking the squares, trying to end up with three of their marked squares in a line (i.e., across, down, or diagonally).

In the Zeroconf version, players register service instances of type _tic-tac-toe-ex._tcp and browse for other players. The game program has two main classes, TicTacToe and GameBoard.

Class TicTacToe browses for other players and displays the list of what it finds. It also opens a listening socket, advertises it with DNS-SD, and then fires off an independent background thread to sit and wait for incoming connections.

Class GameBoard can get instantiated in two ways. If the user clicks on one of the discovered players in the list, then we make a new GameBoard, and start a DNSSD.resolve() running for the named service. When the newly created GameBoard object receives the serviceResolved() callback, it connects to the specified host and port and begins playing the game, listing for messages received over the network from the peer, and sending messages to the peer every time the user clicks in a square. The other way a GameBoard can get instantiated is on the *receiving* end of a connection request. If another user clicks on us in *their* list, then our TicTacToe background thread will receive an incoming connection request. In this case it also makes a new GameBoard object, but in this case no resolve-and-connect is needed, because the TCP connection is already open. A player can have any number of active games, connected to different opponents, at once.

Figure 8-1 shows the TicTacToe class's browser window showing the list of discovered opponents on the network.

*Figure 8-1. Window displaying available opponents*

Figure 8-2 shows a GameBoard window for a game in progress with a player called "Mike."

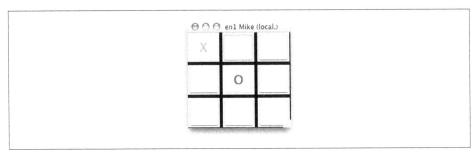

*Figure 8-2. TicTacToe game board*

Note that the purpose of this example is to demonstrate the Zeroconf-related aspects of writing a Java program. As a result, this example does not try to implement the rules of tic-tac-toe; for example, it does not enforce that the players are supposed to take turns clicking squares.

Each time you run the program, it asks the system for a new unallocated TCP port to listen on and then advertises that port number to its peers using DNS-SD. One of the benefits of DNS-SD is that, because it advertises port numbers as well as hostnames and addresses, programs are no longer restricted to using fixed, hard-coded port numbers. This means you can write a program and it can use any available port when run, instead of your having to apply to IANA to get a new well-known port number reserved for every program you write. There are only 65,535 possible TCP port numbers, and they'll run out quickly if every person in the world gets one reserved for every program they write. In addition, even if you get a well-known port number reserved, you get only one, so that doesn't help when you want to run two copies of your program on the same machine. You'll see that, with the TicTacToe program, you can run as many copies as you like on the same machine, which can be very helpful when testing, especially if you're working on your laptop computer on an airplane and don't have a whole network of machines available.

Most Unix systems allocate dynamic TCP port numbers starting at 49152 and working upward. If you have some kind of personal firewall running on your machine, ensure that it is configured to allow incoming connections to high-numbered ports (49152–65535). Otherwise, the firewall will do exactly what it is supposed to do: prevent your networking program from receiving any incoming connection requests. Most firewall programs don't give you any feedback to tell you when they've silently discarded an incoming connection request, so this can be quite frustrating to debug if your program is failing and you don't realize that the personal firewall is the cause. The TicTacToe program window title shows the port number it's listening on, so that you can cross-check with your firewall settings and verify that your personal firewall is allowing the necessary packets through.

Our TicTacToe program calls DNSSD.register without specifying an instance name, so it automatically gets the system default. When it gets the serviceRegistered callback, it updates the window title to show its advertised name. You can try some experiments to see how Multicast DNS name conflict detection works. If you run a second copy of the TicTacToe program on the same machine, you'll see the second copy gets the same name with "(2)" appended. If you plug your Ethernet cable into a network where your name is already being advertised by another TicTacToe program, you'll see your window title update to show a new name. You can also change the system default name while the TicTacToe program is running, and you'll see that it gets informed of the new name and updates its windows. On Mac OS X, you set the system default name by setting the "Computer Name" in the Sharing Preferences.

The TicTacToe program also pays attention to its own advertised name in order to exclude itself from the list of discovered games on the network.

Example 8-7 shows the source code for *TicTacToe.java*, and Example 8-8 shows the source code for *GameBoard.java*. You can compile them both directly on the command line by typing javac TicTacToe.java and then run the program by typing java TicTacToe, or you can use the Makefile shown in Example 8-9. The Makefile builds the classes, placing them in a subdirectory called *classes*, then makes a Java jar file from the classes, and finally runs the resulting jar file with java -jar TicTacToe.jar.

*Example 8-7. TicTacToe.java*

```
import java.util.HashMap;
import java.nio.*;
import java.nio.channels.*;
import java.net.InetSocketAddress;
import javax.swing.*;
import javax.swing.event.*;
import com.apple.dnssd.*;

// Our TicTacToe object does the following:
// 1. It's a JFrame window. It's a DNSSD BrowseListener so it
//     gets add and remove events to tell it what to show in the window,
//     and a ListSelectionListener so it knows what the user clicked.
// 2. It listens for incoming connections. It opens a listening TCP
//     socket and advertises the listening TCP socket with DNS-SD.
//     It's our RegisterListener, so that it knows our advertised name:
//     - To display it in the window title bar
//     - To exclude it from the list of discovered peers on the network

// To safely call Swing routines to update the user interface,
// we have to call them from the Swing event-dispatching thread.
// To do this, we make little Runnable objects where necessary
// and pass them to SwingUtilities.invokeAndWait(). This makes
// their run() method execute on event-dispatching thread where
// it can safely make the calls it needs. For more details, see:
// <http://java.sun.com/docs/books/tutorial/uiswing/misc/threads.html>

public class TicTacToe extends JFrame implements Runnable,
  RegisterListener, BrowseListener, ListSelectionListener
  {
```

*Example 8-7. TicTacToe.java (continued)*

```
public static void main(String[] args)
  {
  Runnable runOnSwingThread = new Runnable( )
    { public void run( ) { new TicTacToe( ); } };
  try { SwingUtilities.invokeAndWait(runOnSwingThread); }
  catch (Exception e) { e.printStackTrace( ); }
  }

public static final String ServiceType = "_tic-tac-toe-ex._tcp";
public String myName;
public HashMap activeGames;
private DefaultListModel gameList;
private JList players;
private ServerSocketChannel listentingChannel;
private int listentingPort;

// NOTE: Because a TicTacToe is a JFrame, the caller MUST be running
// on the event-dispatching thread before trying to create one.
public TicTacToe( )
  {
  super("Tic-Tac-Toe");
  try
    {
    // 1. Make the browsing window, and start browsing
    activeGames = new HashMap( );
    gameList = new DefaultListModel( );
    players = new JList(gameList);
    players.addListSelectionListener(this);
    getContentPane( ).add(new JScrollPane(players));
    setSize(200, 300);
    setDefaultCloseOperation(EXIT_ON_CLOSE);
    setVisible(true);
    DNSSD.browse(ServiceType, this);

    // 2. Make listening socket and advertise it
    listentingChannel = ServerSocketChannel.open( );
    listentingChannel.socket( ).bind(new InetSocketAddress(0));
    listentingPort = listentingChannel.socket( ).getLocalPort( );
    setTitle(listentingPort + " registering");
    DNSSD.register(null, ServiceType, listentingPort, this);

    // 3. If we sit here and hog the event-dispatching thread
    // the whole UI will freeze up, so instead we create a new
    // background thread to receive incoming connection requests.
    new Thread(this).start( );
    }
  catch (Exception e) { e.printStackTrace( ); }
  }

public void operationFailed(DNSSDService service, int errorCode)
  {
  System.out.println("DNS-SD operation failed " + errorCode);
```

*Example 8-7. TicTacToe.java (continued)*

```java
     System.exit(-1);
     }

  // If our name changes while we're running, we update window title.
  // In the event that we're registering in multiple domains (Wide-Area
  // DNS-SD) we'll use the local (mDNS) name for display purposes.
  public void serviceRegistered(DNSSDRegistration sd, int flags,
    String serviceName, String regType, String domain)
    {
    if (!domain.equalsIgnoreCase("local.")) return;
    myName = serviceName;
    Runnable r = new Runnable()
      { public void run() { setTitle(listentingPort + " " + myName); } };
    try { SwingUtilities.invokeAndWait(r); }
    catch (Exception e) { e.printStackTrace(); }
    }

  // Our serviceFound and serviceLost callbacks just make Adder and
  // Remover objects that safely run on the event-dispatching thread
  // so they can modify the user interface
  public void serviceFound(DNSSDService browser, int flags, int ind,
          String name, String type, String domain)
    {
    if (name.equals(myName)) return;  // Don't add ourselves to the list
    DiscoveredInstance x = new DiscoveredInstance(ind, name, domain);
    try { SwingUtilities.invokeAndWait(new Adder(x)); }
    catch (Exception e) { e.printStackTrace(); }
    }

  public void serviceLost(DNSSDService browser, int flags, int ind,
    String name, String regType, String domain)
    {
    DiscoveredInstance x = new DiscoveredInstance(ind, name, domain);
    try { SwingUtilities.invokeAndWait(new Remover(x)); }
    catch (Exception e) { e.printStackTrace(); }
    }

  // The Adder and Remover classes update the list of discovered instances
  private class Adder implements Runnable
    {
    private DiscoveredInstance add;
    public Adder(DiscoveredInstance a) { add = a; }
    public void run() { gameList.addElement(add); }
    }

  private class Remover implements Runnable
    {
    private DiscoveredInstance rmv;
    public Remover(DiscoveredInstance r) { rmv = r; }
    public void run()
      {
      String name = rmv.toString();
```

*Example 8-7. TicTacToe.java (continued)*

```java
      for (int i = 0; i < gameList.size(); i++)
        {
        if (gameList.getElementAt(i).toString().equals(name))
          { gameList.removeElementAt(i); return; }
        }
      }
    }

  // When the user clicks in our list, if we already have a
  // GameBoard we bring it to the front, otherwise we make
  // a new GameBoard and initiate a new outgoing connection.
  public void valueChanged(ListSelectionEvent event)
    {
    int selected = players.getSelectedIndex();
    if (selected != -1)
      {
      DiscoveredInstance x =
        (DiscoveredInstance)players.getSelectedValue();
      GameBoard game = (GameBoard)activeGames.get(x.toString());
      if (game != null) game.toFront();
      else x.resolve(new GameBoard(this, x.toString(), null));
      }
    }

  // When we receive an incoming connection, GameReceiver reads the
  // peer name from the connection and then makes a new GameBoard for it.
  private class GameReceiver implements Runnable
    {
    private SocketChannel sc;
    public GameReceiver(SocketChannel s) { sc = s; }
    public void run()
      {
      try
        {
        ByteBuffer buffer = ByteBuffer.allocate(4 + 128);
        CharBuffer charBuffer = buffer.asCharBuffer();
        sc.read(buffer);
        int length = buffer.getInt(0);
        char[] c = new char[length];
        charBuffer.position(2);
        charBuffer.get(c, 0, length);
        String serviceName = new String(c);
        GameBoard game = new GameBoard(TicTacToe.this, serviceName, sc);
        }
      catch (Exception e) { e.printStackTrace(); }
      }
    }

  // Our run() method just sits and waits for incoming connections
  // and hands each one off to a new thread to handle it.
  public void run()
    {
```

*Example 8-7. TicTacToe.java (continued)*

```
    try
      {
      while (true)
        {
        SocketChannel sc = listentingChannel.accept( );
        if (sc != null) new Thread(new GameReceiver(sc)).start( );
        }
      }
    catch (Exception e) { e.printStackTrace( ); }
    }

  // Our inner class DiscoveredInstance has two special properties
  // It has a custom toString( ) method to display discovered
  // instances the way we want them to appear, and a resolve( )
  // method, which asks it to resolve the named service it represents
  // and pass the result to the specified ResolveListener
  public class DiscoveredInstance
    {
    private int ind;
    private String name, domain;

    public DiscoveredInstance(int i, String n, String d)
      { ind = i; name = n; domain = d; }

    public String toString( )
      {
      String i = DNSSD.getNameForIfIndex(ind);
      return(i + " " + name + " (" + domain + ")");
      }

    public void resolve(ResolveListener x)
      {
      try { DNSSD.resolve(0, ind, name, ServiceType, domain, x); }
      catch (DNSSDException e) { e.printStackTrace( ); }
      }
    }
  }
```

*Example 8-8. GameBoard.java*

```
import java.nio.*;
import java.nio.channels.SocketChannel;
import java.net.InetSocketAddress;
import java.awt.*;
import java.awt.event.*;
import javax.swing.*;
import com.apple.dnssd.*;

public class GameBoard extends JFrame implements ResolveListener, Runnable
  {
  private TicTacToe tictactoe;
  private String name, host;
```

*Example 8-8. GameBoard.java (continued)*

```
private int port;
SocketChannel channel;

// If we're passed in a SocketChannel, it means we received an
// incoming connection, so we should start receiving clicks from it.
// If channel is null, it means our user initiated an outgoing connection,
// so we'll get a serviceResolved callback to tell us when to proceed.
public GameBoard(TicTacToe t, String n, SocketChannel c)
  {
  super(n);
  tictactoe = t;
  name = n;
  channel = c;
  tictactoe.activeGames.put(n, this);
  getContentPane( ).setLayout(new GridLayout(3,3,6,6));
  getContentPane( ).setBackground(Color.BLACK);
  for (int i = 0; i<9; i++) getContentPane( ).add(new SquareGUI(this, i));
  setSize(200,200);
  setVisible(true);
  if (channel != null) new Thread(this).start( );
  }

public void operationFailed(DNSSDService service, int errorCode)
  {
  System.out.println("DNS-SD operation failed " + errorCode);
  System.exit(-1);
  }

// When serviceResolved is called, we send our name to the other end
// and then fire off our thread to start receiving the opponent's clicks.
public void serviceResolved(DNSSDService resolver, int flags, int ifIndex,
  String fullName, String theHost, int thePort, TXTRecord txtRecord)
  {
  host = theHost;
  port = thePort;
  ByteBuffer buffer = ByteBuffer.allocate(4 + 128);
  CharBuffer charBuffer = buffer.asCharBuffer( );
  buffer.putInt(0, tictactoe.myName.length( ));
  charBuffer.position(2);
  charBuffer.put(tictactoe.myName);
  try
    {
    InetSocketAddress socketAddress = new InetSocketAddress(host, port);
    channel = SocketChannel.open(socketAddress);
    channel.write(buffer);
    new Thread(this).start( );
    }
  catch (Exception e) { e.printStackTrace( ); }

  resolver.stop( );
  }
```

*Example 8-8. GameBoard.java (continued)*

```java
// The GameBoard's run( ) method just sits in a loop receiving
// clicks from the opponent and marking the indicated squares.
public void run( )
  {
  try
    {
    while (true)
      {
      ByteBuffer buffer = ByteBuffer.allocate(4);
      channel.read(buffer);
      int n = buffer.getInt(0);
      if (n >= 0 && n < 9)
        {
        try { SwingUtilities.invokeAndWait(new SquareMarker(n)); }
        catch (Exception e) { e.printStackTrace( ); }
        }
      }
    }
  catch (Exception e) { } // Connection reset by peer!
  }

// When we get a message from the opponent, we make a SquareMarker
// object and run it on the event-dispatching thread so it can
// safely do Swing calls to update the user interface
class SquareMarker implements Runnable
  {
  private int num;
  public SquareMarker(int n) { num = n; }
  public void run( )
    {
    SquareGUI s = (SquareGUI)getContentPane( ).getComponent(num);
    s.setText("<html><h1><font color='blue'>O</font></h1></html>");
    s.setEnabled(false);
    }
  }

// Each GameBoard contains nine JButtons displayed in a 3x3 grid
class SquareGUI extends JButton implements ActionListener
  {
  private int num;
  public SquareGUI(GameBoard b, int n) { num = n; addActionListener(this); }
  public void actionPerformed(ActionEvent event)
    {
    // Mark our square with an X
    setText("<html><h1><font color='red'>X</font></h1></html>");
    setEnabled(false);
    // And tell the other end to mark the square too
    ByteBuffer buffer = ByteBuffer.allocate(4);
    buffer.putInt(0, num);
    try { channel.write(buffer); }
```

*Example 8-8. GameBoard.java (continued)*

```
        catch (Exception e) { e.printStackTrace( ); }
        }
    }
  }
```

*Example 8-9. Makefile to build Tic-Tac-Toe example*

```
run: TicTacToe.jar
    java -jar TicTacToe.jar &

clean:
    rm -rf classes TicTacToe.jar

TicTacToe.jar: classes/TicTacToe.class
    @echo "Main-Class: TicTacToe" > Main-Class.txt
    jar cmf Main-Class.txt TicTacToe.jar -C classes .
    @rm Main-Class.txt

# Building TicTacToe.class causes javac automatically
# to find and build other necessary classes too
classes/TicTacToe.class: TicTacToe.java GameBoard.java
    mkdir -p classes
    javac -encoding UTF8 -d classes TicTacToe.java
```

You have now seen how to implement a basic service in Java and advertise it using DNS-SD. The TicTacToe application registers and browses for services of type _tic-tac-toe-ex._tcp. You have resolved services and provided the underlying plumbing to send and receive messages. The remainder of the code managed the GUI elements.

With just a few lines of code, you can add DNS-SD advertising and browsing to your own Java programs.

# CHAPTER 9

# Using the CFNetwork and Cocoa APIs

In the previous three chapters, you have learned about techniques and APIs that work on multiple platforms. In Chapter 6, we covered the general concepts and the *dns-sd* command-line tool, which apply to all the supported platforms. In Chapter 7 we covered the DNSServiceDiscovery C API, which is available on all the supported platforms. In Chapter 8, you saw the Java API, which lets you write a Java program that will run on any supported platform with Java installed.

If you're writing a program in C that's built around a Core Foundation CFRunLoop as its central event-handling mechanism, or a program in Objective-C that's built around a Cocoa RunLoop as its central event-handling mechanism, you have two options. The first option is that you can use the standard C DNSServiceDiscovery API and add those active operations as event sources to your RunLoop, as shown in the Core Foundation and Cocoa examples toward the end of Chapter 7. If you're comfortable mixing standard C in with your Core Foundation-style or Cocoa-style programming, this is fine. However, if you prefer to stick to a single programming style, then you have a second option: Apple has provided additional wrapper APIs that follow the Core Foundation and Cocoa idioms.

In this chapter, you will look at how to perform the basic DNS-SD operations of registering a service, browsing for services, and resolving a service using these Mac OS X–specific APIs, which Apple has provided for the benefit of Core Foundation and Cocoa programmers. As always, the key to creating a good Zeroconf application is in understanding and correctly implementing asynchronous calls. When programming using the CFNetServices API, you pass in a reference to the callback function, much as you did in Chapter 7 with the plain C API. When programming using the Cocoa NSNetServices API, you specify a delegate object that will be notified of interesting events, much as you did in Chapter 8 with the Java API. Just as in the Java API, the delegate or event listener object is usually self. Although the exact mechanisms are different, you use them in analogous ways. If you have not already done so, you will find it helpful to read the section "Asynchronous Programming Model" in Chapter 7 before working with either the CFNetServices or the Cocoa NSNetServices APIs.

# Using the CFNetServices API

You will access Bonjour functionality in CFNetwork using instances of CFNetService and CFNetServiceBrowser objects. There are nearly 40 functions in the API for working with Network Services objects, with descriptive names that convey their purpose. For example, CFNetServiceCreate and CFNetServiceRegister are used respectively to create an instance of CFNetService and then use it to register a particular service. Rather than repeat the details provided in the API documentation for each function, this section provides a summary and a quick example for how you use the CFNetServices API to register, browse, and resolve.

CFNetServices is a component of the CFNetwork framework, and, despite the "CF" prefix, these frameworks actually live within the CoreServices umbrella framework, not the Core Foundation umbrella framework. When creating a new project in Xcode, if you want to use the CFNetServices API, you can either use the "new Core-Services tool" project template or you can manually add the CoreServices framework to your project. CoreServices implicitly includes all of Core Foundation, so you don't need to add both.

## Advertising a Service in CFNetServices

To publish a service using the CFNetServices API, you need to create and register a CFNetService. In the code in Example 9-1 (shown later), you create a service like this:

```
registeredService = CFNetServiceCreate(kCFAllocatorDefault,
    CFSTR(""),                   // Domain
    CFSTR("_example._tcp"),      // Type
    CFSTR("CF Example"),         // Name
    thePort);                    // Port number in host byte order
```

More generally, you call the function CFNetServiceCreate( ) and pass in the CFAllocator to use when allocating memory for the service you are creating. In the example, we use kCFAllocatorDefault. You also pass in a CFStringRef for the domain. Although you cannot pass in NULL, you can and should pass in the empty string unless there is a particular domain on which you want to register the service. You also pass in CFStringRef instances representing the type and name of the service. In this example, they are _example._tcp and CF Example, respectively. Finally, you pass in a UInt32 giving the port number in host byte order. Since the port you get from a sockaddr structure is an opaque identifier in network byte order, this means you have to swap it to host byte order before passing it to CFNetServiceCreate( ). When testing your code on a PowerPC machine, it's easy to get this wrong and not notice, because on a PowerPC, network byte order is the same as host byte order, so the distinction is a purely abstract one. If you have a bug, you will probably discover it when you compile your code for Intel, where network byte order and host byte order are different.

Another common mistake is to get the byte order wrong at *both* ends of the connection. Suppose you have a service listening on port 123. If you forget to convert the sockaddr's sin_port to host byte order before calling CFNetServiceCreate( ), then when you compile your code for Intel, you'll actually be advertising port 31488. If the client at the resolving end also gets the byte order backward, then it will swap 31488 back to 123 and successfully connect, and everything will *appear* to be working correctly. It's only when a PowerPC client tries to resolve and connect to a service on Intel, an Intel client tries to resolve and connect to a service on PowerPC, or you try to interoperate with someone else's client or service that doesn't have your byte order bug, that you'll discover problems. The easiest way to find these problems is using the *dns-sd* tool. After you compile your program for Intel, run it on an Intel-based machine and use dns-sd  -L to verify that you're really advertising the port number you intend, not the byte-swap of the port number. This kind of byte order mismatch problem is not specific to advertising services using the DNS-SD APIs—it can happen any time you're passing 16-bit or larger integer values on the wire between machines.

Once you have a CFNetServiceRef returned by CFNetServiceCreate( ), you then call CFNetServiceSetClient( ) to associate a callback function, which is used to report errors that may arise. In the MyRegisterCallBack( ) function below, you would put in any code needed to handle and report errors and follow it with a call to CFNetServiceCancel( ) to cancel the registration of the service instance. You will usually want the service to run asynchronously and should schedule the CFNetService on a run loop using CFNetServiceScheduleWithRunLoop( ).

The CFNetServiceRegister( ) routine only calls your callback if an error occurs. If you also want to receive a callback on success too (so you can find out what name was registered), you need to use the newer CFNetServiceRegisterWithOptions( ) call, which is available on Mac OS X 10.4 and later (or you can use the lower-level DNS-ServiceDiscovery C API, if your product needs to be able to run on 10.3).

The steps described above are used to create and configure a CFNetService. Registration is accomplished with a call to the function CFNetServiceRegister( ). All of this is shown in Example 9-1.

*Example 9-1. Publishing a service with CFNetServices*

```
#include <sys/types.h>
#include <sys/socket.h>
#include <netinet/in.h>

#include <CoreServices/CoreServices.h>

CFNetServiceRef gRegisteredService;

static void MyCancelRegistration(void)
    {
    CFNetServiceUnscheduleFromRunLoop(gRegisteredService,
```

*Example 9-1. Publishing a service with CFNetServices (continued)*

```
        CFRunLoopGetCurrent( ), kCFRunLoopCommonModes);
    CFNetServiceSetClient(gRegisteredService, NULL, NULL);
    CFRelease(gRegisteredService);
    gRegisteredService = NULL;
    }

static void MyRegisterCallBack(CFNetServiceRef theService, CFStreamError* error, void*
info)
    {
    if (error->domain == kCFStreamErrorDomainNetServices)
        {
        switch(error->error)
            {
            case kCFNetServicesErrorCollision:
                MyCancelRegistration( );
                fprintf(stderr, "kCFNetServicesErrorCollision occurred\n");
                break;
            default:
                MyCancelRegistration( );
                fprintf(stderr, "MyRegisterCallBack (domain = %d, error = %ld)\n",
                    error->domain, error->error);
                break;
            }
        }
    }

static Boolean MyRegisterService(u_short thePort)
    {
    CFNetServiceClientContext context = { 0, NULL, NULL, NULL, NULL };
    CFStreamError error;
    Boolean result;

    printf("MyRegisterService advertising service on port %d\n", htons(thePort));

    gRegisteredService = CFNetServiceCreate(kCFAllocatorDefault,
        CFSTR(""), CFSTR("_example._tcp"), CFSTR("CF Example"), // Domain, type, name
        thePort);
    assert(gRegisteredService != NULL);

    CFNetServiceSetClient(gRegisteredService, MyRegisterCallBack, &context);

    CFNetServiceScheduleWithRunLoop(gRegisteredService,
        CFRunLoopGetCurrent( ), kCFRunLoopCommonModes);

    result = CFNetServiceRegister(gRegisteredService, &error);
    if (result == false) //clean up
        {
        MyCancelRegistration( );
        fprintf(stderr, "CFNetServiceRegister returned (domain = %d, error = %ld)\n",
            error.domain, error.error);
        }
    return result;
    }
```

*Example 9-1. Publishing a service with CFNetServices (continued)*

```
int main(int argc, char* argv[])
    {
    CFSocketRef s = CFSocketCreate(kCFAllocatorDefault,
        PF_INET, SOCK_STREAM, IPPROTO_TCP,
        kCFSocketNoCallBack, NULL, NULL);
    struct sockaddr_in sa = { sizeof(sa), AF_INET };
    CFDataRef addr = CFDataCreateWithBytesNoCopy(kCFAllocatorDefault,
        (const UInt8*)&sa, sizeof(sa), kCFAllocatorNull);
    CFSocketSetAddress(s, addr);
    CFRelease(addr);
    addr = CFSocketCopyAddress(s);
    memmove(&sa, CFDataGetBytePtr(addr), sizeof(sa));
    CFRelease(addr);
    MyRegisterService(ntohs(sa.sin_port));

    CFRunLoopRun();
    return 0;
    }
```

This code can easily be built in Xcode by selecting File → New Project… and choosing the option to make a new CoreServices Tool (near the bottom of the list of options). Open *main.c*, paste in Example 9-1's source code, and click the button to build and run the project. Your program should now be publishing a service of type _example._tcp with name CF Example. You should be able to discover your registered service using the code listed in Example 9-2, or by running dns-sd -B _example._tcp.

## Browsing in CFNetServices

To browse for DNS-SD services, you will need to create a CFNetServiceBrowser. A CFNetServiceBrowserRef is returned by a call to the function CFNetServiceBrowserCreate(). As was the case when programming with the socket-based DNSServiceDiscovery C API, one of the parameters you will need to pass into this function is the callback function. In Example 9-2, the callback function is the MyBrowseCallBack() function.

*Example 9-2. Browsing for services using CFNetServices*

```
#include <CoreServices/CoreServices.h>

CFNetServiceBrowserRef gBrowserService;
CFMutableDictionaryRef gServiceDictionary;

typedef struct
    {
    int refCount;
    char name[64];
    char type[24];
    char domain[1005];
    } MyService;
```

*Example 9-2. Browsing for services using CFNetServices (continued)*

```
CFStringRef MyCreateDictionaryKey(CFNetServiceRef service)
    {
    return CFStringCreateWithFormat(kCFAllocatorDefault, 0, CFSTR("%@.%@%@"),
        CFNetServiceGetName(service),
        CFNetServiceGetType(service),
        CFNetServiceGetDomain(service));
    }

static void MyAddService(CFNetServiceRef service, CFOptionFlags flags)
    {
    CFStringRef dictKey = MyCreateDictionaryKey(service);
    MyService *s;

    // We need to do reference counting of each service because if the computer
    // has two network interfaces set up, like Ethernet and AirPort, you may
    // get notified about the same service twice, once from each interface.
    // You probably don't want both items to be shown to the user.
    // On Mac OS X 10.4 and later, the CFNetServices code does this reference
    // counting for you, so you'll get at most one "add" event for a given
    // name/type/domain, but if your code is also going to run on Mac OS X
    // 10.3, you'll want to implement the reference counting as shown here.

    if (CFDictionaryGetValueIfPresent(gServiceDictionary, dictKey, (const void **)&s) ==
false)
        {
        s = malloc(sizeof(MyService));
        assert(s != NULL);
        s->refCount = 0;
        CFStringGetCString(CFNetServiceGetName  (service), s->name,   sizeof(s->name),
            kCFStringEncodingUTF8);
        CFStringGetCString(CFNetServiceGetType  (service), s->type,   sizeof(s->type),
            kCFStringEncodingUTF8);
        CFStringGetCString(CFNetServiceGetDomain(service), s->domain, sizeof(s->domain),
            kCFStringEncodingUTF8);
        CFDictionarySetValue(gServiceDictionary, dictKey, (const void **)s);
        printf("ADD %s.%s%s\n", s->name, s->type, s->domain);
        }

    s->refCount++;
    CFRelease(dictKey);
    }

static void MyRemoveService(CFNetServiceRef service, CFOptionFlags flags)
    {
    CFStringRef dictKey = MyCreateDictionaryKey(service);
    MyService *s;

    if (CFDictionaryGetValueIfPresent(gServiceDictionary, dictKey, (const void **)&s))
        {
        s->refCount--;
        if (s->refCount == 0)
            {
```

*Example 9-2. Browsing for services using CFNetServices (continued)*

```
                CFDictionaryRemoveValue(gServiceDictionary, dictKey);
                printf("RMV %s.%s%s\n", s->name, s->type, s->domain);
                free(s);
                }
            }

    CFRelease(dictKey);
    }

static void MyBrowseCallBack(CFNetServiceBrowserRef theService,
    CFOptionFlags flags, CFTypeRef service, CFStreamError* err, void* info)
    {
    if (err->error)
        fprintf(stderr, "MyBrowseCallBack %d,%ld\n", err->domain, err->error);
    else if (flags & kCFNetServiceFlagRemove)
        MyRemoveService((CFNetServiceRef)service, flags);
    else
        MyAddService((CFNetServiceRef)service, flags);
    }

static Boolean MyBrowseService()
    {
    CFNetServiceClientContext context = { 0, NULL, NULL, NULL, NULL };
    CFStreamError error;
    Boolean result;

    gServiceDictionary = CFDictionaryCreateMutable(kCFAllocatorDefault,
        0, &kCFCopyStringDictionaryKeyCallBacks, NULL);
    assert(gServiceDictionary != NULL);

    gBrowserService = CFNetServiceBrowserCreate(kCFAllocatorDefault,
        MyBrowseCallBack, &context);
    assert(gBrowserService != NULL);

    CFNetServiceBrowserScheduleWithRunLoop(gBrowserService,
        CFRunLoopGetCurrent(), kCFRunLoopCommonModes);

    result = CFNetServiceBrowserSearchForServices(gBrowserService,
        CFSTR(""), CFSTR("_example._tcp"), &error);

    if (result == false) //clean up
        {
        CFNetServiceBrowserUnscheduleFromRunLoop(gBrowserService,
            CFRunLoopGetCurrent(), kCFRunLoopCommonModes);
        CFRelease(gBrowserService);
        gBrowserService = NULL;
        fprintf(stderr, "CFNetServiceBrowserSearchForServices returned %d, %ld)\n",
            error.domain, error.error);
        }

    return result;
    }
```

---

*Example 9-2. Browsing for services using CFNetServices (continued)*

```
int main(int argc, char* argv[])
    {
    MyBrowseService();
    CFRunLoopRun();
    return 0;
    }
```

For the most part, you will want to perform your searches asynchronously so that your application is not blocked while the search is in progress. You use the returned CFNetServiceBrowser in the asynchronous mode by calling the function CFNetServiceBrowserScheduleWithRunLoop(). Without making this call before searching for domains and services, you will be searching in the synchronous mode and the functions used to search will block until there are search results. The callback function is called when there are search results, but in the synchronous mode you need to stop the search by calling CFNetServiceBrowserStopSearch() from a separate thread.

After starting the browser in asynchronous mode, you search for domains using CFNetServiceBrowserSearchForDomains() and for services using CFNetServiceBrowserSearchForServices(). Be sure to perform the appropriate cleanup of resources. So, for example, if either of these functions returns false, you should call CFNetService-BrowserUnScheduleFromRunLoop() and release the memory for the CFNetServiceBrowserRef.

Example 9-2 shows how you can search for services of type _example._tcp. The MyBrowseService() function follows the steps outlined for browsing for services. The callback function MyBrowseCallBack() uses the functions CFNetServiceGetName(), CFNetServiceGetType(), and CFNetServiceGetDomain() to retrieve the name, type, and domain of the discovered service.

To run the code given in Example 9-2, run Xcode, select File → New Project… and then choose CoreServices Tool. Open *main.c*, paste in the source code in Example 9-2, and click the button to build and run the project. Your program should now be browsing for services of type _example._tcp. To test it, use the code given in Example 9-1 to advertise a service, or else use *dns-sd*:

```
dns-sd -R "CF Example" _example._tcp "" 123
```

Your browser should discover the advertised service and print out:

```
ADD CF Example._example._tcp.local.
```

Kill off the command-line process and your browser should report:

```
RMV CF Example._example._tcp.local.
```

You'll see that this code adds discovered services to a dictionary. If it discovers a service already in its dictionary, then instead of showing it twice, it just increments a reference count. The reason for this is that if your machine has more than one active interface, you may discover the same service via both interfaces. The CFNetServices

API doesn't indicate upon which interface a service was discovered, so although you can't show this information to the user, you can use reference counting to avoid showing the same thing twice. If you want to be able to display the interface index, name, or icon to the user, you can do that using the lower-level DNSServiceDiscovery C API.

You'll also see that this code allows up to 1,005 bytes for a domain name. This is the maximum possible length that a legal domain name can be after escaping non-printable characters using the normal DNS escaping rules. Newer versions of the */usr/include/dns_sd.h* header file define a constant kDNSServiceMaxDomainName for this value.

## Resolving in CFNetServices

To resolve a service, first create a CFNetService object that contains the name, type, and domain of the service you wish to resolve. Unlike registering and browsing, this time you *do* need to give a specific domain. In a real program, you'd be resolving a service you discovered as a result of browsing, so you'd use the name, type, and domain for the service you learned in your browse callback.

Use CFNetServiceSetClient( ) to assign the callback function and use CFNetServiceScheduleWithRunLoop( ) to perform the resolution asynchronously. Pass in the reference to the service to be resolved to the function CFNetServiceResolve( ). When the answer(s) are available, the MyResolveCallBack( ) function is called.

Note that you are very likely to receive IPv6 addresses as well as IPv4 addresses in your callback function. There's no need to be afraid of IPv6 addresses or to take special steps to filter them out. Just pass the sockaddr structure unchanged to the connect( ) system call (or equivalent) and you'll get back a working TCP connection to that address and port, just as with IPv4.

After you've got the information in the callback(s) and used that information to establish a successful TCP connection, remember to cancel your resolve call. If you don't, it will continue to transmit queries on the network, trying to find alternate IP addresses for the target without realizing that you've already succeeded in connecting to it.

The entire process of resolving a service is shown in Example 9-3.

*Example 9-3. Resolving a service with CFNetServices*

```
#include <sys/types.h>
#include <sys/socket.h>
#include <netinet/in.h>
#include <arpa/inet.h>

#include <CoreServices/CoreServices.h>
```

*Example 9-3. Resolving a service with CFNetServices (continued)*

```
static void MyResolveCallBack(CFNetServiceRef service, CFStreamError* error, void* info)
    {
    int count;
    CFArrayRef addresses = CFNetServiceGetAddressing(service);

    assert(addresses != NULL);
    assert(CFArrayGetCount(addresses) > 0);

    // May get more than one reply
    for (count = 0; count < CFArrayGetCount(addresses); count++)
        {
        char addr[256];
        struct sockaddr_in *sa = (struct sockaddr_in *)
            CFDataGetBytePtr(CFArrayGetValueAtIndex(addresses, count));
        // inet_ntop will correctly display both IPv4 and IPv6 addresses
        if (inet_ntop(sa->sin_family, &sa->sin_addr, addr, sizeof(addr)))
            printf("%s:%d \n", addr, ntohs(sa->sin_port));
        }
    }

static void MyResolveService( )
    {
    CFNetServiceClientContext context = { 0, NULL, NULL, NULL, NULL };
    CFStreamError error;

    CFNetServiceRef serviceBeingResolved = CFNetServiceCreate(kCFAllocatorDefault,
        CFSTR("local."), CFSTR("_example._tcp"), CFSTR("CF Example"), 0);
    assert(serviceBeingResolved != NULL);

    CFNetServiceSetClient(serviceBeingResolved, MyResolveCallBack, &context);
    CFNetServiceScheduleWithRunLoop(serviceBeingResolved,
        CFRunLoopGetCurrent( ), kCFRunLoopCommonModes);

    if (CFNetServiceResolve(serviceBeingResolved, &error) == false)
        { // Something went wrong so lets clean up.
        CFNetServiceUnscheduleFromRunLoop(serviceBeingResolved,
            CFRunLoopGetCurrent( ), kCFRunLoopCommonModes);
        CFNetServiceSetClient(serviceBeingResolved, NULL, NULL);
        CFRelease(serviceBeingResolved);
        serviceBeingResolved = NULL;
        fprintf(stderr, "CFNetServiceResolve returned %d, %ld\n",
            error.domain, error.error);
        }
    }

int main(int argc, char* argv[])
    {
    MyResolveService( );
    CFRunLoopRun( );
    return 0;
    }
```

Just as with the other examples, make a new CoreServices Tool, paste in the code, and then compile and run it.

Now advertise a service called CF Example of type _example._tcp:

```
dns-sd -R "CF Example" _example._tcp "" 123
```

As you do, you'll see that your resolve call succeeds and prints out the list of possible addresses for this service. It may appear that CFNetServices is giving you duplicate addresses. In fact, what's happening is that each time CFNetServices gets new results for you, it will call you back again, giving the entire array of addresses, including both the old ones you've seen before and the new ones you haven't. For this reason, you may see the same addresses multiple times as the array grows bigger and bigger with each callback.

There's no guarantee that all the addresses you see will be reachable. Also, some may offer faster performance than others—e.g., an address on Gigabit Ethernet is likely to give a lot faster connection than an address on AirPort. In an ideal program, you'd attempt connections to all of the possible addresses simultaneously to see which one succeeds fastest, and then as soon as one succeeds, cancel the other outstanding attempts.

# Using the NSNetServices API in Cocoa

Objective-C and Cocoa programming are a good fit for the asynchronous DNS-SD programming model. The notion of delegates makes it easy to set up asynchronous calls. All of the Cocoa Bonjour functionality is implemented in the classes NSNetService and NSNetServiceBrowser. When you initiate browsing, for example, you pass in a handle to an object that will act as the delegate. The appropriate delegate methods are called on this object to report on relevant activity that results from browsing. This is very similar to the listener interfaces in Java. As in Java, it's usual for the object making the NSNetServices call to specify self as the delegate to receive event notifications. One difference, though, is that in Java it is mandatory for the listener object to implement all of the methods required by the interface definition, and the Java compiler enforces this. In Objective-C, there's no compile-time check that the delegate object implements the required methods. If you accidentally specify the wrong object as the delegate, the compiler won't warn you that it implements none of the relevant methods. If you specify the right object as the delegate, but when implementing the required methods you mistype one of the method names, the compiler won't complain about that either. Your program won't crash; it just won't work as expected. This is a deliberate feature of the Objective-C language—if you choose not to implement a particular method, then calls to that method automatically become non-operations—but it does mean you have to be careful.

# Advertising a Service in Cocoa

To publish a service, you will create an instance of an NSNetService and pass in the information about the domain, service type, service name, and port with initWithDomain:type:name:port:. You next set the delegate for the NSNetService. Finally, you call the publish method. This process looks something like this:

```
NSNetService *service = [[NSNetService alloc] initWithDomain:@""
                         type:@"_example._tcp."
                         name:@"sample"
                         port:thePort];
    [service setDelegate:self];
    [service publish];
```

There are four delegate methods, which you can implement as you see fit. The netServiceDidPublish: method is new in Mac OS X 10.4.

```
netServiceWillPublish:
netServiceDidPublish:
netService:didNotPublish:
netServiceDidStop:
```

Example 9-4 shows a simple example of publishing a service using the Cocoa API.

*Example 9-4. Publishing a service in Cocoa*

```
#include <sys/types.h>
#include <sys/socket.h>
#include <netinet/in.h>

#import <Foundation/Foundation.h>

@interface MyPublisher : NSObject
    {
    NSNetService *service;
    }
@end

@implementation MyPublisher

- (void)publishService:(UInt16)thePort
    {
    service = [[NSNetService alloc]
        initWithDomain:@"" type:@"_example._tcp." name:@"Cocoa Example" port:thePort];
    [service setDelegate:self];
    [service publish];
    }

- (void)netServiceWillPublish:(NSNetService *)s
    {
    NSLog(@"WillPublish: %@.%@%@\n", [s name], [s type], [s domain]);
    }
```

*Example 9-4. Publishing a service in Cocoa (continued)*

```
- (void)netServiceDidPublish:(NSNetService *)s
    {
    NSLog(@"DidPublish: %@.%@%@\n", [s name], [s type], [s domain]);
    }

- (void)netService:(NSNetService *)s didNotPublish:(NSDictionary *)errorDict
    {
    NSLog(@"didNotPublish: %@.%@%@\n", [s name], [s type], [s domain]);
    }

@end

int main(int argc, char *argv[])
    {
    NSAutoreleasePool *pool = [[NSAutoreleasePool alloc] init];

    // Get a new listening socket...
    int s = socket(PF_INET, SOCK_STREAM, IPPROTO_TCP);
    struct sockaddr_in sa = { sizeof(sa), AF_INET };
    int size = sizeof(sa);
    bind(s, (struct sockaddr *)&sa, sizeof(sa));
    getsockname(s, (struct sockaddr *)&sa, &size);

    // ... and advertise it
    [[[MyPublisher alloc]init] publishService: ntohs(sa.sin_port)];

    [[NSRunLoop currentRunLoop] run];
    [pool release];
    return 0;
    }
```

This code can easily be built in Xcode by selecting File → New Project… and then choosing Foundation Tool (near the bottom of the list of options). Open *main.m*, paste in the source code, and click the button to build and run the project. Your program should now be publishing a service of type _example._tcp with name Cocoa Example. You should be able to discover your registered service using the code listed in Example 9-5, or by running the command dns-sd -B _example._tcp.

*Example 9-5. Browsing for services in Cocoa*

```
#import <Foundation/Foundation.h>

@interface MyBrowser : NSObject
    {
    NSNetServiceBrowser *serviceBrowser;
    }
- (void)browseForServices;

@end

@implementation MyBrowser
```

*Example 9-5. Browsing for services in Cocoa (continued)*

```
- (void)browseForServices
    {
    serviceBrowser = [[NSNetServiceBrowser alloc] init];
    [serviceBrowser setDelegate:self];
    [serviceBrowser searchForServicesOfType:@"_example._tcp." inDomain:@""];
    }

- (void)netServiceBrowserWillSearch:(NSNetServiceBrowser *)aNetServiceBrowser
    {
    NSLog(@"Starting to search . . .\n");
    }


- (void)netServiceBrowser:(NSNetServiceBrowser *)aNetServiceBrowser
        didFindService:(NSNetService *)s moreComing:(BOOL)moreComing
    {
    NSLog(@"Add %@.%@%@\n", [s name], [s type], [s domain]);
    }


- (void)netServiceBrowser:(NSNetServiceBrowser *)aNetServiceBrowser
        didRemoveService:(NSNetService *)s moreComing:(BOOL)moreComing
    {
    NSLog(@"Rmv %@.%@%@\n", [s name], [s type], [s domain]);
    }

@end

int main(int argc, char *argv[])
    {
    NSAutoreleasePool *pool = [[NSAutoreleasePool alloc] init];
    [[[MyBrowser alloc]init] browseForServices];
    [[NSRunLoop currentRunLoop] run];
    [pool release];
    return 0;
    }
```

## Browsing in Cocoa

To begin browsing in Cocoa, you first instantiate NSNetServiceBrowser and assign a delegate to the object with the method setDelegate:. You can then begin browsing by calling the method searchForSevicesOfType: inDomain:, like this:

```
serviceBrowser = [[NSNetServiceBrowser alloc] init];
[serviceBrowser setDelegate:self];
[serviceBrowser searchForServicesOfType:@"_example._tcp." inDomain:@""];
```

Because you have set the delegate to self, you also implement the delegate methods for browsing in the same class. You can track the lifecycle of the search and react to services that have been added or removed using the following methods:

```
netServiceBrowserWillSearch:
netServiceBrowserDidStopSearch:
```

```
netServiceBrowser:didNotSearch:
netServiceBrowser:didFindService:moreComing:
netServiceBrowser:didRemoveService:moreComing:
```

You need to decide whether or not you are interested in each of these events and write the code that performs the actions you want. As a trivial example, you may wish to report on services that have been discovered. Here is a possible implementation of netServiceBrowser:didFindService: moreComing:

```
- (void)netServiceBrowser:(NSNetServiceBrowser *)aNetServiceBrowser
        didFindService:(NSNetService *)s moreComing:(BOOL)moreComing
    {
    NSLog(@"Add %@.%@%@\n", [s name], [s type], [s domain]);
    }
```

A message is printed listing the name, type, and domain of the discovered service. In Example 9-5, you see that other delegate methods are implemented as well.

To run the code given in Example 9-5, run Xcode, select File → New Project…, and then choose Foundation Tool. Open *main.m*, paste in the source code, and click the button to build and run the project. Your program should now be browsing for services of type _example._tcp. To test it, use the code in Example 9-4 to advertise a service, or use the command dns-sd -R "Cocoa Example" _example._tcp "" 123.

Your browser should discover the advertised service and print out:

```
Add Cocoa Example._example._tcp.local.
```

Kill off the command-line process and your browser should report:

```
Rmv Cocoa Example._example._tcp.local.
```

## Resolving in Cocoa

To resolve a DNS-SD service, you begin by creating an NSNetService instance using alloc() and initWithDomain:type:name: or by using a service discovered using NSNetServiceBrowser, as shown when browsing for services in Example 9-5. If you start a resolve running on an NSNetService object handed to you in your didFindService: delegate method, you must be sure to retain it first, or when your didFindService: delegate method returns, the object will be disposed and your program will crash.

Remember that, unlike registering and browsing, to resolve you *do* need to specify a domain. To work asynchronously, you next have to assign a delegate that is used for the callback methods. Finally, you begin to resolve the service by calling resolve. Here's a simple example of how you might resolve a service:

```
NSNetService *service = [[NSNetService alloc] initWithDomain:@"local."
                                    type:@"_example._tcp."
                                    name:@"sample"];
[service setDelegate:self];
[service resolve];
```

---

The delegate methods for resolving services are:

```
netServiceDidResolveAddress:
netService:didNotResolve:
```

Example 9-6 shows a simple example of how you might resolve the service named
Cocoa Example of type _example._tcp.

*Example 9-6. Resolving a service in Cocoa*

```
#include <sys/types.h>
#include <sys/socket.h>
#include <netinet/in.h>
#include <arpa/inet.h>

#import <Foundation/Foundation.h>

@interface MyResolver : NSObject
    {
    NSNetService *service;
    }
@end

@implementation MyResolver

- (void)resolveService
    {
    service = [[NSNetService alloc]
        initWithDomain:@"local." type:@"_example._tcp." name:@"Cocoa Example"];
    [service setDelegate:self];
    [service resolve];
    }

- (void)netServiceWillResolve:(NSNetService *)sender
    {
    NSLog(@"netServiceWillResolve: %@.%@%@\n",
        [sender name], [sender type], [sender domain]);
    }

- (void)netServiceDidResolveAddress:(NSNetService *)s
    {
    NSLog(@"DidResolve: %@.%@%@\n", [s name], [s type], [s domain]);

    // May get more than one reply
    NSArray *addresses = [s addresses];
    int count;
    for (count = 0; count < [addresses count]; count++)
        {
        char addr[256];
        struct sockaddr_in *sa = (struct sockaddr_in *)
            [[addresses objectAtIndex:count] bytes];
        if (inet_ntop(sa->sin_family, &sa->sin_addr, addr, sizeof(addr)))
            NSLog(@"DidResolve: %s:%d \n", addr, ntohs(sa->sin_port));
        }
    }
```

*Example 9-6. Resolving a service in Cocoa (continued)*

```
- (void)netService:(NSNetService *)sender didNotResolve:(NSDictionary *)errorDict
    {
    NSLog(@"didNotResolve: %@.%@%@\n",
      [sender name], [sender type], [sender domain]);
    }

@end

int main(int argc, char *argv[])
    {
    NSAutoreleasePool *pool = [[NSAutoreleasePool alloc] init];
    [[[MyResolver alloc]init] resolveService];
    [[NSRunLoop currentRunLoop] run];
    [pool release];
    return 0;
    }
```

Just as with the other examples, make a new Foundation Tool, paste in the code, and then compile and run it.

Now advertise a service called `Cocoa Example` of type `_example._tcp`:

```
dns-sd -R "Cocoa Example" _example._tcp "" 123
```

As you do, you'll see that your resolve call succeeds and prints out the list of possible addresses for this service. From this point on, you're no longer using the Cocoa NSNetService API. The Cocoa API has done its job. It has resolved the named service to its address(es) and port number. Connecting to the service and using it are done using any of the many networking APIs already available.

There's no guarantee that all the addresses you see will be reachable. Also, some may offer faster performance than others—e.g., an address on Gigabit Ethernet is likely to give a lot faster connection than an address on AirPort. In an ideal program, you'd attempt connections to all of the possible addresses simultaneously to see which one succeeds fastest, and then as soon as one succeeds, cancel the other outstanding attempts.

If you're writing an application that only needs to run on Mac OS X 10.4 or later, then there's a new `resolveWithTimeout:` method you can use that will give up and return an error after the specified interval has elapsed.

# A Cocoa Bonjour Extended Example

Let's use the Cocoa NSNetService API to create a simple application. When the example is complete, you will start up the application and see the window shown in Figure 9-1.

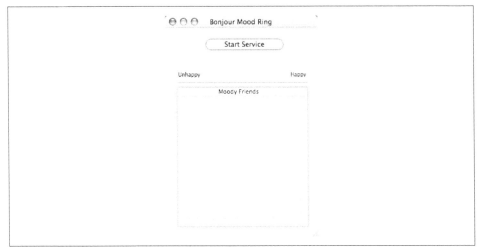

*Figure 9-1. Startup screen for Bonjour Mood Ring*

This is one of the rare examples of an application where there is no actual application protocol. The entire functionality of the application consists of browsing to discover peers on the network and monitoring their TXT record status. All communication happens as a result of updates to the TXT record status, and, consequently, there is no application-layer protocol.

Because TXT record updates have a cost on the network, the mdnsd daemon limits how rapidly a program may update its TXT records in order to help limit the bad impact buggy application software could have on the network. In Mac OS X 10.4, the TXT record may be updated up to 10 times per minute. If you drag the slider around rapidly and exceed this rate, you'll see messages appear in *system.log* saying "Excessive update rate…delaying announcement." Your new mood will be announced eventually, but before sending out the packet, the mdnsd daemon will sit and wait a few seconds to see if you're going to move the slider again. After you've decided what your new mood will be and not changed your mind for a few seconds, the mdnsd daemon will then send out the packet to notify your peers on the local network.

Note that this example application uses some of the newer utility functions, such as NSNetService dataFromTXTRecordDictionary: and NSNetService startMonitoring, introduced in Mac OS X 10.4. It won't work on Mac OS X 10.3.x.

Press the Start Service button and a progress indicator will start to spin until your service is registered. Then the Start Service button will be replaced by a rounded text box containing your full name, with the background color matching your mood. A slider bar also appears, allowing you to change your mood. A list of yours and other discovered services is provided at the bottom of the window, with each name displayed in a text color that matches their mood, as shown in Figure 9-2.

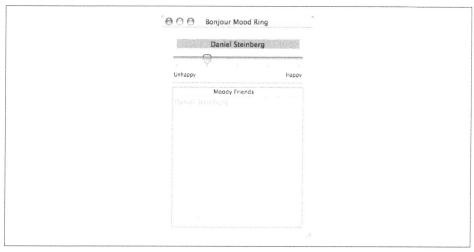

*Figure 9-2. Bonjour Mood Ring with service running*

The application is built on two classes. MoodBeacon advertises the service and is responsible for updating the TXT record when there is a change to the slider position. MoodBrowser discovers other services and is responsible for updating the UI to reflect the current slider setting of other services.

This program is based on an example Ken Arnold demonstrated as a Jini-based application at MacHack 2003, and it is presented with his permission. The noteworthy difference is that with Jini, someone somewhere on the network needs to be running a network service called the "Jini Lookup Service." Clients discover the local Jini Lookup Service by sending a UDP packet to the IP multicast address 224.0.1.85 on port 4160 and waiting for a response. The clients then register their presence with that Jini Lookup Service and query the Jini Lookup Service to find the list of other peers that have registered. For Jini to work, that vital piece of network infrastructure needs to be present and working. In contrast, the Bonjour version needs no infrastructure. For two Bonjour Mood Ring programs to communicate over Ethernet, the only network infrastructure you need is a length of Ethernet cable with a plug at each end. If you use 802.11 wireless, you don't even need the cable. Work is being done to marry the benefits of Jini with the server-less nature of Zeroconf, by defining a mapping from Jini interface specifications to DNS-SD service subtypes. A Jini client can then just perform a DNS-SD browsing query for the specific DNS-SD service subtype that corresponds to the Jini interface specification it's looking for and discover a list of Jini services on the network that implement that desired interface.

## Creating the GUI

If this is your first Cocoa application, the description below may go a little fast for you. You may want to consult the book *Learning Cocoa* (O'Reilly). The key is that with Cocoa applications, there is a strong separation of the View from the Model and Control layers. The result is that there is a lot less actual code in the resulting application than what you might be used to from other languages. You create the view using the application Interface Builder. You create this in two parts: you design the GUI using graphical tools and you create a skeleton outline of the classes that will interact with the GUI.

To begin, double-click on *MainMenu.nib* to open it in Interface Builder. You should see a window. Select the menu item Tools → Show Info to open up the inspector window. You can change the size of the window and text in the title bar of the window and set various other attributes. You can also add other components to the window and configure them. Figure 9-3 gives you an idea of what the final window should look like.

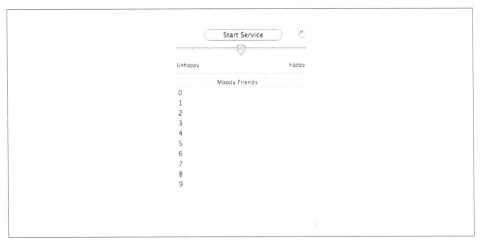

*Figure 9-3. GUI for the BonjourMoods application*

At the top, you can see an NSButton labeled Start Service, which is initially visible. In the same location is a rounded NSTextField and to the right an NSProgressIndicator, both of which are initially invisible. Below is an NSSlider with five markers with values from 0 to 4. The discovered services will be listed in an NSTableView titled Moody Friends.

Create two classes to implement the service. The MoodBeacon class will be used to advertise a service and the MoodBrowser class will be used to discover other services of the same type. In the class view, you will add actions and outlets to your classes. Actions correspond to methods you will create in your class to respond to user input. For example, when the user clicks on the Start Service button, you would like to publish the service. You create an action in the MoodBeacon class named publishService and create an instance of the MoodBeacon. All that remains is for you to implement this method when you are editing the source code. Outlets correspond to variables in your source code that are handles to the GUI object. For example, if you are going to make the Start Service button invisible, you need an outlet in order to refer back to it.

MoodBeacon has five outlets: groupMood (an NSTextField), happinessSlider (an NSSlider), progressIndicator (an NSProgressIndicator), serviceStarter (an NSButton), and userName (an NSTextField). MoodBeacon also has two actions: publishService: and updateMood:. On the other hand, MoodBrowser has no actions and only one outlet, friendView (an NSTableView). The data source and delegate for the NSTableView is the MoodBrowser instance associated with the view. Complete the GUI by using Interface Builder to wire the appropriate GUI component to the corresponding outlet or action and save your work.

## The Generated MoodBeacon and MoodBrowser Header Files

The work you did above in Interface Builder created header files for the two classes. Example 9-7 shows the header file for MoodBeacon. Note the five outlets you created and wired up, followed by the signatures for the two methods you specified as actions.

*Example 9-7. MoodBeacon.h*

```
/* MoodBeacon */

#import <Cocoa/Cocoa.h>

@interface MoodBeacon : NSObject
{
    IBOutlet NSSlider *happinessSlider;
    IBOutlet NSProgressIndicator *progressIndicator;
    IBOutlet NSButton *serviceStarter;
    IBOutlet NSTextField *userName;
}
- (IBAction)publishService:(id)sender;
- (IBAction)updateMood:(NSSlider *)sender;
@end
```

The header file for MoodBrowser is shown in Example 9-8 and contains the outlet corresponding to the NSTableView named friendView. You will also need to add the two NSMutableArray objects friendsList and moodsList as well as the NSNetServiceBrowser object serviceBrowser.

*Example 9-8. MoodBrowser.h*

```
/* MoodBrowser */

#import <Cocoa/Cocoa.h>

@interface MoodBrowser : NSObject
{
    IBOutlet NSTableView *friendView;
```

*Example 9-8. MoodBrowser.h (continued)*

```
    NSMutableArray * friendsList;
    NSNetServiceBrowser * serviceBrowser;
    NSMutableArray * moodsList;
}
@end
```

## Advertising the Service with MoodBeacon

The MoodBeacon class can respond to two actions: publishService: and updateMood:. As you saw above, when the user presses the Start Service button, the publishService: method is called. The first action taken in the publishService: method is to allocate and initialize an NSNetService object of type _moodring._tcp with name equal to the user's full name, as returned by a call to the method NSFullUserName( ). The MoodBeacon object is then registered as the delegate, the service is published, and the updateMood: method is called.

Before discussing the updateMood: method, let's look at how to use the delegate methods to communicate progress to the end user. When the netServiceWillPublish: method is called, the NSProgressIndicator begins to spin to indicate that an action is being taken by the system. Here is all that is required to accomplish this:

```
- (void)netServiceWillPublish:(NSNetService *)sender
{
    [progressIndicator startAnimation:self];
}
```

Similarly, when the method netServiceDidPublish: is called, the NSProgressIndicator stops spinning and the NSButton appears to be replaced with a text area containing the username. The slider with which the user can set his happiness level also appears. If, instead, the didNotPublish: method is called, an error is reported to the user.

The updateMood: method takes the value of the NSSlider, updates the TXT record for the service, and sets the background color of the NSTextField. To update the TXT record, first create an NSDictionary of entries with keys given by the NSStrings @"txtvers" and @"mood". The value corresponding to txtvers is 1 and the value corresponding to mood is the string value of the NSSlider. The method setTXTRecordData: dataFromTXTRecordDictionary: is called to update the TXT record. Example 9-9 shows the complete listing for *MoodBeacon.m*.

*Example 9-9. MoodBeacon.m*

```
#import "MoodBeacon.h"

@implementation MoodBeacon
NSNetService * service;
```

*Example 9-9. MoodBeacon.m (continued)*

```
- (void)netServiceWillPublish:(NSNetService *)sender
{
    [progressIndicator startAnimation:self];
}
- (void)netServiceDidPublish:(NSNetService *)sender
{
    [progressIndicator stopAnimation:self];
    [userName setEnabled:YES];
    [serviceStarter setHidden:YES];
    [userName setHidden:NO];
    [happinessSlider setHidden:NO];
    [userName setStringValue:[sender name]];
}

- (void)netService:(NSNetService *)sender didNotPublish:(NSDictionary *)errorDict
{
    [userName setStringValue:@"Error: did not publish"];
}

- (IBAction)publishService:(id)sender
{
    // Get us a unique listening socket number to advertise
    int s = socket(PF_INET, SOCK_STREAM, IPPROTO_TCP);
    struct sockaddr_in sa = { sizeof(sa), AF_INET };
    int size = sizeof(sa);
    bind(s, (struct sockaddr *)&sa, sizeof(sa));
    getsockname(s, (struct sockaddr *)&sa, &size);

    service = [[NSNetService alloc] initWithDomain:@""
                    type:@"_moodring._tcp."
                    name:NSFullUserName()
                    port:ntohs(sa.sin_port)];
    if ( [[serviceStarter title] isEqualToString:@"Start Service"])
    {
        [service setDelegate:self];
        [service publish];
        [self updateMood:happinessSlider];
    }
}
- (IBAction)updateMood:(NSSlider *)sender
{
    NSMutableDictionary * moodDictionary = [NSMutableDictionary dictionaryWithCapacity:2];
    NSString * txtversKey = @"txtvers";
    NSString * moodKey = @"mood";

    NSString * txtversValue = @"1";
    NSString * moodValue = [sender stringValue];
    [moodDictionary setObject:txtversValue forKey:txtversKey];
    [moodDictionary setObject:moodValue forKey:moodKey];
    [service setTXTRecordData:[NSNetService dataFromTXTRecordDictionary:moodDictionary]];
    float currentValue = [sender floatValue]/4;
```

*Example 9-9. MoodBeacon.m (continued)*

```
    [userName setBackgroundColor:[NSColor colorWithCalibratedRed:3.3 * (1- currentValue)
                                  green:2.0 * (currentValue)
                                  blue:0.0 alpha:1.0]];
}

@end
```

The `MoodBeacon` class is used to announce the availability of the new service and the current state of the mood of the person who the service represents. The next section will detail the actions performed by services receiving messages from `MoodBeacon` objects.

## Finding and Using the Service with MoodBrowser

As you saw in the *MoodBrowser.h* code listing in Example 9-8, the `MoodBrowser` class has two `NSArrayList` objects: `friendsList` and `moodsList`. When a service is discovered, the following callback method is called:

```
    - (void)netServiceBrowser:(NSNetServiceBrowser *)aNetServiceBrowser
                        didFindService:(NSNetService *)aNetService
                        moreComing:(BOOL)moreComing
{
    [friendsList addObject:aNetService];
    [moodsList addObject:[NSColor blackColor]];
    [aNetService setDelegate:self];
    [aNetService startMonitoring];
    if(!moreComing)
        [friendView reloadData];
}
```

The discovered service is added to `friendsList` and initially the color assigned to represent the mood of this service is black. Similarly, when a service is removed, the corresponding entry is removed from both `friendsList` and `moodsList`.

The view is only reloaded once there are no more services coming. This makes the program run a lot faster on a network where there are lots of other MoodRing participants. Instead of updating the window a hundred times, it adds a large batch of participants to `friendsList`, and only when there are no more results waiting to be handled does it update the window.

For active services, the `MoodBrowser` object listens for changes to the TXT record. If there is a change, then the appropriate entry in `moodsList` is updated and the text color of the name of the corresponding entry in `friendsList` is changed to reflect the updated mood:

```
    - (void)netService:(NSNetService *)sender didUpdateTXTRecordData:(NSData *)data
    {
      NSString * temp = [[NSString alloc] initWithData:data encoding:
    NSUTF8StringEncoding];
```

```
    float currentValue = [[temp substringFromIndex:[temp length]-1] floatValue]/4;
    [moodsList replaceObjectAtIndex:[friendsList indexOfObject:sender]
                        withObject:[NSColor colorWithCalibratedRed:3.3 * (1-
  currentValue)
                                        green:2.0 * (currentValue)
                                        blue:0.0 alpha:1.0]];
    [friendView reloadData];
  }
```

Example 9-10 shows the complete listing of *MoodBrowser.m*.

*Example 9-10. MoodBrowser.m*

```
#import "MoodBrowser.h"

@implementation MoodBrowser


- (void) setUpServiceBrowser
{
    serviceBrowser = [[NSNetServiceBrowser alloc] init];
    [serviceBrowser setDelegate:self];
    [serviceBrowser searchForServicesOfType:@"_moodring._tcp."
                inDomain:@""];
}

- (id) init
{
    self = [super init];
    friendsList = [[NSMutableArray alloc] init];
    moodsList = [[NSMutableArray alloc] init];
    [self setUpServiceBrowser];
    return self;
}

- (void) dealloc
{
    [friendsList release];
    [super dealloc];
}

- (int) numberOfRowsInTableView:(NSTableView *)tableView
{
    return [friendsList count];
}

- (id)tableView:(NSTableView *)aTableView
        objectValueForTableColumn:(NSTableColumn *)aTableColumn
            row:(int)rowIndex
{
    return [[friendsList objectAtIndex:rowIndex] name];
}
```

*Example 9-10. MoodBrowser.m (continued)*

```
- (void)netServiceBrowser:(NSNetServiceBrowser *)aNetServiceBrowser
                        didFindService:(NSNetService *)aNetService
                        moreComing:(BOOL)moreComing
{
    [friendsList addObject:aNetService];
    [moodsList addObject:[NSColor blackColor]];
    [aNetService setDelegate:self];
    [aNetService startMonitoring];
    if(!moreComing)
        [friendView reloadData];
}

- (void)netServiceBrowser:(NSNetServiceBrowser *)aNetServiceBrowser
                        didRemoveService:(NSNetService *)aNetService
                        moreComing:(BOOL)moreComing
{
    [moodsList removeObjectAtIndex:[friendsList indexOfObject:aNetService]];
    [friendsList removeObject:aNetService];
    [aNetService stopMonitoring];
    if(!moreComing)
        [friendView reloadData];
}

- (void)tableView:(NSTableView *)inTableView
     willDisplayCell:(id)inCell
       forTableColumn:(NSTableColumn *)inTableColumn
              row:(int)inRow
{
    [inCell setTextColor:[moodsList objectAtIndex:inRow]];
    }

- (void)netService:(NSNetService *)sender didUpdateTXTRecordData:(NSData *)data
{
  NSString * temp = [[NSString alloc] initWithData:data encoding:NSUTF8StringEncoding];
    float currentValue = [[temp substringFromIndex:[temp length]-1] floatValue]/4;
    [moodsList replaceObjectAtIndex:[friendsList indexOfObject:sender]
                    withObject:[NSColor colorWithCalibratedRed:3.3 * (1-
currentValue)
                                       green:2.0 * (currentValue)
                                       blue:0.0 alpha:1.0]];
    [friendView reloadData];
}
@end
```

In this simple example, you saw how to publish and discover services. You also saw
how to update and respond to updates of TXT records. This example shows you
how you might Bonjour-enable your own Cocoa projects.

# CHAPTER 10

# Ruby, Python, and Other Languages

The preceding chapters covered the DNS Service Discovery programming APIs developed primarily by Apple's engineers, which include both cross-platform and Mac-specific APIs. The cross-platform C and Java APIs are available on Macintosh, Microsoft Windows, Linux, FreeBSD, Solaris, and other Unix variants. The Mac-specific Core Foundation API and Cocoa API are available for programmers writing software designed solely for Mac OS X.

Those are just the tip of the iceberg. There exist a range of open source projects (e.g., ones that implement higher-level DNS Service Discovery API layers built on top of the C DNSServiceDiscovery API foundation provided by Apple), some of which complement Apple's work, and some of which overlap or even compete with it. This is made possible by the careful separation of the background daemon and the client library in Apple's own implementation of Multicast DNS and DNS Service Discovery.

The first component is a background daemon, which runs in its own address space and implements all the protocol logic, timing, packet sending and reception, record caching, and similar functionality. The second component is the client library, which client applications link with, in the application's address space, in order to communicate with the background daemon. Apple's background daemon is licensed under the Apple Public Source License 2.0, an FSF-approved open source license. Apple's client library is licensed under an even more liberal three-clause BSD-style license, which allows it to be used in just about anything, from the most secretive proprietary products to the most resolutely open projects using open source licenses such as the GNU Public License (GPL).

This separation into two components offers benefits both technical and legal. The technical benefit is that all the client programs on a machine get the efficiency benefit of sharing a common protocol engine and a common record cache. Also, if a client advertising a service crashes, the daemon detects that and sends the goodbye packet to de-register the advertised service. From a legal standpoint, this separation allows greater freedom for everyone involved. The background daemon is separated from its programming interface, so other independent implementations of the background daemon—with different characteristics and licensing terms—are possible. Meanwhile, the client library, the interface a client program uses to communicate with the daemon, doesn't have to change. Commercial software vendors can link with Apple's client library without the fear of "tainting" sometimes associated with linking GPL libraries, and, at the same time, authors working on GPL programs can also safely link with Apple's client library without fear that they might be violating the strict terms of the GPL.

Similarly, programmers can create their own layers built on top of the C client API, with the freedom to license them as they choose, while users are free to mix and match components as best meets their needs. The key to this flexibility is that as long as all the client layers build on top of the common C API—with its BSD-style license—then all a programmer needs to do to create an alternative daemon implementation is to create a background daemon offering that standard C API, and all of the higher-level client programs and API layers can work with it without change.

In this chapter, we cover two of those higher-level third-party DNS Service Discovery API layers built on top of the C DNSServiceDiscovery API foundation. The first is a language binding for the Ruby programming language. The second is a more general-purpose interface specification written for the Simplified Wrapper and Interface Generator (SWIG), which is used to generate interfaces automatically for a range of languages. That range of languages includes Java and Ruby, which might make you wonder why there are also specific APIs for those languages. The answer is that SWIG does a fairly mechanical translation of the C interface into other languages, yielding an interface with the same basic operating model. For example, just as calls in the C interface hand you back a file descriptor, which you add to your event loop, the SWIG-derived interfaces do the same. In contrast, the specific APIs for Java and Ruby both take advantage of those languages' inherent multithreading support to provide callbacks that are invoked automagically on some other thread. We explore the SWIG interfaces from the perspective of the Python programming language, which doesn't have its own handcrafted API at this time.

Finally, this chapter wraps up with a brief mention of the *mDNSEmbeddedAPI.h* interface, used by hardware devices that don't really need the benefits of an independent mdnsd background process and instead use a monolithic piece of software dedicated to advertising the services of that device, using the core Multicast DNS functions directly.

# Ruby

At publication time, the current version of the Ruby DNS Service Discovery (DNS-SD) interface is 0.6.0. If you use RubyGems to install and manage your Ruby libraries, then you can install Ruby DNS-SD by typing:

```
sudo gem install dndsd
```

If you don't use RubyGems, you can get Ruby DNS-SD by downloading the *dnssd-0_6_0.tar.gz* file from *http://rubyforge.org/projects/dnssd/* and running the three commands shown in the *README* file:

```
ruby setup.rb config
ruby setup.rb setup
ruby setup.rb install
```

In future versions of OS X and other operating systems, it may come preinstalled by default. You can tell if it's already preinstalled with the following command:

```
ruby -e "require 'dnssd'"
```

If there's no error message, then you have the Ruby *dnssd* package already installed. If it prints "No such file to load…," you will need to install it. Once you have the Ruby DNS-SD API installed, you can experiment with registering, browsing, and resolving from a Ruby program.

## Registering a Service in Ruby

The Ruby code to advertise a service is just a few lines:

```
require 'dnssd'
registration = DNSSD.register("", "_http._tcp", nil, 8080) do |register_reply|
  puts "Registration result: #{register_reply.inspect}"
end
puts "Registration started"
sleep 30
registration.stop
puts "Registration stopped"
```

This code:

- Tells the Ruby language interpreter that it requires the *dnssd* package
- Registers a pretend service of type _http._tcp using the computer's default service name
- Prints out the advertised name when the service is successfully registered
- Waits for 30 seconds, then stops the registration and exits

If you save this file as *register.rb* and run it, you should see something like this:

```
% ruby register.rb
Registration started
Registration result: #<DNSSD::RegisterReply Stuart\032Cheshire's\032PowerBook\032G4._
http._tcp.local.>
Registration stopping
```

If you're new to Ruby, some explanation is called for. Ruby supports code blocks as first-class entities, much like integers or strings in other languages. The block of code from do to end is not equivalent to a similar block of code enclosed within curly braces in C. In C, lines of code in a routine execute more or less sequentially. The body of an if or for statement enclosed within curly braces may be executed zero, one, or more times, but it's always executed *before* the lines that appear later in the routine. In Ruby, the block of code from do to end is actually a *parameter* passed to the DNSSD.register() routine. It doesn't execute at all until DNSSD.register() decides it's time to execute it, asynchronously, on an automatically created background thread. If you save the program above as *register.rb* and then run it by typing ruby register.rb, you'll see that it prints the "Registration started" message *before* the "Registration result..." message.

Following the "do" keyword, you'll see an identifier enclosed between a pair of vertical bar symbols (the same character as the Unix "pipe" symbol), which names the parameter that is passed to the code block when it executes, rather like the parameter list enclosed in parentheses when you declare a C function.

In some ways, a Ruby code block is somewhat similar to passing a function pointer in a C program—there's some code to execute and a parameter that's passed to that code—but there's one important difference. A Ruby code block is what computer scientists call a *closure*. It's not just the code but also its *environment*. Similar to the way the body of an if or for statement may access local variables declared in the enclosing function, the Ruby code block passed to DNSSD.register() may access local variables declared in the enclosing function, even though the code block might not even get to execute until after the function that created it has exited. The Ruby interpreter knows that there's a code block that has access to those local variables and makes sure that they continue to remain valid even after the function that declared them has exited.

If you want to register a service with TXT record attributes, Ruby DNS-SD supports that too. The full signature of the DNSSD.register() function is as shown here:

```
DNSSD.register(name, type, domain, port,
    text_record=nil, flags=0, interface=DNSSD::InterfaceAny) {|reply| block }
```

Ruby supports automatic default values for unspecified parameters. In this example, we didn't specify anything for text_record, flags or interface, so they automatically got the default values nil, 0, and DNSSD::InterfaceAny. If you want to register a service with TXT record attributes, you just need to pass a hash (key/value) or a string in the proper format for the text_record parameter.

## Browsing for Services in Ruby

The general structure of the Ruby code to browse for services follows the same outline as the code to register a service:

```
require 'dnssd'
browser = DNSSD.browse('_http._tcp') do |browse_reply|
  if (browse_reply.flags.to_i & DNSSD::Flags::Add) != 0
    puts "Add: #{browse_reply.inspect}"
  else
    puts "Rmv: #{browse_reply.inspect}"
```

```
    end
  end
  puts "Browsing started"
  sleep 30
  browser.stop
  puts "Browsing stopped"
```

If you save this file as *browse.rb* and run it, you should see something like this:

```
% ruby browse.rb
Browsing started
Add: #<DNSSD::BrowseReply Stuart\032Cheshire's\032PowerBook\032G4._http._tcp.local.
interface:lo0>
Browsing stopping
```

## Resolving a Service in Ruby

When you've browsed to discover available services, and the user has picked one, the next step is to resolve the named service to its target host and port number:

```
require 'dnssd'
name = ARGV.shift
puts "Resolving: #{name}"
resolver = DNSSD.resolve(name, "_http._tcp", "local") do |resolve_reply|
  puts "Resolve result: #{resolve_reply.inspect}"
end
puts "Resolver started"
sleep 30
resolver.stop
puts "Resolver stopped"
```

If you save this file as *resolve.rb* and run it, you should see something like this:

```
% ruby resolve.rb "Stuart Cheshire's PowerBook G4"
Resolving: Stuart Cheshire's PowerBook G4
Resolver started
Resolve result: #<DNSSD::ResolveReply Stuart\032Cheshire's\032PowerBook\032G4._http._
tcp.local. interface:en0 target:chesh7.local.:123>
Resolver stopped
```

In a real program, you'd take the resolve results you get and use them to initiate connections, and as soon as one succeeds, you'd then cancel the ongoing resolve operation.

# Python

Python programmers can access DNS-SD functionality via the SWIG interface definition created by Tom Uram, Argonne National Laboratory. At time of writing, you can get it from *http://www.mcs.anl.gov/fl/research/accessgrid/bonjour-py/bonjour-py.html* or from the link on the DNS-SD web site *http://www.dns-sd.org/*. All of these examples are included in the bonjour-py package, along with a more involved example: a graphical service browser built using the wxPython GUI toolkit. To build the Python interfaces using SWIG, you'll need to have SWIG installed; you can get that from *http://sourceforge.net/projects/swig/.*

## Registering a Service in Python

The Python code to advertise a service is a little longer than the Ruby code, but it's still quite simple:

```python
import sys
import time
import select
import socket
import bonjour

# Callback for service registration
def RegisterCallback(sdRef, flags, errorCode, name, regtype, domain, context):
    print "Service registered:", name, regtype, domain

if len(sys.argv) < 4:
    print "Usage: register.py servicename regtype port"
    sys.exit(1)

servicename = sys.argv[1]
regtype = sys.argv[2]
port = int(sys.argv[3])

# Allocate a service discovery reference and register the specified service
flags = 0
interfaceIndex = 0
domain = ''
host = ''
txtLen = 0
txtRecord = ''
userdata = None
serviceRef = bonjour.AllocateDNSServiceRef()
ret = bonjour.pyDNSServiceRegister(serviceRef,
                                   flags,
                                   interfaceIndex,
                                   servicename,
                                   regtype,
                                   domain,
                                   host,
                                   port,
                                   txtLen,
                                   txtRecord,
                                   RegisterCallback,
                                   userdata)


if ret != bonjour.kDNSServiceErr_NoError:
    print "error %d returned; exiting" % ret
    sys.exit(ret)
```

```
# Get the socket and loop
fd = bonjour.DNSServiceRefSockFD(serviceRef)
while 1:
    ret = select.select([fd], [], [])
    ret = bonjour.DNSServiceProcessResult(serviceRef)

# Deallocate the service discovery ref
bonjour.DNSServiceRefDeallocate(serviceRef)
```

This code:

- Defines the callback function to be invoked when the registration succeeds

- Calls bonjour.pyDNSServiceRegister to register the service

- Accesses the serviceRef's file descriptor, adding it to a select( ) set and calling bonjour.DNSServiceProcessResult( ) each time data arrives on that socket

If you save this file as *register.py* and run it, you should see something like this:

```
% python register.py "" _http._tcp 123
Service registered: Stuart Cheshire's PowerBook G4 _http._tcp. local.
```

In this case, we're just using an empty string name to advertise the service using the system default name, but as with the other APIs, if you want something else you can specify an explicit name instead.

## Browsing for Services in Python

It should be little surprise by now to see that the outline of the browsing code looks a lot like the service registration code:

```
import sys
import select
import bonjour

# Callback for service browsing
def BrowseCallback(sdRef, flags, interfaceIndex,
    errorCode, serviceName, regtype, replyDomain, userdata):
    if flags & bonjour.kDNSServiceFlagsAdd:
        print "Service added:    ", serviceName, regtype, replyDomain, interfaceIndex
    else:
        print "Service removed: ", serviceName, regtype, replyDomain, interfaceIndex

if len(sys.argv) < 2:
    print "Usage: browse.py regtype"
    sys.exit(1)

regtype = sys.argv[1]

# Allocate a service discovery ref and browse for the specified service type
flags = 0
interfaceIndex = 0
domain = ''
userdata = None
```

```
serviceRef = bonjour.AllocateDNSServiceRef( )
ret = bonjour.pyDNSServiceBrowse(serviceRef,
                                 flags,
                                 interfaceIndex,
                                 regtype,
                                 domain,
                                 BrowseCallback,
                                 userdata)

if ret != bonjour.kDNSServiceErr_NoError:
    print "ret = %d; exiting" % ret
    sys.exit(1)

# Get socket descriptor and loop
fd = bonjour.DNSServiceRefSockFD(serviceRef)
while 1:
    ret = select.select([fd], [], [])
    ret = bonjour.DNSServiceProcessResult(serviceRef)

# Deallocate the service discovery ref
bonjour.DNSServiceRefDeallocate(serviceRef)
```

This code:

- Defines the callback function to be invoked when results are found
- Calls bonjour.pyDNSServiceBrowse to start the browse operation running
- Accesses the serviceRef's file descriptor, adding it to a select( ) set and calling bonjour.DNSServiceProcessResult( ) each time data arrives on that socket

If you save this file as *browse.py* and run it, you should see something like this:

```
% python browse.py _http._tcp
Service added:    Stuart Cheshire's PowerBook G4 _http._tcp. local. 4
```

This browse operation will run indefinitely, reporting as services come and go, until you press Ctrl-C to stop it.

## Resolving a Service in Python

When you've browsed to discover available services, and the user has picked one, the next step is to resolve the named service to its target host and port number:

```
iimport sys
import select
import bonjour

# Callback for service resolving
def ResolveCallback(sdRef, flags, interfaceIndex,
                    errorCode, fullname, hosttarget,
                    port, txtLen, txtRecord, userdata):
    print "Service:", fullname
    print "is at", hosttarget, ":", port
```

```
if len(sys.argv) < 4:
    print "Usage: resolve.py serviceName serviceType serviceDomain"
    sys.exit(1)

serviceName   = sys.argv[1]
serviceType   = sys.argv[2]
serviceDomain = sys.argv[3]

# Allocate a service discovery ref and resolve the named service
flags = 0
interfaceIndex = 0
userdata = None
serviceRef = bonjour.AllocateDNSServiceRef( )
ret = bonjour.pyDNSServiceResolve(serviceRef,
                                  flags,
                                  interfaceIndex,
                                  serviceName,
                                  serviceType,
                                  serviceDomain,
                                  ResolveCallback,
                                  userdata);

if ret != bonjour.kDNSServiceErr_NoError:
    print "ret = %d; exiting" % ret
    sys.exit(1)

# Get socket descriptor and loop
fd = bonjour.DNSServiceRefSockFD(serviceRef)
while 1:
    ret = select.select([fd], [], [])
    ret = bonjour.DNSServiceProcessResult(serviceRef)

# Deallocate the service discovery ref
bonjour.DNSServiceRefDeallocate(serviceRef)
```

If you save this file as *resolve.py* and run it, you should see something like this:

```
% python resolve.py "Stuart Cheshire's PowerBook G4" _http._tcp. local.
Service: Stuart\032Cheshire's\032PowerBook\032G4._http._tcp.local.
is at chesh7.local. : 123
```

In a real program, you'd take the resolve results you get and use them to initiate connections, and as soon as one succeeds, you'd then cancel the ongoing resolve operation.

# Embedded Responders

On most general-purpose computers, there may be several different services advertising their presence via DNS-SD and several different clients browsing or resolving. On such computers, it makes sense to have a single shared daemon that all the clients and servers talk to.

However, if you're making a very simple single-purpose hardware device, then another API choice is available. If your device offers one and only one service or a small known set of services, and it offers those services from the moment it's powered on and boots up to the moment it's powered down, then you can save a bit of memory by dispensing with the background daemon and just having a single monolithic process that advertises your service(s). To write such a monolithic DNS-SD advertising process, you use the source code from Apple's Darwin mDNSResponder project, adding some code of your own to advertise the appropriate service(s). That code of yours interfaces directly with the core Multicast DNS functions defined in the *mDNSEmbeddedAPI.h* file. The mDNSResponder project's *mDNSPosix* folder contains some example code showing how to do this. For example, *Responder.c* builds a binary called *mDNSResponderPosix*, a single monolithic process that advertises one or more services.

If you're building a hardware device with very limited memory, then one of the benefits of using the raw *mDNSEmbeddedAPI.h* API is that it's malloc-free. That means that there is never a case where the code can suffer intermittent failures because the mDNSCore implementation calls malloc( ), and sometimes malloc( ) returns NULL because memory is so limited that no more is available. Instead, all the memory needs are precisely known in advance, and for each mDNSCore call, the caller is responsible for passing in a pointer to the storage that will be used in the execution of that call, in the form of a C structure defining that required storage. That storage can be a global variable, a local stack variable, a member of another enclosing structure, or allocated any other way the caller chooses. It can even be allocated via malloc( ) if the caller wishes, but the important point is that the decision about how to allocate that memory is in the hands of the caller. Because of this, all the mDNSCore calls (when called with correct parameters) are guaranteed to succeed, with no errors like "out of memory," "no more resources," or something similar. In the simple case of a device advertising a few known services, the easiest thing to do is just to declare each advertised service structure as a global variable, and then you know with certainty that there can't be any runtime failures because of memory shortage. At compile time, you know whether it's going to work, because you either have enough space for your declared globals or you don't. There's no runtime uncertainty.

This malloc-free operation is ideal for devices that need to have precisely known fixed memory requirements, with absolutely no uncertainty or runtime variation, but that certainty comes at a cost of more difficult programming. Generally, if your device has enough memory and runs a conventional general-purpose operating system like Linux, then using the standard mdnsd background daemon is the best choice. However, if that choice doesn't fit your product, then embedding mDNSCore and calling it directly with your own code may be attractive. If you do choose that route, you won't be alone. Most of today's Zeroconf hardware devices, such as printers and network cameras, do exactly that.

.

# Index

We'd like to hear your suggestions for improving our indexes. Send email to *index@oreilly.com*.

## H

hardware
   addresses, 18
   naming, 6
header files, Cocoa, 204
HINFO (host info), 47
hostnames, 5
   wide-area Bonjour preferences, 75
HTTP GET commands, 57

## I

infrastructure, 95
installing Bonjour
   Linux/Unix, 94
   Macintosh, 93
   Windows, 93
interfaces
   BrowseListener, 157
   listener, 150
intranets, names, 40
IP addresses, 5
   announcing claim, 26
   availability, probing for, 23–26
   conflicts, late, 27–30
   defending, 27
   DHCP
      provided, 17
      servers and, 17–20
   direction, 35
   dotted decimal format, 13
   link-local range, claming, 22
   manual assignment, 13–16
   mDNS and, 32
      temporary, 32
   private, 20
   public, NAT, 87
   selecting, link-local range, 20–22
   subnet mask, 13
IP Multicast, DNS and, 33
IPP printing client, _ipp service type, 56
_ipp service type, 56

## J

Java APIs, 145
   asynchronous operations, 145
   browsing for services, 157–159
   Callback Interface Classes, 145
   DNSSD class, 147–149
   DNSSDException class, 150
   DNSServiceDiscovery C, 148
   Factory Class, 145
      listener interfaces, 150
      service registration, 151–157
      service resolution, 160–162

## K

key/value pairs, TXT records, 67

## L

late binding, 65
lb._dns-sd._udp query (Domain
      Enumeration), 72
lexicographically later rdata, 48
link-local address range, 20–22
   claiming IP address, 22–23
link-local addressing, xvii
links, subnets and, 15
Linux, Bonjour installation, 94
listener interfaces
   BrowseListener, 157
   Java APIs, 150
   RegisterListener interface, 152–154
local domain, 39
local, definition, 33

## M

MAC addresses, 18
Macintosh, Bonjour installation, 93
manually assigning IP addresses, 13–16
mappings
   creating, 89–91
   destroying, 89–91
mDNS, 42
   address, 43
   IP addresses, 32
      temporary, 32
   IP Multicast and, 33
   message structure, 49
   queries, 44
      one-shot, 44
      ongoing, 44
   small networks and, 71
   traffic reduction, 45
mDNSResponder, 33
message format
   DNS-LLQ, 80
   DNS-UL, 78
MFC (Microsoft Foundation Classes), event
      handling, 141–143
monitoring, dns-sd tool, 105
Multicast DNS, xvii

## N

name resolution, 36
named services, 8
names
    service instance names, 60
    uniqueness, 46
    visibility, 62
namespaces, 34
    Zeroconf, 38
NAT (Network Address Translation), 85
    overview, 86
    public IP address, 87
NAT gateway, 86
NAT-PMP (NAT port mapping
        protocol), 84–91
Network Address Translation (see NAT)
Non-authoritative answer, 37
nslookup, 37
NSNetServices API, 194–200

## O

one-shot query (mDNS), 44
    with multiple responses, 44
ongiong queries (mDNS), 44

## P

port mapping, NAP-PMP, 84–91
Preference Pane, 74
preferences, wide-area service discovery
    browsing, 76
    hostname, 75
    registration, 75
private IP addresses, 20
_presence._tcp service type, 70
probing for address availability, 23–26
protocols
    application protocol name
        registration, 60
    flagship protocols, 63
    NAT-PMP, 84–91
    service discovery and, 56
proxies, dns-sd tool, 104
pseudo-TLD
    local, 39
    multicast, 40
PTR records, rdata, 37
Python, 214
    browsing for services, 216
    service registration, 215
    service resolution, 217

## Q

queries
    Domain Enumeration, 71–73
    mDNS, 44

## R

r._dns-sd._udp query (Domain
        Enumeration), 72
rdata, lexicographically later, 48
refresh messages, DNS-UL, 79
refreshes, DNS-LLQ, 83
registering services, 98–102, 124
    DNS TXT record attributes and, 162–165
    Java APIs, 151–157
    Python, 215
    Ruby, 212
    testing program, 156
    wide-area service discovery
        preferences, 75
RegisterListener interface, 152–154
resolving services, 102–104
    CFNetServices, 192–194
    Cocoa, 198–200
    Java APIs, 160–162
    Python, 217
    Ruby, 214
resource records (DNS), 36
rrclass, resource records, 36
rrtype, resource records, 36
Ruby, 211
    browsing for services, 213
    service registration, 212
    service resolution, 214
RunLoop (Cocoa) event handling, 133–137

## S

Safari, xxi
search time, 108
secure shell (ssh), 39
select( ) function, 110
select( ) loop, event handling and, 109–114
service design, protocols and, 56
service discovery, 1
    available services, 3
    DNS-SD and, 58
    DNS-ServiceDiscovery
        APIs, 109
        error codes, 109
    error codes, 113
    hostnames, 5
    IP addresses, 5

# About the Authors

**Stuart Cheshire** is currently a senior scientist with Apple Computer, specializing in Internet protocols. He's published papers in the areas of wireless and networking and Mobile IP, and previously worked on IBM Token Ring with Madge Networks in the U.K. Stuart received B.A. and M.A. degrees from Sidney Sussex College, Cambridge, U.K., and M.S. and Ph.D. degrees from Stanford University.

**Daniel H. Steinberg** is the editor of ONJava and java.net for the O'Reilly Network. He's been working with Java on the Mac since it first appeared, but also enjoys coding in ObjC and other languages. Daniel is a longtime technical writer, trainer, and developer with Dim Sum Thinking, Inc. and recently coauthored the book *Extreme Software Engineering: A Hands-on Approach* (Prentice Hall).

# Colophon

Our look is the result of reader comments, our own experimentation, and feedback from distribution channels. Distinctive covers complement our distinctive approach to technical topics, breathing personality and life into potentially dry subjects.

The animal on the cover of *Zero Configuration Networking: The Definitive Guide* is a turtle dove. Originally from the arid woodlands of Africa, turtle doves were once domesticated birds, but escapees from aviaries have resulted in a wide distribution over many areas, including southern Africa, eastern Asia, Europe, and North America. Today, these doves are a migratory species that tend to live in clusters in savannas and grasslands. They are also still bred in captivity and often used for scientific experiments. Currently, the turle dove population is in steady decline due to hunting and constant changes in farming practices, which deplete its food supply of weeds and shoots.

The turtle dove is brownish, slightly darker than other doves, and can be recognized by striped feathers on its neck. Its wedge-shaped tail has distinctive white borders that are highly visible when the bird takes flight. It has a black bill and red rims around the eyes.

Males and females both incubate a clutch of eggs. In captivity, female doves group together and take turns caring for their clutches. However, one female eventually adopts the chicks and nourishes them with regurgitated "dove milk."

The bird's name has nothing to do with actual turtles. The arrival of turtle doves in northern Europe at the end of each April is accompanied by a deep, cat-like purring song that sounds like "trrrr, trrrr," hence the bird's Latin name, *turtur*.

Matt Hutchinson was the production editor, and Derek DiMatteo was the copyeditor for *Zero Configuration Networking: The Definitive Guide*. Chris Downey proofread the book. Adam Witwer and Claire Cloutier provided quality control. Johnna Dinse wrote the index.

Karen Montgomery designed the cover of this book, based on a series design by Edie Freedman. The cover image is a 19th-century engraving from *The Riverside Natural History*, Volume IV. Karen Montgomery produced the cover layout with Adobe InDesign CS using Adobe's ITC Garamond font.

David Futato designed the interior layout. This book was converted by Keith Fahlgren from Microsoft Word to Adobe FrameMaker 5.5.6. The text font is Linotype Birka; the heading font is Adobe Myriad Condensed; and the code font is LucasFont's TheSans Mono Condensed. The illustrations that appear in the book were produced by Robert Romano, Jessamyn Read, and Lesley Borash using Macromedia FreeHand MX and Adobe Photoshop CS. The tip and warning icons were drawn by Christopher Bing. This colophon was written by Matt Hutchinson.

Milton Keynes UK
Ingram Content Group UK Ltd.
UKHW030638051024
449225UK00007B/135

9 780596 101008